The All-American Sport of Bipartisan Bashing

Common Sense Rantings
from a Raging Moderate

WILL DURST

Illustrated by Max Kornell

Ulysses Press

For Miss Frozen Toes
from the Blanket Hog

Published in the U.S. by
ULYSSES PRESS
P.O. Box 3440
Berkeley, CA 94703
www.ulyssespress.com

ISBN10: 1-56975-656-2
ISBN13: 978-1-56975-656-0
Library of Congress Control Number: 2007907737

Aquisitions/Developmental Editor: Nick Denton-Brown
Copy Editor: Mark Woodworth / editmarks.com
Design/Production Director: Steven Zah Schwartz
Cover design: Double R Design
Cover photograph: Pat Johnson
Book design: Sara Glaser Graphic Design / saraglaser.com
Illustrator: Max Kornell / maxkornell.com

Printed and bound in Canada by Transcontinental Printing

10 9 8 7 6 5 4 3 2 1

Contents

1

Republicans
Democrats
Independents

We all know who's who and what's what here. This is a not-so-in-depth examination of the Petri dish of true believers. No matter how well they clean up, you can still spot the chalk dusting their shoes from a long history of drawing thick party lines. The vast right-wing conspiracy. The liberal media elite. And those wacky, raging moderates.

Good guys versus bad guys versus the guys in between. And we can pretty much tell who stands where on what, based on how they miscut their hair. The middle is a bit of a muddle.

In California we call ourselves "decline-to-states." Or, if you're inclined to cut to the chase, the philosophical shortcuts are: conservatives who smoke pot and liberals who own handguns.

The World of Wrongevity

George Bush is as wrong as Wyoming sushi. And he seems determined to continue to be wrong, in a tank-with-no-brakes-headed-down-a-hill-toward-a-Boy-Scout-camp-at-the-break-of-dawn sort of way. He was wrong about Saddam's weapons of mass destruction. He was wrong about Iraq's ties to Al-Qaeda. He was wrong when he told the UN that a mobile weather van was a chemical lab on wheels. He was wrong to call an invasion of a country that had nothing to do with 9/11 part of his war on terrorism. He was wrong to squander our national goodwill on a neocomical ideological misadventure. He was wrong about being greeted with flowers and candy, unless by "flowers and candy" he meant suicide bombers and improvised explosive devices. He was wrong about how long it would take, how much it would cost, how many troops would be needed, what kind of armor required. He was wrong about eating a pretzel without dunking it in beer first.

Firing the Iraqi Army and allowing the looting of an ancient civilization's artifacts while protecting the Oil Ministry...ill-advised. "Mission Accomplished"? Misguided. "Bring it on"? Wrongo exponential factor 13. When Omar Bradley talked about fighting the wrong war, at the wrong place, at the wrong time, and with the wrong enemy, he was predicting Bush. Expecting a democracy to spring up from soil drenched with the blood of ancient sectarian hatreds: a critical goof. "The insurgency is in its last throes"? Extremely erroneous. The rest of the world supporting us? Inaccurate. Creating more terrorists than he's killing? Iniquitous (which means "wicked wrong").

Counting on Iraqi Prime Minister al-Maliki to exhibit the will to succeed? Delusional. "They hate us for our freedoms"? Nope, sorry, that's counterfactual: They hate us for our guns and our bombs and the fact we act like our God hid our oil under their sand. Declaring anybody who disagrees with him is "comforting the enemy"? Not right. He was mistaken about Iraq's falling into sectarian strife, then denying it's a civil war. And when he says we are actually winning, ooh, buddy, that's so, what do you call it?, imprecise. So far, the only thing he's gotten right is being born a Bush and not hunting with Cheney.

He was dead wrong when he suborned torture, stupid wrong for spying on Americans and just plain wrong declaring that wartime gave him special powers, unless he's been bitten by a radioactive spider and hasn't exhibited any detectable symptoms yet. He was wrong with "stay the course" and wronger still when he argued he was never a big fan of "stay the course." He was disingenuous to ignore the November 7th election wake-up call loud enough to have rolled Pete Townsend right out of bed. And incorrect to reject the suggestions of the Iraq Study Group so completely that you wonder if he even read them or had anybody read them to him, wide-eyed with his chin under the covers.

But now he speaks to the nation to announce his next plan— The New Way Forward—which involves…sending more troops. Are you kidding me? That's how he gets out of a hole? More shovels? Some therapists maintain the definition of "insanity" is doing the same thing over and over while expecting a different result. Describing exactly what we can expect for the next two years living in the president's wild and wacky, not-so-wonderful world of wrongevity.

Contract on America 2.1

Oh sure, the calendar calls it the end of autumn, but for the Democratic Party, this is high noon, dead-solid summer. And I'm shocked every single time I see a high-ranking Democrat on television and he slash she is not twirling and spinning and throwing spears of asparagus into a mesquite bonfire wearing only a stringed necklace of extravirgin acorns...or however it is that godless secularists make sacrifices to celebrate good fortune. There should be meteoric fireworks. Organic fireworks, if need be, but fireworks. For this is a good time. A *fabulous* time. A time of comeuppance. A time that calls for slow-motion skipping on the beach with bouquets of ribbons attached to helium balloons trailing in the breeze over sun-kissed shoulders.

Why? Because the GOP is in deep doo-doo. How deep the doo-doo? Real deep the doo-doo. Reeking heap of steaming feces deep the doo-doo. So deep the doo-doo that every Republican member of Congress will soon be issued a three-foot length of bamboo to use as a breathing tube. So deep that watching Saddam Hussein plead "not guilty" is just a grim reminder that it won't be long before Karl Rove, Scooter Libby and Bill Frist get the chance to do the same. So deep the doo-doo that the best news the Republicans can look back on this fall was that their chief, the House Majority Leader, avoided a nationally televised perp walk by surrendering to Houston authorities on his own. Deep enough doo-doo that one more revelation is going to trip the Environmental Protection Agency filing requirement.

One would think the Democrats' reaction would be to capitalize on their adversaries' miseries. To issue sermons and wax eloquent on how poorer the nation is, due to this tragic loss of public trust. To bite through the twine that binds their hands and keeps them from punching back. To kick like they've been kicked and to kick back like they've never kicked before. To grab the feet of the majority party and run screaming down the stairs of the Washington Monument with their opponent's head bouncing off each of the 897 cement steps with a soft wet thud. One would think this would be the Democratic response...and one would be as wrong as plaid velour. Instead, the Dems have adopted a policy that redefines the word "lackluster."

In response, and I use the term loosely, the Democrats have mustered up a simmering series of platitudes. Oooh. Stand back. In a lame attempt at replicating Newt Gingrich's 1994 Congressional coup blueprint, Nancy Pelosi announced the Dems have written their own Contract with America. And in synch with their recently perfected castrated style, they are in the process of mucking it up worse than a three-legged pig on roller skates spinning china plates with greased hocks. Instead of easy-to-comprehend slogans designed for ordinary voters like you and me, the leaders of the shadow opposition are contemplating such reforms as "Support Fair Wages with Good Benefits So No One Goes to Work Every Day and Comes Home Poor and Dependent on Public Services"—and doesn't *that* lilt trippingly off the tongue like a diseased cattle truck off the side of Bryce Canyon? Let's not forget "An End to a Culture of Cronyism, Incompetence and Corruption in America"—a slogan about as sexy as Alan Greenspan naked with pom-poms. And 20 bonus points to anyone who can get that image out of their head in under an hour.

So I racked my brain, working my fingers to the bone on my hands and knees, and came up with a list of contract items the Democrats can use to ingratiate themselves with their supposed base. No need to thank me, I'm here to help.

The Democrats' New, Improved Revised
Contract with America (Version 2.1)

1. The "It's the Economy, Stupid, Part 2" Act.
2. The "Stop Shooting Ourselves in the Foot, Especially When Our Foot Is in Our Mouth" Act.
3. The "Common-sense Don't Invade Countries That Had Nothing to Do with 9/11" Act.
4. The "We Don't Hire Our Buddies' Roommates (Kennedys Excepted)" Act.
5. The "Health Care: Good / Oil Companies: Bad" Act.
6. The "Clinton Aura Restoration" Act.
7. The "Stop Whining Already" Act.
8. The "Fiscal Responsibility—No, Really!" Act.
9. The "We Promise to Grow Some Cojones and Remember We Are Not Republicans" Act.
10. The "Never, Ever Run Another Effete Intellectual from Massachusetts for President Ever Again" Act.

Put the Hammer Down

The adage is, "Any halfway decent prosecutor can convince a grand jury to indict a ham sandwich." And that old saw may just be true, because this week a grand jury in Travis County, Texas, indicted a hammer. Not just any hammer but "*The Hammer.*" House Majority Leader Tom DeLay was indicted on a single count of criminal conspiracy as well as multiple counts of "cranky old man" and "doesn't work well with others." To say he's not happy now is like saying barium enemas are not highlighted on many resort spa service menus. And ironically enough, when I speak of a barium enema I think of Tom DeLay.

In his press conference denying the charges, Teflon Tom

channeled some stoic Beast from the Bible, probably named Balthabazary or something. His righteous indignation was enough to smite evil-doers right through the TV screen as he characterized his indictment as one of political motivation. What? Politically motivated? In D.C.? No! You can't be serious. What next? Lobbyists with tassels on their loafers? What's ludicrous, in terms of being politically motivated, is that Tom DeLay wrote the book. District Attorney Ronnie Earle may actually be responsible for royalties being paid to the subject of his indictment.

DeLay went on to call Earle's indictment of him "one of the weakest, most baseless indictments in American history." Wow. In American history!?! Say what you will about DeLay's faults, a lack of self-esteem is not among them. Although it does seem a bit histrionic, coming from the man personally responsible for reigniting Bill Clinton's impeachment train just when it seemed most everybody was willing to shut up, go home and launder their own blue dresses. "Lying to a grand jury is an impeachable offense" was The Hammer's exact quote. Hmmm, interesting. How 'bout bribery, extortion and general venality?

What I'm delicately hinting at here is Mr. DeLay and ethical lapses are not unfamiliar dance partners. They go together like Chaplin and jerky film. Like grease and skids. Like Spiro Agnew and brown paper bags full of cash. The guy is a walking "12 Days of Corruption" song. "Fiiiiive trips to Palm Springs, four admonishments, three reprimands, two censures…and an indictment in the Lone Star State."

September. Not a good month for Republicans. Bush's spiritual advisor, Karl Rove: still under a cloud in the Valerie Plame leakage. GOP lobbyist Jack Abramoff: indicted in one case and under investigation in umpteen others. Top White House procurement official David Safavian: charged with obstruction in the Abramoff probe. Majority Leader Doctor Senator Indian Chief Bill Frist: under investigation due to questionable stock sales. And in his talk to the nation from New Orleans, President Bush misbuttoned his work shirt. That's right, the president of the United States can't even dress himself anymore.

This is not to say that DeLay is screwed dead in the water. For all we know, he could pull a Martha Stewart and come out of this smelling like a rose. I.e., go to prison, lose some weight and end up with a spinoff of *The Apprentice*. Instead of Trump's "You're fired," or Stewart's "You don't fit in," DeLay could lift the favorite kiss-off of his ideological twin, Dick Cheney: "Go f*** yourself." I smile every time I imagine him practicing that line in front of a mirror.

The Official George W. Bush Vice Presidential Prospect Questionnaire

In an attempt to narrow his search for a running mate, George W. Bush has sent out background questionnaires to prospective candidates. Due to my string of incredibly well-placed inside sources, whose sole compensation is simply the peace of mind they get from full public disclosure (and, of course, my regular contributions to their yeast-deficiency containment regimen), I am now able to leak portions of that questionnaire directly to you, with no hidden obligations on your part. Although a six-pack of Anchor Steam is never a bad investment.

Questionnaire

Please type or print neatly, using black or blue ink only.

Name: _____

Address: _____

Age: _____

Occupation: _____

Marital Status: _____

Blood type: _____

1. The most important quality I would bring to a national ticket is:
   A. A fierce dedication to uphold the Constitution of the United States.
   B. The electoral vote guarantee of an important swing state.
   C. Respect and dignity.
   D. Money. Lots and lots and lots of money.

2. Which of these statements is truest?
   A. "Blood is thicker than oil."
   B. "Oil is thicker than water."
   C. "Blood is thicker than water."
   D. "Oil and blood have approximately the same viscosity, but oil is easier to use as leverage."

3. The investment of portions of the Social Security trust fund in the stock market is:
   A. A good idea.
   B. A great idea.
   C. A great idea the public will come to trust after I've talked to them about it.
   D. The worst idea since oyster-flavored popsicles.

4. Please spell "potato." Both singular and plural.

5. True or false: Hunting is better than golfing.

6. Did you ever know, or work with, or have as a good friend, Jack Kennedy?

7. Jeb Bush's children are:
    A. Black.
    B. Red.
    C. Brown.
    D. Short.

8. Complete this statement: Women...
    A. ...should be seen barefoot and pregnant but not heard.
    B. ...are best served with lemon butter and capers.
    C. ...got to learn to relax for the inevitable.
    D. ...deserve to be executed, just like normal people.

9. As an impressionable youth, I experimented with:
    A. Pot.
    B. Coke.
    C. Acid.
    D. Campaign finance reform.

10. Electric shock therapy:
    A. Apparently happens frequently to guests of Jerry Springer.
    B. Should be utilized only as a last-ditch effort.
    C. Is like drinking three triple shots of bourbon real fast.
    D. Can be fun.

11. If you cannot answer yes to A, please complete B.
    A. I have many children.
    B. Why not?

12. The "W" in George W. Bush stands for:
    A. Wimp.
    B. Wussie.
    C. Walker.
    D. What-the-f***-do-I-stand-for?

13. Please answer the following question to the best of your ability: "Who am I, and why am I here?"

Scarlet Service Threat

It is my duty as a patriotic American to fire this warning flare up to the Republican Congress. Their very lives are in peril. *This is not a test!* They have unknowingly stumbled into a perilous situation that menaces them to a degree of which they are blissfully unaware. The fact that none of them will heed my advice saddens me a little, but not as much as it makes me giggle. Let me explain. They just barely missed pushing through a bogus minimum wage bill that also would finally accomplish their thickheaded goal of eliminating the estate tax, thus making sure that Paris Hilton gets every damn penny she deserves. Well, perhaps that's imprecise phrasing.

Anyway, that's not the scariest part. As part of the bill, the majority passed, on straight party lines, an amendment to the bill mandating a *drop* in the minimum wage for workers who live in the seven states with a higher minimum wage for tipped employees, meaning that in California the pay for bartenders, waitresses, bellmen and valets would have fallen from $6.75 an hour to $2.65. In other words, the minimum wage hike would have cut the yearly pay of tipped employees by about $9,600 each. Besides being more cynical than dyeing oval-shaped rocks and passing them off as Easter eggs to Special Olympics contestants, this situation would place thousands of Americans at risk. Especially members of our distinguished Congress.

Now, it goes without saying that these privileged lords and ladies have the same working relationship with the service industry that a giant cephalopod has with the gear ratio of a Toyota Camry, but my question is: Are they out of their mother-freaking minds? Do they harbor a secret death wish? What, exactly, is their long-term plan—to never eat in a restaurant or drink in a bar or park their car again? Back in Milwaukee, at a classy joint known as Century Hall, I was Will the Cosmic Waiter for a year and a half, and remain eminently knowledge-able of how very, very, *very* lengthy that journey between the kitchen and the table actually is. Many a drop twixt cup and lip doesn't even begin to cover the circuitous trip that a stray appe-tizer may be subject to. Quick-and-dirty detours to the smoke hole are always just three steps away. What lies at the bottom of the murky depths of your soup? You don't want to know.

I'm not just talking about ptomaine and salmonella and *E. coli* and hepatitis C, I'm talking about foreign objects such as grated pencil shavings and excess pocket lint in the béarnaise sauce. How many of our distinguished representatives are pre-pared to wear diapers full time to guard against the surrepti-tious drop of Visine in their vodka cran? And good luck getting the bathroom attendant to hand you more paper. You might want to ask the Senator in the next stall for change for a five.

A Republican leader posited the bill may be scuttled for now, but plans are to revisit it as soon as possible. Someone, please, for the sake of humanity, warn these simpletons that a minimum wage bill is supposed to *raise* the wages of our needi-est. And they do not want to put themselves in jeopardy by even *considering* such a regressive measure. I am only thinking of their welfare, at this point. To root out every possible sabotage would be like picking out a pubic hair in a sprout sandwich. Does a dead fish under the passenger seat of your Town Car have no meaning here?

The Pork Barrel Protection Act

So the Flag Desecration Amendment fell a single vote short of passing in the Senate. And the liberals are celebrating way too long into the night, if you ask me. I imagine the Republicans are laughing so hard right now, their drool guards are spilling over capacity. Because they get to bring it up again and again and accuse Democrats of dooming Old Glory to an ignominious fate, over and over. The only problem is flag desecration is so 1987. Might as well be wearing patchouli-scented elephant bellbottoms. There's a plethora of American icons in danger of being bespoilt that Republicans can exploit. Let's take a look, shall we?

Operation: Baseball Preservation

I don't want to hear another word about these commie pinko soccer moms. If they can't figure out how to be good old American baseball moms, maybe they should turn in their minivans and consider raccoon adoption.

The Thanksgiving Turkey Protection Act

No ham. No beef Wellington. No turkey-shaped tofu loaf. It's Thanksgiving. You'll eat turkey and you'll damn well like it. And the Dallas Cowboys game had better be on your television, too. And you'll be rooting against them, thank you very much.

Cheeseburger Antidesecration Crusade

The only proper cheese on a cheeseburger is yellow. Either Wisconsin cheddar or good ol' American. That's it. You can take your Mexican pepper gorgonzola and your baby emmenthaler and your aged Stilton and shred them where the sun never shines. Like on a salad. And it better be a butter-grilled sesame seed bun, not some basil balsamic olive focaccia bread foolishness.

Chocolate Simplification Act

It's chocolate, for crum's sake. It don't get more basic than a Hershey chocolate bar. If it was good enough for our brave boys in WW II, it should be good enough for those attention-deficit rug rats of yours.

Katie Couric: America's Sweetheart Proclamation

There's absolutely no reason why anybody should be watching Brian Williams or Charlie Gibson, to begin with. None. It's Katie's world—we just live in it. I want my news perky.

The Mandatory Rose Bowl Parade Viewing Order

Everyone should start the year off by watching the Rose Bowl Parade. And if it takes closing all the bars at 10 p.m. on New Year's Eve to make sure it gets done, then that's what we'll do.

Apple Pie Protection Bill

It's apple pie. 'Nuff said. Ordering any other kind is like throwing mud in your mother's face. Can you imagine Jimmy Stewart ordering a slice of Turkish-coffee chiffon raspberry torte? I thought not.

"Superman Is the Only Superhero" Acceptance Act

Did you ever hear the X-Men talk about Truth, Justice and the American Way? There's a reason for that.

Holiday Fruitcake Proliferation Compact

I don't care whether you like it or not. This is a generational thing, and a lot bigger than just you or me. Eat it or pass it on, then shut the hell up.

The Official Veneration of Snowboarding as a Winter Sport

In America, we don't give a real rat's ass about the four-man luge or whether some 14-year-old figure skater nailed her triple lutz. If HBO were smart, they'd get Jonny Mosely together with that girl who lost the gold by celebrating too early and just have the two of them make out for a six-part miniseries.

Pork Barrel Politics Protection Bill

"Pork is bad." "Pork is bad." How else you supposed to pay back contributors from your district? Bridge builders gotta work too, you know. Who cares if there's no river?

Pabst Blue Ribbon Celebration Act

Screw Heineken. It's Pabst Blue Ribbon. Beer comes in brown bottles. Shampoo comes in green bottles.

2-Dollars-a-Gallon Gas War

Oh, wait a minute. We already lost that one. And moved on to the 3-Dollars-a-Gallon Gas War. We're losing that one too. 4-Dollar?

Scientist Suspects Bush Has Syphilis!

President Bush is a stone-crazed loon suffering from a deterioration of his brain due to a tertiary case of syphilis and is liable to become incapacitated at any time and accidentally start World War III, according to a noted Baltimore psychotherapist. Or he could die. Or both.

In a shocking revelation, famed Johns Hopkins scientist Dr. Robert Musckovitz has diagnosed George W. Bush as suffering from stage 3 syphilis, after examining the president's increasingly erratic behavior. Dr. Musckovitz and his team of physicians, who have not seen or treated the president, have identified telling characteristics of the dreaded sexually transmitted disease in him by closely studying tapes of his mannerisms, speech patterns and eating habits. Candidly, the doctor cautioned, "He's really starting to creep me out."

Specifically, the doctor, a graduate of the University of Michigan–Escanaba Medical School, detailed incidents of the president's peculiar behavior, such as his frozen indecision on 9/11, his inability to escape a Chinese press conference, the weird growth on his back during the first debate with John Kerry and his trademark smirk, which could be a symptomatic rictus disguising telltale muscle contractions.

Citing the STD's devious ability to hide undetected for many years, the doctor refused to speculate on where or when Dubyah, constant companion of Condoleezza Rice, may have become syphilitic. He did rule out contracting it by performing a back rub, clearing German Chancellor Angela Merkel and avoiding a potentially nasty international incident. An intern working in Dr. Musckovitz's reception room did hazard a guess that Bush, a former Yale cheerleader, may have carried it for years. "I bet he picked it up at Stumpy's Bar in New Haven from a waitress. Hell, that's where *I* got it."

Various experts selling plasma at local free clinics in the District of Columbia maintain syphilis is a disease contracted through sexual contact, although rare instances of spontaneous contraction have been reported, as ascertained in the hospital logs of numerous Catholic seminaries.

A really respected medical book with pretty gold leaf on the cover says the late stages of syphilis can damage internal organs, including the brain, nerves, eyes, heart, blood vessels, liver, bones and joints. Signs and symptoms of the late stage include difficulty coordinating muscle movements, paralysis, numbness, blindness, dementia and pronouncing "nuclear" as *NU-kew-lerr*. This damage may be serious enough to cause death and/or the inability to speak with your mouth full.

A high-level White House source, requesting anonymity for fear of physical recrimination from what he considers an increasingly unstable Commander-in-Chief, also spoke of bizarre conduct, e.g., the president cupping a hand under his armpit and making flatulent noises during intelligence briefings, as well as dancing on the South Lawn in triple-digit heat wearing heavy winter clothing. "He was rocking out like he was listening to an iPod, but he had earmuffs on at the time. The Day-Glo blaze-orange kind. He even tied a string around them that went into his parka pocket but wasn't connected to anything. I'm not even going to talk about the squirrel, the spatula or the candle wax."

Asked to estimate how long the country has before its president descends permanently into the depths of dementia, Dr. Musckovitz muttered, "It may already be too late." Responding to a query as to whether he thinks Bush is still capable of handling the responsibility of having his finger on the nuclear button, the doctor shook his head and said, "At this point, I wouldn't trust him with a garage door opener."

Republicans Gone Wild 2!

If you're one of the millions still rolling on the floor in amazement at the greed and hypocrisy featured in last year's surprise hit, *Republicans Gone Wild,* throw that DVD away. Because you're not going to believe the extreme and hilarious action we've compiled for you in the brand-new *Republicans Gone Wild 2.*

You'll laugh. You'll cry. You'll kiss any chance of their recapturing Congress goodbye. But you'll never forget this brand new, never-before-seen footage featuring their patented wide stances and narrow minds. You've seen their unseemly breakdowns on television. You've read about their scurrilous exploits in the newspapers. You've witnessed their Family Values blustering for years. Now relive their blathering and blubbering at your leisure.

Here it is...the ultimate collection of the most crazed and sexed-up elected official footage ever accumulated on one DVD. *Republicans Gone Wild 2* has it all! At the malls, inside stalls, even in the halls of the Capitol. It will have you saying "Jiminy."

You may think the Republican Party needs this the same way a three-legged armadillo needs a rabid badger gnawing at his last remaining front paw on the gravel shoulder of I-95 in the dead of night. And you'd be right! Conduct unbecoming a Senator? Conduct unbecoming a weasel.

All the hilarious escapades you loved in *Republicans Gone Wild* are back, only they're bigger and better and sleazier than ever in *Republicans Gone Wild 2*. The crazy, zany antics of Jack Abramoff, Mark Foley, Duke Cunningham and Bob Ney will *pale* next to this madcap collection of weird and wild wackiness.

100 percent raw, real and uncut! Riotous solo gaffes aplenty. Congressman-on-Congressman action. 2008 presidential candidates hiding their faces behind their hands, mumbling for Idaho's Republican Senator Larry Craig to "Just go away. Please, go away!" Plus much, much more. See them lie, deny and just plain cry.

All your favorite 2007 moments are here:

- Gasp as chastised Louisiana Senator David Vitter, southern regional chair of the Giuliani campaign, admits to frequenting a house of prostitution, but avoids any further questions by saying the matter is between his family and God.

- Inhale as newly elected millionaire South Carolina Treasurer Thomas Ravenel, chair of the state's Giuliani campaign, is charged with conspiracy to distribute a quantity of cocaine, carrying a possible sentence of 20 years.

- Guffaw as Robert W. Allen, co-chair of Senator John McCain's Florida legislative leadership team, is arrested for soliciting prostitution from an undercover police officer posing as a transvestite in a public park restroom but says he was intimidated into it because he was the only white guy in the area.

- Thrill as Idaho Senator Larry Craig, Mitt Romney's 2008 GOP Senate coordinator, announces to the world, "I am not gay. I have never been gay." Then repeats it about 87 times and thanks those in attendance "for coming out today."

Become a member of the *Republicans Gone Wild* Pioneers Club and enjoy instant access to a special website and the *Republicans Gone Wild* archives, 24/7. Republicans don't sleep. Why should you? Get exclusive clips not available anywhere else. Updated hourly.

Republicans Gone Wild 3 is being compiled by assistant DAs all over the country, as we speak.

Act within the next 48 hours and get your free FOLEY/ CRAIG '08 bumper sticker!

Stalking the Hypocritical Oafs

I'm a little worried about the Republicans. I am. It's my job to mock and scoff and taunt, but these days it's almost too darn easy. I was taught not to kick people when they're down. Which I'm sure qualifies me as a weenie-ass pussy, in their book. Hence the famous retractable eight-penny serrated hobnails in the toes of Karl Rove's boots. But to imply that, lately, they're a tad disorganized is like supposing Don Imus might not be first choice to play Santa at the 2007 Apollo Theater Christmas Gala. Not only isn't this your father's Republican Party. It's not even George Bush's father's Republican Party anymore. You could go so far as to say that this Republican

Party is mighty disconnected from the Republic, and it sure ain't no party.

Over at the White House, the president's head is in danger of snapping right off at the third vertebrae as he swivels to and fro explaining why he won't sign the $120 billion supplemental war funding bill about to be sent to him by the Democratic Congress. Initially, he claimed his threatened veto was due to the bill's surfeit of Democratic earmarks. Then some of his earmarks were found stapled to it, not to mention hundreds of Republican legislative Post-it notes attached to the $94 billion supplemental war funding bill he did sign last June. These discoveries caused him to switch tactics faster than it takes a fifth-year art school undergrad to disrobe at Burning Man. Now he says he won't sign the bill because of its artificial timetable for Iraqi troop withdrawal. Apparently he's interested in an organic timetable. An heirloom tomato and bathtub tofu timetable.

Meanwhile, in another part of town, Republicans jumped all over House Speaker Nancy Pelosi for speaking to Syrian President Bashar al-Assad, totally ignoring the fact that three Republican Congressmen made the exact same trip and spoke to the very same Syrian president in Damascus on April 1. Must have been written off as an April Fool's Day prank. Next, I suppose, they'll complain Pelosi traveled on a bigger plane than the Republicans. Or she usurped frequent-flyer miles that rightfully belong to Condoleezza Rice.

On Capitol Hill you got Connecticut Senator Joe Lieberman. And don't bother with that "Independent" stuff. The man is such a lapdog of the Administration, if you listen real close to C-SPAN, you can hear his toenails echo off the marble floors of the rotunda. Referring to Moqtada al-Sadar's rally where hundreds of thousands burned American flags and chanted "Americans Leave Now!" Lieberman called it a good thing. "He's striking a nationalist chord...acknowledging that the surge is working," he remarked, going a long way to convince sane people that some nefarious government agency has replaced his brain with two quarts of Campbell's Navy Bean Soup with Ham.

Speaking of Iraq, that's where Representative Mike Pence put his foot in his mouth so deep his Kevlar loafer was in danger of wrapping around his own lower intestine, when he talked about a heavily fortified trip to a market in Baghdad as being like "a normal outdoor market in Indiana in the summertime." Funny, I grew up in the Midwest. Totally missed the whole armored Humvee, roof sharpshooters, bulletproof vest market-shopping deal.

And then there's the candidates. John McCain echoing yet distancing himself from his buddy Pence. Rudy Giuliani telling Alabama he sees nothing wrong with flying the Confederate flag (and those hotel pillowcases with the eye holes cut in them...snazzy!). Mitt Romney bragging about being a lifelong hunter, then admitting he's only been hunting twice. Those wacky Republicans and their fuzzy math. "Lifelong" is twice? Logic like that qualifies George W. Bush as a lifelong reader. But it definitely prolongs the GOP tradition of painting themselves as lifelong targets for my sophomoric sniping. Long may they hypocrize.

Al Gore and the Blue Sky Theory

So Al Gore got the Nobel Peace Prize for his incessant blabbing about "global warming." Big deal. The committee that hands those things out is the most motley collection of Norwegian Marxists you ever did see. Previous Peace Prize nominees have included Adolf Hitler, Joseph Stalin, Benito Mussolini, Satan, Michael Moore and Mother Teresa. But the worst part is the encouragement this Scandinavian Cracker Jack prize has given the former crime confederate of Hillary Clinton's husband to proselytize his other harebrained speculations.

Now Mister Global Gloomy Gus is going around trying to convince people the sky is blue. He doesn't call it an opinion. He neglects to cite scientific evidence linking other colors to the sky. Nope. The sky is blue. Why? Because Al Gore says so. And we're supposed to take his word for it and shut the hell up. I don't think it's any big secret why Tipper's old man wants the sky to be blue. Certainly can't have the sky being red, now can we, like Florida in 2000?

Exactly where does this guy get off? Who voted *him* Mister Science Expert of the World Guy? He's a failed politician who blew his last race and apparently can't get over losing the limelight. What does he know about skies? Just Googled his bio: not surprisingly, no degrees in "Sky." Although, to be fair, there were no degrees in "Manure Spreader" either, and I have to admit, he's one of the best.

Correct me if I'm wrong, but isn't the sky often full of *clouds?* When he looks up, does he see blue clouds as well? Makes sense when you consider all the hallucinogenics he must have swallowed at Harvard with his East Coast Ivy League, a-little-light-in-their-loafers buddies. All of whom, I'm sure, still see green pigs and polka-dot trees under those liberal blue skies of theirs.

To hear the way Gore and his cabal of elite environmental extremists tell it, you'd think general scientific consensus has signed off on the whole "sky is blue" hypothesis, but they'd be dead wrong. What they don't want you to know is that several highly respected Texas-based scientists who haven't drunk from Gore's pitcher of socialist Kool-Aid vehemently dispute this contention, calling his laughable theory just that: the "blue sky *theory.*" According to them, there's not enough evidence either way. Jury is still out.

So what if, on occasion, the sky is bluish? Who's to say that it isn't turning back to its original color of green or magenta or cerulean real soon? Has Hollywood's favorite political mascot ever thought of that? Or is he too busy trying to divert billions of dollars to his good friend Osama bin Laden and the Islamofascists by scuttling important domestic oil research and instead trotting out his lame and spurious "blue sky" campaign?

By ramming these irrational beliefs down the throats of ordinary people, Al Gore and his Goth band of America-haters revel in their disdain for the hard-working men and women of this country, while at the same time flagrantly endangering the safety of our brave freedom-fighting troops in Iraq. I imagine the next piece of junk-science propaganda nonsense this world-class snake-oil salesman will try peddling to a gullible public is that water is wet or war is bad. God help us all.

He's Back!

Hey guys, guess what: He's baaaack! Yes, dear friends, Tom DeLay has crawled out from under the rock where he's been hiding for the last couple of months, prematurely completing all those important pieces of personal business he needed to attend to, like filing his teeth and sucking hundreds of pints of virgin Mormon blood so that he's refreshed and ready to jump back into electoral politics. Whether he wants to or not, DeLay seems to have acquired a tertiary case of the Michael Corleones: Every time he tries to get out, they pull him back in. And if the "they" in question have a lick of commonsense, they're wearing protective rubber gloves while doing it.

Right now, a dilemma is facing down the Republican Party like a stampeding herd in a dead-end alley of Pamplona. This is trickier than a magician's junk drawer, so follow closely. Because this King of K Street retired from public service after winning the GOP primary for Congress in Texas's 22nd District last spring, unless the decision to keep his name on the ballot is overturned on appeal he's going to have to mount a campaign to run for the same seat he resigned and, if he gets elected, he'll have to resign again, then let the governor of Texas call a special election to name his replacement. The upshot is, either he's going to run or he's going to run. And I'm putting my money on the former.

Or, the Republicans could decide to put together a write-in campaign. Which might prove to be a mite ticklish, especially when you consider voters in "Texas 22" are about as bright as a 15-watt bulb buried at the bottom of a briefcase full of marked $100 bills to begin with, which can be verified by their perpetual requited love affair with Mr. DeLay. So, teaching an entire district to learn how to write is going to be about as easy as untying the shoes of a greased-up millipede while wearing oven mitts.

If he's really serious about keeping us from having Tom DeLay to kick around anymore, there are a variety of new interests he could pursue. For instance, he could become a conductor on that new Beijing-to-Tibet railway, contract a severe case of elevation sickness (causing his neck to bloat up to the size of an overinflated soccer ball) and escape detection that way. Or maybe he'll just pull a Ken Lay, fake a heart attack, fly to some uncharted desert isle and play a quick couple of rounds in a foursome with William Casey, Tupac Shakur and Elvis.

In any case, this has *got* to be good news for the Democrats, putting DeLay, symbol of Congressional corruption (not to mention poster child of smug self-satisfaction), flush front blunt back in the crosshairs of the national spotlight. Again. Maybe this time, that negative of him and Jack Abramoff and Karl Rove naked under a goat at a Junkie Hookers for Satan convention will finally surface. Of course, with the Democrats' luck, Louisiana Congressman William Jefferson will be bent

over in the background pulling a couple of cold ones out of the
fridge. And I ain't talking about brewskies, either.

FAQ: 2004 Democratic Primary

Q. What's happening with the Democrats?

A. Well, as you may have guessed, it's boiled down to essen-
tially a two-man race in their attempt to pick which rich
white guy they think has the best shot against Bush in
November.

Q. Which must be a good thing. More time for the top dogs
to stand out, right?

A. Well, it certainly is good for Edwards.

Q. Meaning it's bad for Kerry?

A. Not necessarily. As long as he's winning, he gets to pretty
much dictate the terms of the race. Like his decision to
participate in only two debates before Super Tuesday
instead of the 348 that Edwards wanted, and Dennis
Kucinich and Al Sharpton get to keep their shovels and
buckets and play in the sandbox as well.

Q. So, that's good?

A. Some good, because the opposition party now has fewer
voices on the nightly news attacking the president's
policies on a regular basis, and it needs Sharpton and
Kucinich to keep the attacks strident. Which Edwards
and Kerry can't do because they're too busy sounding
presidential.

Q. That's bad?

A. Could be good too, because most recent polls show both
Senator Johns leading Bush.

Q. Sounds excellent, but then again, probably not—right?

A. Not all that good, since at this time eight years ago the
living sarcophagus, Bob Dole, was ahead of Bill Clinton.

Q. I see your point, but still, it can't be that bad, can it?

A. You're right, it's not, since it puts Bush on the defensive.

Q. Which is good?

A. Well, could be good. Could be bad, too. Just like Dean made Kerry and Edwards better candidates, the Democrats have to worry about awakening the sleeping beast inside Bush, and yes, I do mean Dick Cheney.

Q. Ooh, that's bad, right?

A. Well...

Q. Wait, wait, let me.... It's good in a way, but in other ways it's bad, right?

A. You know, I think you're getting the hang of it here. Yes, it's a little of both. As long as Edwards keeps his "Happy Face" campaign going strong and avoids the temptation to attack Kerry, it's a good thing. But something happens to people who get this close to the residents' entrance of the White House. The mind starts to unravel. They begin to explore all their options, and if one of them includes the slinging of mud, well, best to keep a supply of dirt and water handy.

Q. Which would be bad, right?

A. Well, for those of you who think we need a barometric reading on how Kerry reacts under pressure, sooner might be better than later, if you know what I mean.

Q. So, it's good that Edwards continues to imitate the Energizer Bunny?

A. Well, you *do* want the eventual winner to have enough time to prepare for the general election.

Q. Right. Everyone has been so polite lately. You sure these are Democrats?

A. After seeing Dean and Gephardt both eat big beige banana slugs in their murder-suicide pact in Iowa, it's obvious what the Democratic party faithful want, and that's electability, which is hard to get from a bleeding stump of a candidate clinging to life support.

Q. Are you calling Kerry the most electable Democrat?

A. No, *Kerry* is calling Kerry the most electable Democrat.

Q. Is the general impression that Edwards should drop out or stay in?

A. Well, Super Tuesday is coming up, and it would be nice to have California involved for once—if for nothing else than letting the media see the sun, which might put them in a better mood.

A Horror Movie Sequel, Inaugural 2: This Time It's Really Personal

Exhibiting his mastery of faith-based weather, President Bush's second coronation carnival slipped smack dab between two Washington, D.C., snowstorms amid the most oppressive security setup since some old Chinese guys reclaimed Tiananmen Square. Like every circus worth its weight in pork, it started with a parade. However, the battalion of armored limousines and two-hour waits to stand on 10 degree street corners behind about 10 million gun-strapped law enforcement officers proved this to be a parade without a lot of laughs. No balloons, cotton candy or deep-fried bananas. The only animals were sniffy drug dogs, and the few clowns in attendance were all on the reviewing stand.

In his 21-minute, 1,430-word speech, the president called for an end to tyranny, but I have a funny feeling that does not extend to the Republican majority's behavior toward the Democrats in Congress. He managed to mention the word "freedom" 27 times, but surprisingly the word "Iraq" was AWOL, failing to make a single appearance. Probably holding off till the State of the Union for its formal commencement. The point is,

George Bush is profreedom and antityranny. Wow. Can't wait for his position paper on irritable bowel syndrome.

Sporting the lowest approval rating of a second-term president in 50 years, the president defended the pomp and circumstance of his $40 million coming-out-again party to the critics who called it excessive: "You can be equally concerned about our troops in Iraq and those who suffered in the tsunami while celebrating democracy." Other concerns he neglected to mention that one can still hold while celebrating democracy are the heartbreak of psoriasis, curtain rod drawstring finger burns, windborne *Ebola,* the critical international shortage of ethical show-business agents, and huge meteors on extinction-level trajectories.

The Evangelist of Freedom actually went on to say his second inauguration should serve as an inspiration to fledgling democracies in Iraq and Afghanistan. I'm sure both countries are salivating over the opportunity to hold an event featuring dozens of exclusive feasts, such as the one with 21,000 enchiladas, 20,000 quesadillas and 3,000 pounds of barbecued beef, as was found at Texas State Society's Black Tie and Boots Ball. I am guessing that in the Middle East the pulled-pork sand-

wiches will be replaced with a couple of bowls of red pepper humus, but an emphasis on fiber is probably not a bad thing.

Although a member of the Bush family has been part of the ruling presidential ticket in five of the last seven contests, both 41 and 43 went out of their way to say they don't appreciate the term "dynasty." Yeah, well, you know what? Neither do we, and it's probably not because of an allergic reaction to Joan Collins. The only silver lining for Democrats is Dubyah can't run again, unless Karl Rove starts a clandestine push to jettison the 20th Amendment, in which case Bill Clinton can head a ticket, too. To which you can hear all the blue states shout as they rise in unison: "Bring it on!"

2

Left
Right
Center

Scientists tell us the brain is split into two halves.

Scientists tell us a bunch of stuff, like buffalo semen cured in birch barrels and shipped upside down within 30 days of an equinox makes for tastier bison burgers. Then they argue among themselves over half of what they tell us, but most of them do agree on this whole separated-brain deal. The primordial right side controls the creative and instinctual parts, activating the sensors that make us want to cavort with Pamela Anderson or George Clooney. The upstart left brain is more linear and analytical, calculating how feasible is that fantasy, restraining many of us from making complete and utter asses of ourselves.

Many. But not all. And the synaptic bridges that connect the two lumps of gray are adorned with the remnants of millions of cells martyred to various barleycorn deities. And the memories of Ron Paul and Dennis Kucinich have gone to live under those synaptic bridges like trolls. This chapter addresses other things.

Spanking the Diaper

I don't know if you've heard about this, but it's exactly the kind of news that compels perfectly sane people to throw their arms up in the air, bang their foreheads against brick walls and devote the rest of their lives to eating raw cookie dough out of plastic tubs in the basement while watching Jessica Fletcher overturn police incompetence in Cabot Cove on the Biography Channel. And what the hell is *Murder, She Wrote* doing on the Biography Channel in the first place? But that diatribe is best left for another day.

Today's harangue concerns Democratic California Assemblywoman Sally Lieber and her plan to introduce a bill to the Legislature ("Hello, Bill," "Hello, Legislature") that will make parental spanking a crime if the child is three years old or younger, labeling it misdemeanor child abuse. That's right, "Spank your kid, go to jail" is about to become law. "Neglect to stroke a pony, pay a fine" is on the docket for next year. And the "Polyester Banky Ban"? Still stuck in conference.

Now, don't get me wrong, I understand Lieber's motivation. As a card-carrying member of the Nanny Party, she is unable to control her insatiable urge to protect us from ourselves. And she's seriously against child abuse. But then again, aren't we all? And that's a good thing. But come *on*. Do we really need a law here? Aren't most slaps to the bottom more of a Pavlovian response training exercise, anyway? Throw a tantrum, get a smack. Repeat till salivation occurs. Besides, unless it's full, spanking a diaper is like dropping a dime on a pillow. And when it *is* full, it's a revolting exercise that neither the spanker nor the spankee is likely to forget. Or, more importantly, anxious to duplicate.

I'm curious as to exactly how the honorable Assembly-woman proposes parents discipline their darling nippers in the event that they toss the toaster into the tropical fish tank. Perhaps a squirt gun to the back of the head, like veterinarians recommend to keep cats off the furniture? Or temporary exile to a kid terrarium upholstered in an array of bubble wrap? Or replacing *Teletubbies* with tapes of last season's *The Apprentice*? If Donald Trump doesn't constitute cruel and unusual, I don't know what does.

Mostly, though, what worries me is misdemeanor rug-rat abuse creep. How soon before the Legislature is asked to outlaw stern looks, unseemly scents and substandard nose-nuzzling? All potentially very traumatizing to our miniature progeny. Doesn't the simple act of an adult walking past a crawling moppet constitute sheer intimidation through sizism? Walking past a toddler? Get down on all fours, mister. And put that beer in a sippy cup. "A pacifier for all my friends." Not to mention that the booming adult voice has to be a terrifying thing, so infractions of the decibel meter will be financially penalized via a complex geometric formula involving frequency and frequency.

Once you cross the cherub-protection threshold, a gibberish translator to protect the little angel's fragile sense of self-esteem, easily compromised by formalized language, seems to be a logical leap. And picking up a wee bairn and thrusting them toward the ceiling with extended arms or riding them on one's shoulders? Flagrant reinforcement of an overwhelming sense of powerlessness. All I'm saying here is, it's a slippery slope, Sally Lieber. One that involves hunching way over and whispering and squirt guns and rampant sheep-shearing and grown men sucking on nipples. And who wants that?

Wimp II

Wimps, rejoice! The glittering realm of wimpdom is vacant no more. "Long live His Wimpiness, King George II." Yes, friends, the wimp is back and he's wimpier than ever. As the Arnold is wont to say: "He's a girlie-man." Punked-out mamma's boy. You know, if he were in prison, he'd be shaving his legs, wearing mascara and calling his cellmate "Sushi Lips." Not that there's anything wrong with that. I'm just saying.

Got to admit, it's not completely the 43rd president's fault. This whole wimp thing is obviously a congenital condition inherited from 41. A slow-motion victory by one of the more recessive of Episcopalian genes. Like all bad history, bound to repeat itself. I hear you querying, "What remarkable wimp-like activity has the president perpetrated to reclaim his long-lost family heritage?" Well, to be fair, it wasn't a single feeble pander on his part, but a catalog of pathetic grandstanding that placed Daddy's long-unclaimed crown on his head. But now that you mention it, yes, one particularly nasty piece of business does stand out like a quarter-sized hairy mole on the airbrushed cheek of a *Playboy* centerfold.

I'm referring to the sorry spectacle of the president flying back to D.C. from Texas to jump on the holy-roller bandwagon that was busy entangling a brain-damaged coma victim's feeding tubes in its spokes. Don't know if he was trying to energize his base or distract folks from his Social Security debacle or just plain happy to get his face next to a headline that contains the word "coma."

But any way you cut it, it's rare to see this kind of world class brown-nosing from a termed-out politician. His staff loves to say Bush is a man who doesn't know the meaning of the

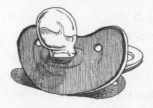

word "quit." Well, apparently he's not all that conversant with the word "shame," either.

I can understand Bill Frist and Tom DeLay orchestrating these weasel moves, as they're still ambitious, poisonous little suckups with big Christian Right butts and their big bucks in their crosshairs. But shouldn't George be working out of the downtown plaza of Legacy City right now, cleaning up his contribution to a presidential library by shredding documents? And, as it turns out, he's just a big fat sissy-boy like his dad. Isn't that sweet?

Sanctimoniously justifying his attempt to intercede on behalf of a supine human pawn, Bush intoned, "Always err on the side of life." Of course, the obvious exception would be those darn Iraqis. Didn't "err on the side of life" with that one, did you, George?

Instead of waiting for the UN inspectors to do their work, his beliefs were a mite more secular then, listening instead to his whispering generals: "If we don't get there in eight weeks, it's going to get wicked hot, which will make our troops' flak jackets itchy." That time he decided to "err" on the side of wardrobe. This time, the newly crowned King of Wimps erred on the side of political expediency. Not the first time and (I got a funny feeling) not the last.

Satan's Filibuster

"Hey, you crazy faithful, how 'bout a hand for the Doctor Senator Reverend Indian Chief Bill Frist! Could that guy sweet-talk the chrome off the bumper of a '57 Ford, or what? And one more time for little Bonita Gonzalez for channeling the Spirit of Ronald Reagan. Should have trusted the Lord to find a way for the Great Communicator to lend a hand in our just cause. And while you're at it, give yourselves a huge hand for not staying home and watching *Davey and Goliath* but instead filling the Sugar Bowl in TODAY'S NATIONALLY TELEVISED JUSTICE SUNDAY RALLY 2 SPONSORED BY EXXON-MOBIL! A follow-up, or should I say a sequel, to our fabulously successful first Justice Sunday Rally, which frightened the liberal media like a little schoolgirl with hairy spiders down her pants.

And just why are the liberals frightened? Yes, because they're doomed to spend all of eternity in damnation, of course, but also because they're afraid of God's righteous retribution. Afraid of the resolve and conviction the Lord filled us with in our triumphant crusade to wrestle the Devil's pitchfork, the filibuster, to the ground. Afraid of getting their asses kicked in the '06 midterm elections just as sure as God made little acorns to grow up into mighty oaks and topple over onto the picnic blankets of the godless, pinning them to the ground in writhing agony. Afraid that George Bush will appoint more judges that are too conservative. "Too conservative"? What does that mean, ladies and gentlemen? It's like saying the sky is too blue. Or the grass is too green. Or Dennis Hastert is too bland.

Today's JUSTICE SUNDAY RALLY 2 is a celebration of the destruction of the judicial tyranny that kept Beelzebub's foot on the neck of people of faith: Satan's Filibuster. But we can never get so comfortable that we think our job here is done. So let us turn our attention to other forms of repression the inhuman hater of life utilizes to grease the skids for him and his liberal acolytes in Washington and Hollywood. Including but not limited to:

- The so-called Miranda Law. If the guilty really want to know their rights, all they need do is read the Bible. I suggest the unabridged books-on-tape version, read by Charlton Heston. His Leviticus rocks. That whole "innocent before proven guilty" silliness—a truly spiritual man is able to tell who's guilty just by looking at them.

- Perhaps it's time to rethink that term "innocent." Rather outdated, isn't it? For, in God's eyes, aren't we all sinners?

- Habeas corpus. You want to know whether someone is imprisoned lawfully? The Lord will tell you when someone is imprisoned lawfully. You'll meet them in Hell.

- The First Amendment, which we intend to change to read: "Congress shall make no law respecting an establishment of religion, EXCEPT THE ONE TRUE RELIGION, WHICH IS ALLOWED TO SMITE ALL OTHER MAJOR RELIGIOUS BUTT, SINCE THEY'RE DOOMED TO SPEND ALL OF ETERNITY IN DAMNATION, ANYWAY."

Also, we'll take a few shots at activist school boards and anybody who makes fun of Rick Santorum's hair. But first, let's welcome Tom DeLay, who will explain how to find Satan's secret subliminal messages in the *New York Times*.

That Mythical Ethical High Ground

In an effort to regain the ethical high ground in Washington, D.C., which admittedly is lower than a parasite on the belly of a flounder on the floor of the Marianas Trench in the Pacific Ocean, Republican Party leaders announced a series of lobbying reforms to counteract the publicity they've received due to the Jack Abramoff contretemps ("scandal" is such an ugly word). This is kind of like a skulk of foxes calling for a new collection of locks to be placed on the hen house. Which they get to install. And reference their brother-in-law as vendor. Shockingly, the prospective reforms don't really reform much. One of them is a bill that calls for a cap on gifts. Or is it a bill calling for a cap on gift caps? Or does it cap the bill length of gift caps? No matter. Another calls for filing more disclosure reports. As if there's anybody in place to read the ones that aren't being filed now! As in most grandstanding Congressional efforts, these policy changes are so mostly for show, they make the Golden Globes look like Nobel Laureate biochemical research. You have to understand, inside the Beltway it is much more imperative to give the appearance of doing something than actually doing it. Outside of massive and continuous fund-raising, that's pretty much their job description. So, in a similar spirit of appearing as if I'm helping, I've come up with some further reforms that don't do much but look good set in embossed type and will serve to pad out their list.

Possible New Republican Congressional Ethics Reforms

- Footrests in all Congressional motor pool limousines to be reconfigured to Naugahyde from leather.

- While assisting with writing legislation, lobbyists required to keep their jackets on in committee meetings. Ties may still be loosened.

- Oil companies no longer get extraspecial treatment. From now on they will only receive special treatment.

- To lessen the appearance of ethics violations in Congress, the Congressional Ethics Committee is to be disbanded.

- Campaign contributions no longer allowed to be directly deposited to offshore accounts. Must be deposited to onshore banking institutions. Pseudonyms are discouraged.

- A frivolity tax to be levied on all tasseled loafers sold in the 202 area code.

- Persons or organizations revealing instances of Congressional ethics violations to be prosecuted under the full penalty of the law.

- Congressional shredders to be upgraded to units employing motors of a minimum of 8 horsepower.

- Exlawmakers hereby prohibited from making cameo appearances on television shows like *24* and *Lost*. But *Dancing with the Stars*? OK.

- Six-drink maximum to be strictly enforced when flying on corporate jets during trips of fewer than 1,000 air miles.

- When procuring the services of an escort, American-born hookers will be given right of first refusal.

- Henceforth, all no-bid contracts to Halliburton will be delivered through the first-class mail services of the U.S. Postal Service rather than being FedEx'd.

Simple Is as Simple Does

"Your calls are important to us. For quality control and training purposes the rest of your life will be monitored."

While we were all distracted by Scooter, the Looter and the Shooter, big-time conservatives tried to sweep Bush's whole warrantless wiretapping scheme under a rug of complications. First they claimed it's a matter of the president's prerogative: "He wants to bug somebody. He bugs them. That's what a Commander-in-Chief does." Then they applied a legal paint job: "Congress said he could, when authorizing his use of force against terrorism." Then they hammered it down with the big gun. The golden oldie. Their game-saving Hail Mary—national security: "If you disagree with listening in on Al-Qaeda, you're endangering the troops and giving the terrorists a back rub."

Next they'll tell us he was just assuaging Democratic concerns that he never listens to them.

It's not complicated at all. He broke the law. Peed on the Constitution. Flipped off the Founding Fathers. Nobody knows why. All he had to do was notify the FISA court within three days of when he started eavesdropping. In previous trips to the court, 18,000 wiretaps were OK'd and 5 turned down. Eighteen thousand out of eighteen thousand and five. Not a bad return. We're talking a .999 batting average here. As an old baseball hand, he should be aware that they keep you in the "bigs" with that.

I don't know why he didn't go to the court. Maybe he worried they wouldn't buy these specific warrants. Maybe he stretched the definition of "terrorist" to include Michael Moore's dog walker. Maybe he suspects NBC White House correspondent David Gregory has a mole in the Justice Department. Or maybe he just really believes he is above the law. I know he claims during wartime to possess special powers. "Special powers": I love that. He can't even ride a bicycle without falling off. I guess his special powers don't include balance. I don't want a president with special powers, I want a president to uphold the Constitution. I never knew King George the Third. I didn't work with King George the Third, but from what I read about King George the Third, I feel safe to say, you, sir, are no King George the Third.

He's starting to make less sense than a polar bear in golf cleats sipping a sloe gin fizz on an escalator. Said he didn't want any interval standing in the way of fighting terrorism. Hello! George! Tutor Time! Go ask Condoleezza; she went to school and actually studied. Have her explain to you about the whole space–time continuum deal. How what happens afterward doesn't affect the speed of what went on before. In other words, if you kill a chicken, it does not alter how many eggs it has laid in its lifetime. Might put a slight crimp in the number to be laid in the future, but the past tense is finite. Hell, you said it yourself: "The past is over." It's a reality thing. They may not have lived in the real world at Yale, but I'm pretty sure they referenced it once in a while.

And stop with the silly charge that the person who told the press about the program is the bad guy. That they brought the plan to the attention of Al-Qaeda. Any terrorist who doesn't know that talking on an open, unencrypted line is a fast track to 72 perfumed virgins is probably not trusted by the big turbans to do anything more important than run out to get the scorched coffee and day-old baklava, anyhow. Kind of what Dubyah would be doing if his dad hadn't made his bones with Reagan. Besides, we're never going to understand the mind of Al-Qaeda. These guys spell their name with a "Q," it's not followed by a "U"; they play by rules we don't even understand. That's a grammar thing.

Impeachment? Hell, No—Impalement

I don't know about you guys but I am so sick and tired of these lying, thieving, holier-than-thou, right-wing, cruel, crude, rude, coarse, crass, cocky, corrupt, coercive, criminal, crooked, dishonest, dissolute, degenerate, debauched, delusional, jingoistic, homophobic, xenophobic, xylophonic, racist, sexist, ageist, fascist, cashist, arrogant, ignorant, inept, inbred, insipid, insolent, impotent, incompetent, incontinent, ineffectual, insufferable, pompous, gutless, spineless, shameless, noxious, poisonous, avaricious, malicious, brutal, brutish, inhuman, inhumane, spiteful, vengeful, persistent vegetative state grandstanding, nuclear-option threatening, evolution denying, irony-deprived, depraved, erectile dysfunctional, ethnic cleansing, ethics eluding, preemptory invading of a country that had absolutely nothing to do with 9/11, 35-day-vacation-taking, greedy exponential factor 15, domestic spying, CIA-outing, medical marijuana busting, union-busting, infrastructure destroying, roommate appointing, clear-cutting, torturing, jobs outsourcing, torture outsourcing, Constitution shredding, collateral damaging, Duke Cunninghaming, brush clearing, bicycle falling, pretzel choking, monkey-faced, hunchbacked, smirking, trust funding, draft-dodging, Moslem baiting, hurricane disregarding, oil company fellating, nonsense spewing, education ravaging, faith-based math and science advocating, anybody who disagrees with them slandering, ally-alienating, God and Flag waving, scaremongering, your hand under the rock the maggoty remains of a marsupial, just won't get off the Arctic National Wildlife Refuge drilling, two-faced, lawyer shooting, voting-machine tampering, sociopathic, psychopathic, consensuspathic, partisanpathic, pathicpathic, air and ground and water and media polluting (which is pretty much all the polluting you can get), vile, venal, vulgar, venomous, villainous, vomitus, vituperative, virulent, mephitic, bloodthirsty, yellow-bellied, oedipal (not edible), hypocritical, evil, not sure if I've said "evil" yet and I want to make damn sure I said evil, evil, cretinous, fool, toad, buttwipe, lizardstick, corporate, imperialistic, cowardly, slime bucket tools of the Bush Administration that I could just spit. Impeachment, hell no. Impalement. Upon the swift and righteous sword of the people's justice. Screw the sword, make it a curtain rod. 'Cuz it'll hurt more.

The Party of No Ideas vs. the Party of Bad Ideas

The Republicans are fond of accusing the Democrats of being a party without ideas. Well, after watching the GOP trot out the trite tripe it passes off as ideas for the last couple of years, I'll tell you, no ideas seem like a pretty damn good idea at this point. Estate taxes and gay bashing and flag burning seem to be their front-burner issues. Which, if you think about it, is pretty cynical on their part. Bashing gays while spending the bulk of their time down on their knees blowing the rich…kisses.

Since the beginning of the year, the best idea President Bush has come up with was a secret mission to capitalize on the death of Abu Musab al-Zarqawi. Think of it as the less-hyped and budgeted straight-to-DVD sequel to *Mission Accomplished*. A midnight run into the Green Zone startling Prime Minister Nouri al-Maliki like the honoree of a surprise 110th birthday party in a fireworks factory. All Dubyah ended up doing on his surreptitious secret-agent strike was cutting the Iraqi leader's autonomy off at the knees. That, and racking up about 24,000 Air Force One frequent-flyer miles. Which means that on his next trip the president gets a free movie. Maybe he'll finally get to see *An Inconvenient Truth*.

Instead of belying fears that the new Iraqi government is just a collection of American puppets, Bush's trip drew marionette strings above their heads with one of those four-inch-wide black Magic Markers. The industrial-strength kind with the indelible ink. And, with the ultimate puppet master, Karl Rove, convinced that the only way for Republicans to win the midterm elections in November is to focus on the war and to portray Democrats as congenital cut-and-runners, we can expect to see a lot more of these cynical surgical strikes into the heart of pseudoreality. When the going gets tough, the tough arrange photo-ops.

Recently, GOP Congressional candidates were given a 74-page briefing book to provide ammunition for a focused attack against Democrats for the midterms. One of the main tenets is that "withdrawal" means thousands of troops died for nothing, conveniently laying a perpetual base for eternal occupation. Like refusing to throw a vine to a guy halfway stuck in quicksand because his pants are already wet and it would insult his launderer.

Right now the Pro-War Boys' metabolisms are fluttering on high-speed alert, heartened by the spectacle of a semi-nonfierce battle raging among the Democrats over when to bring the troops home—now, later or subsequently. But maybe, just maybe, Mister Unindicted Co-Conspirator has gone to the well of fear one too many times. Let's face it, Democrats arguing among themselves is about as unusual as finding sand in the waistband of your shorts after a day at the beach.

Speaking of sand, one thing you can say now is that there's a line drawn in the hot Iraqi-Weapons-of-Mass-Destruction-Free sand for the voters. If you're looking for a party whose big, bad idea is to call anyone who disagrees with them "sending our boys to die for nothing" cowards, who you going to call? The Republicans. But if you just want to be entertained by people who have no idea how to stop fighting with each other, it's those wacky, peace-loving Democrats you want.

Demagogic Whistle-Stop

Oh, for crum's sake, people. It was a joke! "If you don't study in school you'll end up getting stuck in Iraq." Get it? *Like the president!* He can't get out of Iraq. He didn't study. He's stuck. John Kerry was talking about George Bush. He wasn't talking about our troops. John Kerry *was* a troop. Anybody who can't figure that out either is a cynical oaf hiding their scurrilous ass behind the troops, or is pretending they're dumber than they already are. From all appearances, the president falls into one of those categories, and if it's the latter, that's a very scary proposition indeed.

Right before Senator John Kerry blew the joke about how dumb people get stuck in Iraq, he blew another about how President Bush comes from the state of Texas but now lives in the state of denial. See, it's a pattern. That's ostensibly a joke, too. Didn't get much of a laugh on that one, either. In the "stuck in Iraq" joke, he left out the word "us." It was supposed to be "you'll end up getting *US* stuck in Iraq," which is funnier on paper, especially if you read the "US" as "U.S.," making it work on a couple of different levels. Both of which are way beyond the cognitive range of most college students in Pasadena. One reason why only dogs think John Kerry is funny.

Granted, the man has the timing of an end table. Part of the problem is, even when he tells a joke with all the words intact, it still doesn't sound like a joke. He's just not good at talking. He's good at thinking. Probably reads, too. I even bet he studied. But talking: not his strong suit, which, be honest, we've known for some time now. So he botched a joke. The president botched a war. Nobody ended up dead because of Kerry's botch. Except for a few Democratic Congressional campaign managers in Indiana, Pennsylvania and Ohio.

Where is our modern-day Joseph Welch to ask: "At long last, Mr. Bush, have you no sense of decency?" Because this grasping for the discarded shoe of a verbal slip on the campaign shoulder with election day looming like a stalled 18-wheeler in the fast lane of the voters' windshield is nothing but a cheap, expedient political ploy. Earlier on the campaign trail, the president called a vote for the Democrats a vote for the terrorists. Why didn't the fabled liberal media focus on that demagoguery? Because he does it all the time. Not what you call your new news. Kerry, however, was fresh meat, so the media voraciously jumped so far down his throat, all you could see coming out of his mouth was the cuffs of their pants and the soles of their shoes, being the only souls they possess. (Another joke that doesn't work on paper.)

And even though he's being attacked for something he didn't mean to do, I'm still pissed at Kerry for falling into the trap. For proving to the whole world he is such a bad politician that he almost blew an election he wasn't even running in. I just hope and pray this thing comes back to bite Bush in the butt bad. That the American people studied. And that, by keeping Iraq in the spotlight, those same plenty-smart Americans will be reminded how this Administration lied and spied and stole and sold and cheated and tortured and killed and ignored intelligence and promoted incompetence and defied international cooperation and incited religious intolerance and eschewed bipartisanship and exploited the very same troops they pretend to be offended on behalf of—and that, my friends, is no joke. Go vote.

San Francisco Values

Hope you were hanging onto something solid last week, because this country lurched so hard to the left that half of Washington woke up with a wicked case of whiplash. No, make that *most* of Washington. And all of K Street. The Republicans should be grateful. Because if it weren't for such Democratic persistence they wouldn't still be able to file for protection under the Endangered Species Act.

The semielectoral tsunami means the new Speaker of the House, Nancy Pelosi, is next in line after Dick Cheney in presidential succession. In other words, she's only two chicken bones away from the presidency. And Bush does not look like a picky eater. Does the term "unchewed pretzel" have any meaning here? Not to mention one loud noise takes Cheney out like *that*, leading to…President Pelosi. To conservatives, that's got to be scarier than a raw-meat bathing suit in a shark tank.

Since she's the human embodiment of what right-wing talk-show hosts refer to as (cue theme music from *Psycho*) the extreme agenda of San Francisco values, people all over the

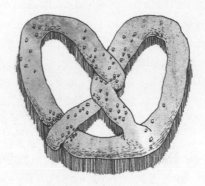

country are curious as to what exactly are these alarming values? Glad you asked. Pull up a chair, plop the kids in front of *CSI: Topeka* and let me tell you about Pelosi and the den of iniquity she represents that serves as my home, the city on the bay named for Saint Francis of Assisi.

For those of you who can't wait to get Nancy Pelosi down on the ground to shave her head and expose her horns, I regret to inform you, they aren't there. She's a kindly old grandma now, and although her smile does look like some fiend is twisting a knobby pole inserted up her butt, the ironic part is, in San Francisco, this supposedly frighteningly extreme liberal is considered a moderate and frequently protested by leftist factions for planting herself too deep in the mainstream and selling out. And yeah, some of those factions also believe the same is true of Fidel.

The best way to analyze "The City," as we in San Francisco presumptively call ourselves, is to look to the movies. Like in *The Wizard of Oz,* when Dorothy says, "We're not in Kansas anymore," that's our motto. Then, at the end of *Peter Pan,* when Tinkerbell almost dies and the only thing that can save her is audience applause? Well, that's us, too. We're not Kansas and we clap for fairies. So what? Big deal. Who cares?

San Francisco beliefs center on the rights of the individual. Our biggest moral flaw is that we hate judgmental people—a bit of an internal fallacy, I'll admit. We go out of our way not to place restrictions on people or their actions or religions or appearances. When you think about it, what right-wingers are really afraid of is the freedoms the citizens of San Francisco enjoy. That's right, they hate us for our freedoms.

We may be part of America, but we're the exception that proves the rule. You've heard of "thinking outside the box"? Well, we outlawed corners. We're as far beyond that whole red/blue thing as a sperm whale is beyond a toothpick. We're not blue. We're indigo. Eggplant. Plum. Aubergine. Periwinkle. And yes, we do know the difference. Recent revelations seem to suggest that a large percentage of Americans *do* know the difference between hope and hopeless. And here in the 415 area code, we revel in the fact that we are no longer the last pocket of resistance.

Who's the Comeback Kid Now?

Guess who the Republicans snuck in as Senate Minority Whip? Trent Lott. Yes, *that* Trent Lott. Welcome back, buddy! You're a breath of stale air. And just the shot of smack in the arm the GOP needs. A return to the good old high-flying junkie days of yore when votes stayed counted and people had priorities. Winning. At all costs.

Don't worry about those silly racist slur charges. Hardly anybody remembers how or why you were unceremoniously bounced from your Majority Leader position in the first place. That was four long years ago, which, in politics, is measured via carbon dating. It was so long ago we hadn't discovered the phantom nature of weapons of mass destruction yet. When President Bush had a higher approval rating than the puppy-eating-snake level he's at now. Back when he acted like he was better than you. And acted to reclaim a position of power right after the midterms that he fumbled away like a running back wearing ham mittens…a genius move. As was the secret ballot. (Need more of those in the Senate.)

As per your controversial speechifying about how better off America would be if Strom Thurmond's presidential bid on the Segregationist Dixiecrat ticket had been successful: Don't sweat it, man, people already forgot. Most Americans are hard pressed to recall anything before the last *Lost*. And your 25-to-24 vote margin in the Asleep at the Wheel Party Sweepstakes is especially delicious, considering that these are the same folks who insist they're doing all they can to reach out to minorities. Apparently they still don't realize you were arguing that integration is bad. Besides, you did apologize, and if nobody could quite understand what you were saying because of the hood muffling your words, tough.

Trust me, time heals all wounds. Your explanation of the Thurmond gaffe—that you were just trying to make an elderly gentleman feel good, and that it was a mistake of the mouth not of the heart—was brilliant. Didn't matter if no one knew what you were talking about. It was so zen. A much hipper proposition today than back in 2002. And no, no, no, *nobody* recollects that this incident was so serious even President Bush felt compelled to weigh in: "There's no room in the Republican Party for racists." Gee, we knew there were a lot of them, didn't think all the slots were full. Must be some sort of alternative affirmative action program going on somewhere. Don't let Scalia hear about this.

Then, last year, when you wondered aloud about the Sunnis and the Shiites and their penchant for killing each other: "How do they tell the difference? They all look alike to me," you know what that was? That was you channeling the American public.

All those swarthy people *do* look alike. Just as all the Republican leadership looks alike. Overly groomed, mirthless, clueless and whiter than the inside of small-bore cottage cheese.

The good news for the Republicans is that, after less than two weeks of wandering in the wilderness, there's a light at the end of the tunnel. The bad news for the American people is, the light being produced just might be coming from the flames emanating from a fiery cross.

The Center Left, Right?

Does anybody know what happened to the center? I remember hearing about it in the old days, but it seems to have disappeared like a wisp of mist in a solar wind. All anybody talks about is the left and the right. On CNN: "From the left. And from the right." On Fox News: "From the right. From the righter." We're so polarized these days, I'm surprised our compasses still work. They should be stuck on due daft. To paraphrase Ronald Reagan speaking about the Democratic Party: I didn't leave the center, the center left *me*. And you can blame Uncle Ronnie for triggering the seismic shift that shoved the center to the right. For instance:

Q. What did they call the homeless before Reagan?
A. Mental patients.

Bush One wallowed in Ronnie's footsteps and kicked the center a bit more rightwise, and even Bill Clinton nudged it not less than a little. Then Bush Two…fugetaboutit. He attached a rocket booster to the edge of the center and shot it so far west of Texas you can't see it anymore due to the curvature of the earth. Now, I grew up a moderate. A raging moderate, perhaps, but a moderate nonetheless. Yet these guys keep moving the center. I stay in the same place, and suddenly I'm a Marxist. Just because I believe a society should be based on how it treats its least fortunate, not its most fortunate. And that makes me a commie pinko yellow rat bastard? How the hell did that happen?

Think about it. Nixon: civil rights, the Environmental Protection Agency. He'd have problems getting the Democratic nomination for Lieutenant Governor in Massachusetts. Goldwater, who said about gays in the military, "You don't have to be straight to shoot straight," would be written off as an enemy of our troops and a close personal friend of Nancy Pelosi's hairstylist, if you know what I mean.

Twenty percent of the country is, has been and always will be far left. And 20 percent is far right. The rest of us are in the middle. Between the fringes. You could say we are average, ordinary or even, God forbid, normal. Me, I'm just a middle-aged, middle-class, Middle American of medium height and medium build who likes his steaks medium rare. And that's the only thing exemplary about me.

Like a lot of us, I'm just a guy—a regular guy tired of having to pick either Anne Coulter or Sheryl Crowe as my spokesperson. These women have as much to do with me as a Madagascar hissing cockroach has to do with the United Auto Workers Pension Fund. Crowe is a great singer but, as an activist, she's a bit much. Wants to restrict all Americans to one square of toilet paper per bathroom visit. All right, lady, but you're doing my laundry.

I blame Starbucks for instigating semantic size corruption. Selling America a medium-sized coffee and calling it "grande." Their small is known as "tall." Everybody expects to be special. Extraordinary. Everything has to be extreme. The only thing I want extreme is the action of my laxative. And even that has to be under severely controlled conditions.

We're not just losing the middle, we're losing the middle class, which is not a good thing. 'Cuz when the middle class disappears, you start to hear things like "Eat the rich," and, trust me, nobody wants that. The rich are way too stringy. All that free time to exercise. They can afford the good machines. Let me tell you, the fat poor is where it's at. Mmmmm. The fat poor...tastes just like chicken. So if you see the center or know what happened to it, please contact me ASAP. Reward on return.

God's Only Party

Earlier this week, a clandestine cadre of controlling conservative Christian captains (bunch of right-wing religious nut jobs, is what I'm getting at) threatened to run from the GOP like ducks from an alligator the size of a Buick if any infidel they don't anoint is nominated for president. And yes, specific former New York City mayors were mentioned. Funny you should ask.

At a meeting in Salt Lake City (where else—you thought Vegas, maybe?), Heaven's Soldiers collectively decided they would rather support a burned-beyond-recognition, duck-billed platypus with wire coat-hanger hands than a certain Mr. Rudolph Giuliani. Apparently, they do not consider the mayor of 9/11 to be the answer to their prayers.

Oh, they have their reasons. Giuliani's serial inclination to appear at fundraisers in drag, resulting in his being photographed wearing a dress more often than Hillary Clinton, could be one. His brazen courting of the pro-choice, pro–gay rights, pro–gun control wing of the Republican Party might be another. The fact that the whole Rudy clan, including both ex-wives (two too many), is campaigning for other people doesn't help much, either. A bit of a sticky wicket, that: trying to swing Independents with your Family Value bona fides, when your own family hates you. With megaphones.

The Zealot Heads went so far as to talk out loud about forming their very own party if Giuliani *does* weasel his way to the top of the ticket. And since white Protestant evangelicals make up a third of the electorate in the early primary states of Iowa and South Carolina, they believe the threat of mass defection is too big a bluff for the GOP leadership to call. Because, as we all know, a Republican Party without Christian conservatives is like a snake handler with no snake. A scorpion minus the stinger. Hell without dental surgery.

You might think this is one of those cut-off-your-nose-to-spite-your-face kind of deals, because, well, it is. But evangelicals are sick and tired of being taken for granted, and count on party bigwigs to remember how Ross Perot threw the '92 and '96 elections to Bill Clinton. Which in those kinds of Kool-Aid circle jerks is like handing the keys of your children's soul to Satan for a bucket of deep-fried Twinkies. But let's leave Bush's fiscal policy out of this.

Not only are some dogmatic noses severely out of joint from having the door of implemented policy change slammed in their apostolistic faces, but they also have a few canonistic bones to pick with some of their recent higher-profile disciples like Mark Foley, David Vitter, Larry Craig and the Creator's own personal mouthpiece, Ted Haggard. Guys whose newsreels feature more extracurricular sexual footage than you'd run into at the Moonlight Bunny Ranch during an after-hours party for the Adult Video Awards.

Of course, if they *do* form a third party, the big question is what to call it. "The Holier Than Thou Party" is a bit offputting. "God's Only Party" would be confusing, especially if the media tried to acronym it. "The Everyone Has to Live Like We Think They Should Live Party" is probably too long. I did come up with what I think could be the perfect name, but I'm pretty sure "The Taliban" is already taken.

Eight Reasons It Would Behoove All American Guys to Be Pro-Choice

There's a huge Pro-Choice March in Washington next weekend, and thousands of women are expected to swarm the Capital from all over the country to demonstrate en masse how they're as distressed as a wedding party in the gondola of a hot air balloon approaching electrical wires. Distressed over the future of *Roe v. Wade* due to some cranky, self-proclaimed righteous members of Congress equipped with minuscule members. These, my friends, are women who are determined they will not be trifled with, especially for the sake of energizing some phantom political base. They are concerned women. Alarmed women. Women anxious over the prospect that the Bush Administration has plans up its collective sleeve to continue the slow dissolution of rights over controlling what happens to the female body. I would rather dance naked in the aisles between the fry bins of a Popeyes Chicken during rush hour than mess with these women. What has happened is the edges of a woman's right to choose are being nibbled away to where it won't be long before no right will be left at all. Think of a cheeseburger with no burger, cheese or bun.

What's missing in all this righteous indignation is one important segment in the bridge to real choice. And that chunk of asphalt is…us: the Y chromosomes. Because, hey guys, this isn't just a Women's March, this is a Rights March, and we too have a lot riding on the future where this train wreck of a policy is headed. Unless something as drastic as a 180-degree turnaround in the Executive, Legislative and Judicial branches is looming over the horizon, unhappy women will be roaming this land of ours. And just as unhappy men make for unhappy women, unhappy women make for unhappy men. It's a yin-yang thing. So I'm here to convince dudes all over this great country how our best interests are at stake here as well.

Reasons for All American Guys to Be Pro-Choice

- It's only a matter of time before some smart-ass scientist figures out how to get men pregnant. And then what?
- If the Administration gets away with this, what keeps it from outlawing the use of maple syrup in the bedroom?
- An empowered woman is a limber woman.
- Fewer children equals less congestion at sports bars.
- If we aren't successful, it'll get to the point where abortions are still legal, but there's a 10-month waiting period.
- More romantic candlelit picnics, fewer Huggie runs.
- Pro-choice rallies a lot more fun than anti-choice rallies, especially to those with hair spray allergies.
- Child support is not tax deductible.

Leading the Pack Away from the Leader

"Welcome back to *Meet the Press*. In this segment, our guest is the distinguished Representative from the Third District of Wyoming. Congressman, welcome. As you know, the D.C. Police have announced today that the House Majority Leader has been found naked in a bathtub next to a dead prostitute, hugging a bloody axe, the suspected murder weapon, to his chest, with the words 'Yes, I did it. Me.' written with the victim's blood on the bathroom mirror in the Congressman's own handwriting. We've just heard a senior member of the Minority delegation voice his argument as to why the Leader deserves to have at least one, if not both, of his hands slapped. Do you, sir, agree with this punishment, which would involve the admonishment of a member of your own party?"

"Thank you, Tim. With all due respect to my good friend of long standing and esteemed associate from across the aisle,

I condemn this character assassination of our revered Leader, so obviously a scurrilous partisan attack, solely meant to distract us, the party of ideas, from accomplishing the tasks that the good and hard-working people of America sent us here to Washington to achieve. I will tell you who the true victim is here, and it's not this alleged 'prostitute.' It's America, Tim. And America's crying, because it is abundantly clear this is simply an assault by the radical left-wing press as part of their fundamental agenda to tear down the Leader's leadership in which he excels by leading.

"Blood was found? What does that mean, Tim? Are we certain it is blood or could it possibly be just a bloodlike substance? Ketchup, perhaps? Heinz ketchup, perhaps? And let's say the jackbooted goons from *CSI: DC* do indeed find it to be blood—might it not have come from one of the apes my distinguished adversary and his godless ilk are so certain we evolved from? Isn't the planting of this so-called blood just another example of the lengths to which the liberal media conspiracy and treacherous cadre of Al-Qaeda sympathizers will go to railroad the man they hold responsible for many of the American freedoms they hate so much?

"I was under the impression, Tim, that this was still a free country, where a man is innocent till proven guilty. Have the Communists taken over? Has the Supreme Court suspended the 21st Amendment while I wasn't looking? I have seen nothing, outside of a few grainy, misleading photos of a naked woman hacked to bits, that leads me to believe this is anything but a conscientious civil servant trying to lead our country out of the darkness we were plunged into on 9/11. We must not leap to conclusions. How do we know the Leader wasn't trying to warm the woman with his body heat after her ill-fated attempt at suicide?

"I'll tell you one thing: Our Leader is a fighter, and if the spineless cowards in charge of this politically motivated lynching think he is going to run away and hide because of one dead prostitute, they got another think coming. I, for one, trust the fine and hard-working American people to see through this transparent fabrication as nothing but the fever dream of a bankrupt party striking out with their tiny little girlie-fists whose marching orders for this bogus partisan witch hunt can be traced directly to the sticky desk of Hillary Clinton's felonious husband. Thank you, Tim. Oh…and how 'bout those Nationals?"

Ethics Bye-Bye

Well, I hope you enjoyed last year's ethics investigations of Tom DeLay, because they are the last ethics investigations you will likely ever see conducted by the House of Representatives. Did I say "ever"? Because I meant to say, "ever." Or let me state it in a classical sense: Nevermore.

Permit me to explain. The House Ethics Committee consists of an equal number of members from each party: three Democrats and three Republicans. Under the old rules, a tie committee vote meant an investigation would ensue. That is, if all three opposing-party committee people voted for an inquiry of a Representative, it went through, no matter what anyone from the member's own party thought. Because what the members of their own party usually think is "Hey, I don't care what you said he did, leave our guy alone, you big creepy hypocritical bullies." And you know what: They're right.

Now, however, the rules have changed. With their first piece of business on the first day of the 109th Congress, Republican leaders of the House modified the rule so that a deadlock of the Ethics Committee ends up with no action taken. Which means somebody from the same party as the member under scrutiny has to vote for an investigation, which means…no investigations. Ever. Again. The era of ethics investigations in the House of Representatives is over. It is history. A memory. Expired. Dodo City. In the archives. It's gone. Wave bye-bye.

Not that I mean to suggest the House Ethics Committee was ever that effective, in the first place. As a matter of fact, among us comics, it became a shorthand generic joke meaning "oxymoronic," as in "House Ethics Committee." That's a lot like saying "military intelligence" or "Swedish banana farm" or "Soviet fashion plate" or "Henry Kissinger Fact-Finding Commission." It goes on, but you get the idea.

Yet there was always the appearance of a self-regulating body. Hands got slapped. But apparently now Republican House leaders believe their people are so corrupt, they can't afford the pretense of propriety anymore. Hand slapping is off limits.

The Democrats whined and sputtered, as they always do, "They can't *do* that!" Well, not only *can* they do that, but they *have* done that, and here's the real irony: The Republicans are just tracing the playbook written by the Dems back in the '70s on how to play hard-ball "powertics" on the Hill. Of course, power goes in cycles, and getting stuck with the very stick you whittled is an old tradition in D.C. As bad as it is now for the Democrats might be exactly how bad it will be for the Republicans in another 20 years. When that very same high-pitched whine may be coming from *them*. Ain't life odd?

3 | Upper
Lower
Middle

That darn class warfare is rearing its ugly head again, as it tends to do now and then (and this is most definitely now). Exacerbating the conflict is the disappearance of one of those classes, which is on the verge of total evaporation before our very eyes. No, no, no, it's not the lower one of which I speak. That class seems to be doing just fine, in terms of size.

You could say it's flourishing faster than Chinese child-labor camps can pump out counterfeit Louis Vuitton bags. And speaking of the upper class...well, I guess the simplest way of putting it is, not doing too badly over the last seven years. So which class is it that is disappearing? We'll let you do the math. No checking your neighbor's paper!

An Important Message from Your Family at YourBank

We here at YourBank realize you and yours might be a little worried about the recent legislation removing burdensome regulations on financial institutions voted into law by both houses of Congress and signed by the president. Well, we don't blame you. You'd have to be dumber than a bucket of bacon-and-cheese potato skins not to figure out that the economic jungle out there is growing so thick, it's a wonder Ben Bernanke can tell the difference between interest rates on a three-year Treasury Bond and yellow paint.

Let us take this time to put your mind at ease. You know what these changes are? They're good. And overdue. Real good and way overdue. Eensy teensy tiny little corrections designed solely with you, our most valued assets, in mind. These minor adjustments, a fine-tuning if you will, are simply one additional way for the YourBank family to streamline and modernize our operations to provide a wider path for you, YourBank's most precious collateral, to navigate today's labyrinth of modern-day financial frontiers in your never-ending search for fiduciary freedom. Available, as always, with an interest-free smile.

An extensive battery of concerned focus groups has informed our marketing department that you don't want a lot of perplexing "decisions" slowing down your day, so we're doing our best to make sure that, when the smoke clears, Your-Bank remains standing as your one and solitary choice when seeking fiscal security. YourBank understands what every North American family (soon to include the Virgin Islands) knows: that blocking growth and communication leads to such problems as isolation, shrinking market shares, diminished quarterly dividends and external audits.

That's why we're proud to take this opportunity to announce the introduction of the new "One-Rate" convenience fee from YourBank. Tired of all those confusing, ever-changing charges for automated banking? Who wouldn't be? One institution tacks on a user fee for each online service dial-up, while another nails you even more, just for utilizing their ATM, while your bank (not YourBank!) adds another equally outrageous fee. If you're not worried those security cameras might be pointing the wrong way, we are.

Now YourBank takes the guesswork out of banking. Our new "One Rate" convenience fee guarantees that each and every transaction you make will always be the same special low user-friendly price of...$5.00. That way, you'll always know you're getting the same beneficial easy-to-remember rate no matter when or why or how you attempt to try to do business with us. No hassles. No confusion. No hidden surcharges. Just the same convenient price. Anytime. Anywhere. For anything. You'll never have to wonder if you're being ripped off again.

Remember, YourBank is committed to doing only what *you* would do if you were in our shoes. YourBank. Where our only job is to work as hard as we can to make your money...*our* money. The new, one-stop marketplace for your every monetary, insurance, brokerage and pawn requirements. Join the YourBank Family Today.

Coming soon: YourBank Preowned Autos, YourBank-Managed Residential Care, and YourBank Protein Breakfast Bars. YourBank: a division of Tyco.

Blue Collar Decathlon

OK, so a large number of us normal folk are screwed to the screen right now watching large men with muscles in places we don't even have places and miniature, elastic-boned, aeronautically designed women compete in the Olympics, in which most of us can imagine ourselves contesting with the same grace, speed and élan as a three-legged armadillo wind surfing. Sometimes you see a sport like baseball or basketball and go, "I could do that!" Yeah, right. But here, that's not going to happen without the help of Industrial Light & Magic. I'd need a blue screen and animated assistance just to run 100 meters. But we *do* do stuff I'm not sure athletes even understand. People who work for a living have mastered events that so far have not received medal status. So I've come up with the Blue Collar Decathlon, games in which we can all contend.

1. Pouring a Cup of Coffee While It's Still Brewing Free-style.
2. The Three-Bus Crosstown Transfer Dash.
3. Family-of-Five Theme Park Weekend for Under $200 Scramble.
4. The 45-Second Breakfast Sprint.
5. Day Before Payday Grocery Run.
6. The Three-Job Individual Medley.
7. Broken Basement Bulb Midnight Obstacle Crawl.
8. Tax-Day Crunch.
9. Biting Your Tongue in Front of Your Boss Marathon.
10. Retrieving a Corncob Holder from the Garbage Disposal Clean and Jerk.

Welcome! Kneel!

Like a Doberman with a chew toy, the Republican Party loves to wave its bloody new divisive social issues in front of the electorate, accomplishing the dual mission of energizing its base and placing Democrats on the defensive like a mongoose in a cobra cage. And they got themselves a doozy this time. An issue guaranteed to drive a stake deeper into the American consciousness than a six-state-wide red, white and green backhoe. The only problem is this particular division is so effective it's starting to get stuck in the hearts of fellow Republicans as well. It's called immigration. And to witness the wailing and the flailing, it has reached a state of crisis. A situation building since 1492. "Can't let those damn immigrants in—they'll ruin everything." A popular modern refrain taken from the original Iroquois. And, as it turns out, the Iroquois were right.

Counting the president, who is trying to shepherd through his own plan, there are approximately 536 separate immigration bills running around Capitol Hill these days. Bush's plan includes a provision for "guest workers," which is political shorthand for "Think of it as a five-year slumber party, and when it's over, everybody calls their parents and gets a ride home in their jammies." If you ask me, the term "guest worker" is a bit of an oxymoron. Another way of saying, "Welcome! Kneel!"

Senator Doctor Indian Chief Bill Frist has floated the most draconian proposal. His is the moral equivalent of corralling immigrants onto meat farms, to be ground up and served as frozen enchilada filling. Never mind the fact that U.S. undercover agents announced they were able to use fake documents to sneak the makings of a dirty bomb across our border. And yet all we can talk about is the wanton lawlessness of the people picking our vegetables and vacuuming our office cubicles.

Congress did reach a compromise. They agreed to build a 700-mile-long fence. On a 1,952-mile-long border. Because, God knows, nobody will ever think of going around. Or bringing a ladder. Besides, in this day and age, logistically, exactly how *do* we plan to build a 700-mile-long, 16-foot-high fence along the Mexican border without using Mexican labor? What's the plan here? Draft housewives from La Jolla?

I got to be honest. I fail to understand the fear here. "You let all these Mexicans in, they're going to take all those fruit-picking jobs I've dreamed of all my life. Working outdoors, sleeping in my car, fighting with dogs for food. Just like camping, only different." I do understand this is an emotional subject, not always rooted in what you call your logic. A couple of years ago, I was in Billings, Montana, and actually saw rednecks hassle some Native Americans: "Go back to where you came from." Talk about unclear on the concept.

"Give me your tired, your poor, your huddled masses yearning to breathe free." That's not just an archaic inscription on a big green lady, that's a philosophical summons to heroism. The United States of America that we know and love. A country in which we're all immigrants. And when you look at the big picture, with California as a former part of Mexico, in essence, immigrants are going back to where they came from. Maybe it's we Anglos who should be carrying the green cards. Who wouldn't just love to take a bullhorn into the Capitol Rotunda, yell "*Migra!*" and watch Congress scatter? OK. Just me.

Gouging? What Gouging?

HHHHHHHHHHEEEEEEEEEEEEEEEEYYYYYYYYYYYY! Sorry. Didn't mean to startle you. I'm just tired of talking to myself here. Worried about shredding my vocal cords shouting into a vacuum. Apparently some of you have been nodding off.

And don't give me that "who, me?" crap. You know who you are. Yes, you. The ones who are waiting for the president to do something about this gas price thing. The ones who mistook that lame B.S. oozing out of his "Gosh, gas prices are getting high, aren't they?" press conference as sincere. When are you going to get it through your tiny little heads? He's not here to help.

Let me go through this one more time. Stay with me. It's not that complicated. The president is a Texas oilman. His father is a Texas oilman. His vice president is a Wyoming oilman who shoots Texas lawyers. All the rich people he knows, his father knows and Dick Cheney knows have 30-weight running through their veins. *All the people who gave him the money that put him in the White House are oilmen.* Does this clear anything up? Maybe a little? His major priority is to pay them back in spades, then they tell him what a good job he's doing and give him *more money*.

So if you're waiting for him to grow a spine or learn to read or ever, ever, *ever* go so far as erecting a single, solitary obstacle in the way of folks' making obscene profits on fossil fuels…you'd best be advised not to hold your breath unless you enjoy that certain bluish look most often associated with people no longer eligible for Social Security benefits due to the fact that they've become altogether much too skinny and dead. Get it? Got it. Good.

The president says, "There's no magic wands." No kidding. Neither are there talking fish or fairy wings or giant toadstools upon which Donald Rumsfeld can perch naked eating flies with his bifurcated tongue. What's your point? Bush plans to investigate possible collusion or price fixing and the good news is, the report is already finished and it turns out everything is okey-dokey, folks. Everything is on the up and up, and George knows because his buddies assured him it is.

He also plans to relax environmental rules, which you could see coming like an 18-wheeler full of concrete blocks rolling off a 45-degree ramp straight up the driveway toward your front door. He wants to boost domestic supply, which is code for *Arctic National Wildlife Refuge, baby,* and he's delaying deposits into our Strategic Petroleum Reserve, which might save a thimble's worth. Measures destined to be about as effective as cross-country skis on a duck.

I've come up with a few other things the president could do that would be as effective to cut gas prices.

- Run around in circles till he gets dizzy and falls down.

- Bang a walking stick on the ground real hard, like Nanny McPhee.

- Get the entire House of Representatives to sing "Jeremiah Was a Bullfrog" in the key of off.

- Lay a wreath of $80 gas receipts at the tomb of the unknown SUV driver.

- Shoot a 78-year-old Texas lawyer in the face with a gun.

- Propose a bill that gives more tax incentives to oil companies.

- And the last thing the president can do that will be as effective as what he's doing now in cutting gas prices: mandate that the oil companies change their accounting practices to base 12 so those profits don't look so big.

The First Green President

In the middle of the president's midwinter publicity tour, NBC's Brian Williams asked him whether the federal government's faltering response to Hurricane Katrina was due to racial indifference. For half a second you could almost hear Dubyah's vertebrae fuse together as he perceptibly grew about a quarter of a millimeter and his reedy twang trembled and he snarled, with a noticeable lack of TelePrompting, "You can call me anything you want, but do not call me a racist."

Which was not the point, but it is true. It's not fair to call the president of the United States a racist. This is not a man who gives the tiniest whit about black or white. This is a man who only cares about green. And whether or not you have any. He doesn't judge people by the color of their skin. He judges people by the size of their wallet. In George Bush's America, if you're wealthy, you'll get taken care of. If you're not, you won't. Pretty much as simple as that. And for the rest of this diatribe I will mostly restate that argument in increasingly creative ways, so please feel free at any time to skip on over to the commie pinko yellow rat bastard book reviews.

Not only is Bush not a racist, he is neither an ageist nor a sexist nor a fascist nor a typist. Nor a homophobe. Nor a xenophobe. Rather, he is a cashist. The first green president, but about as friendly to the Sierra Club as a patch of thistles is to nylon stockings. The only whales he's interested in saving are the kind that get comped 2,500-square-foot Jacuzzi suites in Vegas.

Look at his record. Tax cuts for the wealthy. Economic stimuli for the wealthy. Legislative amendments for the wealthy. Overseas incentives for the wealthy. Judicial appointments designed to nurture favorable decisions for the wealthy. Secret winking clandestine loopholes for the wealthy. Complimentary all-you-can-eat seafood buffets with a pearl in every oyster for the wealthy. No-bid contracts for his buddies. Who just happen to be, say it with me now...*wealthy*.

For the poor: You got your cuts. Winter heating subsidy cuts for the poor. Student aid cuts for the poor. Medicaid and Medicare cuts for the poor. Food stamp and nutritional cuts for the poor. Education cuts for the poor. Outlandish dress codes at State Dinners to further disenfranchise the poor. Outsourcing jobs to create more poor. With George Bush in charge, it's a bull market for poor. On the other hand, it's not fair to accuse him of not knowing how poor people live. You see pictures of him looking out the windows of Air Force One as he flies over them, all the time.

To boil it down, if you got money, just sit yourself back in a comfy chair and prepare to get showered with more. If you ain't got nothing, expect him and his people to throw up roadblocks, Plexiglas, guard dogs, razor wire, enough red tape to wrap a moose: whatever it takes to keep you from getting any of theirs.

I know that on paper the theory is "trickle down." That rich people will spend their money, which eventually will trickle down to the poor. But my theory is that theory is crap. And not just on paper. Rich people hang onto their money. That's how they got rich. You give us poor people money and we'll spend every damn penny we get our grubby little hands on. Why do you think we're poor? Blowing it on silly, superfluous stuff like food and rent and medicine and gasoline. Foolish, profligate us. Besides, I don't know about you, but I'm tired of being trickled on.

So, let's be straight about this. Kanye West, although a wonderful singer and deserving of the Best Song Grammy for "Gold Digger," is dead wrong about the president. George Bush doesn't hate black people. George Bush doesn't hate poor people, either. He just *loves* rich people. A whole lot. We're talking love of operatic magnitude. Like a fellow waiter back in Milwaukee used to tell me, "It's not that I like the rich more than the poor, it's just that they tip so much better."

Not Your Species, Monkey Boy

In response to what hopefully is the final tail-slapping video of *The Frenzied Errant Whale Saga: The Sequel,* I have some advice for the people in charge that might come in handy the next time a couple of oceangoing behemoths appear in waters in which you don't think they belong. *Leave them alone. Get out of their way. Don't even look at them.* Let the immense beasts go their own way without your questionable assistance. They are not your species, monkey boy. You are helping the same way silverware helps a garbage disposal.

Especially when your idea of help consists of poking them with sticks, banging on pipes, spraying with fire hoses and piping underwater recordings of killer-whale noises near where you think they might be. Pretty much the watery equivalent of throwing crap against a wall and seeing what sticks. You had no idea what you were doing. You had no idea if it helped. You had no idea if you made it worse. Why? Because, listen closely, You Are Not a Whale.

And I know you can't control the urge to anthropomorphize everything to cute and cuddly Beanie Baby status, but come on: Delta & Dawn? Gag. You don't give solemn, ancient, behemoth creatures punny, adorable names. Their real monikers are probably elegant mournful sounds like *Errraauuuuuuuuuugh* and *Meeeeaaaraaauuuugh.* How would you like it if a whale called your daughter *Reeeuuuuubaaaaaaag* on TV?

No, we don't know why they're here. Who cares? Maybe they had a telepathic message for Nancy Pelosi to get her act together or they were changing the batteries on the Delta's pollution monitors, or maybe fresh water annoys the barnacles on their dorsals. Then again, maybe their ancestors regaled them with heroic humpback tales of the Delta and they were moseying around looking at the legendary sights; just really big tourists. Like the Germans at Yosemite. With blowholes. And yes, that is funny and, no, it's not redundant.

Could be they're related to that whale who made the same trip about 20 years ago. Remember him? You named him Humphrey. He meandered around the Delta for a month and nothing you did deterred him. And you banged on the same pots and shot off the same fire hoses this time around. What, did you think using Teflon pots was going to make the difference? Or maybe this year's sticks were pointier. Wait, I got it: These recorded orca sounds were high-def CDs.

Here's another tip: *You don't speak humpback.* Be careful of your communication attempts. For all you know, the sounds you were making got translated as "Anchovy Bar: Straight Ahead," or "Special humpback discount on all things krill!" Or, "Danger, danger. For the sake of the planet, swallow the entire boat in front of you *now!*"

I have a theory as to why they returned to sea. Either they were distressed at all the diesel fuel you were wasting exhibiting your extreme concern, or they were afraid your concern might turn taxidermic. Does the term "hunting for blubber" have any meaning here? "Save the Whales," my ass. They're whales. Save yourself.

Free Speech Ain't Free. Oh, Wait a Minute. Yeah, It Is.

After all the brouhaha in New York City this week, this seems like a good time to have us a little chat about free speech. Not restricted free speech. Not partial free speech. Not pseudo-semi-counterfeit-limited-free speech. Not free speech on Wednesdays between 2 and 3 p.m. EDT. Not free speech zones and not free speech reserved for the people we like and kept from the ones we don't. No, my friends, I'm talking about your total, unfettered, full-throated, in your face, front-row death metal rock concert, spitting in the wind, 24/7, every square inch of your big white furry butt, gushing like runoff from a rain gutter off a cantilevered roof during a Force 5 hurricane in the tropics free speech.

There's no whining about who gets to speak at what college. We're supposed to be setting an example. Doesn't matter out of which holes the free speech is coming. The mouths of an opposition politico or the biggest little two-bit dictator in the world or the personification of Lucifer himself, replete with red horns and forked tail and cloven hooves. But let's leave the vice president out of this one.

Everybody gets to say their piece. That's the deal. Even if half the world considers that "piece" total B.S. Face it, half of what *we* believe usually turns out to be total B.S. Beliefs have this nagging tendency to mutate over time. It wasn't long ago they burned people as witches for not thinking the world was flat. Wasn't it Cardinal Richelieu who said treason is just a matter of dates?

The same way it's better to let 100 guilty people go free rather than convict 1 innocent person, it's better that we let 100 cretinous, fool, toad, buttwipes reveal themselves as boneheads, just so a safe platform for the idealistic visionary is guaranteed. Given enough rope, idiots are notoriously susceptible to hanging themselves from the noose of their own ridiculousness.

And yes, Mr. Iranian President Mahmoud Ahmadinejad, I'm talking about you. Admittedly, you got a lousy intro at Columbia University, but when you agree to a Q & A, the general routine is to answer the questions you get asked. And yeah, OK, the crowd laughed at you, and no, you can't execute them like the gays you say your country doesn't have. Our crowds enjoy free speech, too. Democracy is a bitch, isn't it? And next time, for crum's sake, wear a tie.

If free speech isn't what this country is all about, what the hell are we fighting for? Free speech ain't free. Oh, wait a minute. Yeah, it is. As we witnessed at the UN when both Presidents Bush and Ahmadinejad got to exercise their rights on the same day. Think of it: On one hand you got a religious fanatic who sponsors secret prisons and has antagonized the entire world, and on the other hand you got an Iranian. And you know why I get to say that? That's right. I think you're finally getting the hang of it.

Paris Hilton Paid for George Bush's Sins

Poor, poor Paris. OK. Admittedly, she's as likable as fingernails on a blackboard. Fingernails that have never been chipped in the normal pursuit of an actual day's work *and* brandishing an exclusive, not-for-sale Chanel-sparkle-enamel sheathing a recent $300 French manicure. But holy moley. People have jumped on the Kick Paris When She's Down train as if there were free stacks of $100 bills secreted in the seatback pockets.

Oh sure, I get the whole schadenfreude as a spectator sport. Our fascination with the train wreck of supercilious celebrity. Build them up to tear them down. It was cumulative. Year after year of exposure to her pirouetting down the runways of the world collecting obscene amounts of cash for supplying a face to "smug." Perfecting the art of being famous for being famous. My theory is part of this gleeful piling-on can be traced to our built-up frustration with Dubyah. We've got blue balls for accountability and are kicking this poor poodle of a person as a presidential proxy.

Last September she blew the illegal minimum of .08 after being caught driving erratically on what she described as a midnight burger run. Yeah. Right. Burger run. Redeeming her maxed-out frequent-burger card at the Fatburger on La Cienega, I'm sure. She was fined $1,500, given 36 months' probation and had her license suspended. Then in January, she was caught driving on that suspended license…twice. The second time clocked doing 70 in a 35. Should have been enough right there.

The 26-year-old wannabe pop star or spoiled heiress or fledgling actress or whatever the hell she is pleaded ignorance about the whole driving with a suspended license thing being illegal, apparently unfamiliar with the definition of "suspension" or, like Leona Helmsley, convinced the law only applies to us little people. Either she wasn't a good enough actress to sell the stupidity defense or she ran into a judge who just didn't like her attitude. Probably not the first time, but quite possibly the first time anybody was in a position to do something about it.

So, 45 days in prison. Reduced to 23 days, which she surrendered to serve but then the sheriff released her after 3 days due to an undisclosed medical condition. Which remains undisclosed. General consensus is she suffers from an allergy to icky coupled with a severe aversion to yuck. Whereupon all kinds of Hollywood hell broke out. The judge flipped out. Sent her back to jail. And much doubling over with undisguised merriment ensued. News anchors couldn't hide their delight: "Ha ha, rich girl. Welcome to the real world." Which they are familiar with how? Oh, that's right—by regularly reading stories based in it.

We're guilty as well, of pasting George Bush's face onto her emaciated frame. He is the Paris Hilton of presidents. The two of them share the smirk and the obliviousness and the trust funders' undying belief in their eternal impunity from culpability. If you were asked who better fit the definition of "clueless upper-class twit marinated in an overwhelming sense of entitlement and never held accountable for a single thing they ever did," would you pick Paris or George or both? Payback is a bitch. Especially proxy payback. Pardon Scooter Libby? Hell with that, Bush should pardon Paris. After all, she's paying for his sins.

George & Attila

When a ton of crap is dumped from way high above into the lake of our lives, we rarely worry about the tiny arcing droplets splashing on our face, mainly because we're too busy keeping our boats afloat and our breathing apparatuses above water. But I would like to spotlight a seemingly insignificant drop of moisture pooling at the end of our nose that is destined to affect us for the rest of our natural-born days. Namely: the name George. Which is getting such a bad rap these days, it will soon qualify for 12-step status. "Hi, my name's George and I'm a George." "Hi, George."

Even though this honorable moniker stands as a symbol of our country's birthing struggle, due to the father of our nation wrestling its honor from the crazed clutches of King George III, parents must be having second, third and no thoughts whatsoever about naming their kids George lest it be seen as a tacit approval of the ways and means of the current Administration. Hell, I bet the names Mothra, Dweezil and Philomena get better placement in the baby-name books than George and/or Georgette do over the next couple of decades. Wouldn't be surprised to hear Prince George, British Columbia, attempts to change its handle to Margaritaville.

Like the demise of free buffalo chicken wings during happy hour, all it takes is one or two little snortie pigs stuffing the plastic-bag-lined pockets of their overcoats to ruin it for everybody. Well, in this case, everybody named George. No, scratch that, I was right the first time: Ruin it for everybody. And for lowering the bar on this whole Jorgé thing so deep you'd have to dig about six feet underground just to get a sonar detection on it, the responsibility lies with the usual suspects: presidents numbers 41 and 43. But God knows, they are not alone.

Earlier this month, the alleged Boy George was busted for allegedly imprisoning an alleged male prostitute (triple extra credit for anybody who can hold that image in their head for more than 15 seconds), and now...*now*...along comes Medal of Freedom–winning (hack) former head of the CIA, George Tenet, who writes a book saying he was never that big a fan of the Iraq war and was a reluctant player, simply going along to get along, and now he's not sure if it was a good idea or not and enh, enhhhh enhh, weh weh weh weh weh, all the way home, and hey! What's that noise? Oh, it's the sound of the final nails being hammered into the George coffin. Dearly beloved, it is my sad duty to inform you that George, as we know it, is over. Exists no more. Elapsed. Expired. It's gone. Say bye.

This might even prove to be a fatal blow. A death knell for the venerable name of George. Kind of like what happened to Attila and Adolf and Maynard. Of course, pets will still be called George, based on the modern children's classics *George of the Jungle* and *Curious George.* While we grown-ups can only fantasize about how truly marvelous this world would be, if only we were blessed with a president whose mind had a predilection toward the latter rather than the geography of the former.

"Stupid People Love Bush," New Study Proves

According to the prestigious Southern California think tank The Gluton Group, stupid people prefer President George W. Bush over Senator John Kerry by a 4-to-1 margin. As Chief Resident Dr. Louis Friend characterized the results of the research, "The less intelligent you are, the more you like Bush." This landmark study, conducted over a five-month period, involved 2,400 likely voters bridging all economic strata in the 17 states generally considered up for grabs on November 2. Participants were tested for intelligence, then asked to fill out a 12-page series of questions involving the presidential candidates, with results released earlier this week.

The consensus: The higher the IQ, the less that people trust Bush and respect the job his Administration has done. The lower the IQ, the more that people admire his steadfastness. "It was pretty much a slam dunk. There's no nice way to say this. Dumb people like him. They think his unwavering nature is a positive personality trait. They venerate him for never admitting mistakes, even when he's wrong. On the other hand, smart people think he's a lying bully. I mean, c'mon, you have a deserter accusing a decorated veteran of treason. Who's going to buy that besides stupid people?"

Preliminary results:
IQ Above 140: Kerry 80%. Bush 20%.
120–140: Kerry 65%. Bush 35%.
100–120: Kerry 54%. Bush 46%.
80–100: Bush 54%. Kerry 46%.
60–80: Bush 60%. Kerry 15%. Dale Earnhardt Jr. 25%.

Apparently Bush's good–evil, black–white philosophy resonates on an inverse relationship with higher education, whereas it became evident over the period of analysis that John Kerry's nuanced arguments are only understood by people who paid attention in any class above the fifth grade. Dr. Friend elaborated: "It has to do with intellectual curiosity. Folks see Bush in front of a stream talking about the environment and they assume he's in favor of it, even though, if you read his legislation, I'd be surprised to hear him endorse shade. This also explains why Bush gets away with pretending he doesn't know how the Senate works, allowing him to call Kerry a flip-flopper."

Friend released evidence that this type of disconnect exists across the board: education, foreign policy, the economy, post-9/11 security response and State Dinner entertainment choices. Also discovered was a direct correlation between the number of preset country-western stations on car radios and Bush's approval rating. Dr. Friend attributes this phenomenon to the simplicity inherent in the messages indigenous to both. Classical music listeners were preponderantly Kerry supporters, but surprisingly, on heavy metal, the two split down the middle.

Spotting a trend, Dr. Friend cautioned, "Because of the deterioration in public education, larger and larger segments of the population are creeping downward IQ-wise, cementing the hold Republicans have on the electorate." However, if the election were held today, Bush would have a lead of 52 to 48 in the popular vote, but would be virtually tied in the Electoral College, which Bush supporters argue against because the word "College" angers them. When contacted, a Kerry spokesman just chuckled. No Bush spokesperson was made available for comment. It was also found that Ralph Nader supporters were the brightest of all political proponents tested, but Dr. Friend dismissed them as "too smart for their own good."

In a related study, smart people prefer baseball because the pace is such that there's time to read.

The Cheeseburger Bill

Well, I don't know about you, but I'm breathing a whole lot easier today. Whew. Oh yeah, I'll admit, I was a nervous wreck there for a while: anxious, sweating and just plain shivering like a shaved poodle nailed to the foul pole of Pac Bell Park on a night game in April. Now it's starting to look like it might be OK to exhale. Yeah, sure, the world is spinning out of control and our personal security is threatened every time John Ashcroft takes off his bedroom slippers, but we should thank our lucky stars our elected public officials are on the case. Guarding our best interests. No matter how much evidence you may think you have to the contrary, and admittedly, it is a huge, freaking

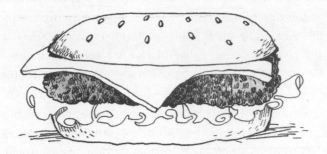

amount, I think it is safe to say that we, as a country, are finally back on track.

And exactly what leads me to this impression? How is Congress manning the watchtower, you ask? Perhaps by closing the tax loopholes to keep corporations from skipping out on paying millions of dollars by claiming offshore residency? No. By clamping down on the Justice Department's sleazy invasion of our bedrooms? Unh, no, sorry, no. Plugging the Wyoming-sized leaks in our oxymoronically named intelligence agencies? Sorry, no, not that, either. See, what they've managed to do is isolate the terrorist scourge threatening to tear the fabric of our country apart and they're taking the appropriate steps to end it, by readying to pass the "Cheeseburger Bill."

This piece of legislation seeks to indemnify fast food restaurants from "obesity" lawsuits. And no, I'm not kidding. How this issue rose to the top of the country's priority list so quickly is a question only a politician's contributions director in an election year could answer. The bill is sponsored by Representative Ric Keller, R-Fla., and imagine that—a Republican standing up for the rights of that traditionally downtrodden group of Americans, huge corporations. What next? Mustard on hot dogs? Hookers in Hollywood? Aloof cats?

"We got to get away from this new culture where people

always try to play the victim and blame others for our prob-lems." And you know what, I don't disagree with him. Yeah, I know, two thirds of all adult Americans are overweight, and Ronald McDonald keeps shoving quarter pounders in our face, but c'mon, nobody's forcing them down our throats. House Minority Leader Tom DeLay, R-Tex., says the debate is about "personal responsibility," but do we really need to immunize the food industry against lawsuits? You know, if we spent a cou-ple of bucks on school lunch programs, maybe kids wouldn't need to pig out on Happy Meals. Sorry. Got a little strident there. At ease.

Bush to Poor: Drop Dead

You know what surprises me most about Bush's new Budget Proposal? I'll tell you what surprises me most about Bush's new Budget Proposal. What surprises me most about Bush's new Budget Proposal is that the front gates of the White House aren't being knocked down by legions of outraged clergy armed with spiked bats and pitchforks and acetylene torches screaming for the head of any of the leering corporate lackeys possessing even the remotest of roles in submitting this moral crime against humanity to Congress. And that the ruling class lets Bush get away with this potentially revolutionary inciting crap. *That's* what surprises me most about Bush's new Budget Proposal.

And I don't use the term "ruling class" lightly. His tax cuts for the rich: Not only do they remain in defiance of the larg-est deficit *ever*, but King Leer intends to fight to make them permanent. *However*, for any program involving anybody who isn't rich: Oh yes, there will be cuts. Severe cuts. Cuts o'plenty. Cuts to the bone, unless those bones happen to be located in the vicinity of the cholesterol-laden limb of a fat cat.

Apparently the plan is to balance the budget on the nutritionally deprived uninsured backs of the inadequately medicated poor. That's the deal: tax cuts if you are rich, budget cuts if you're not. Less money for those who don't have any, and more for those who do. That's how President Fredo wants to get out of the giant deficit hole he's dug. You can't put it any more simply. Rich people richer. Poor people poorer.

Here's just a sample of what he plans for our future, with a handy reminder of why. *Because you can't hear it too much.* For those of you with a strong stomach and a low threshold of infuriation, feel free to read on. For the rest of you, this might be a good time to check out your horoscope or some of the cheerier comic strips like "Family Circus." No kidding.

- Tighter restrictions on Food Stamp eligibility so rich people can have more money.

- Federal Drug Administration meat inspection teams sacked so rich people can have more money.

- Highway and infrastructure improvement budgets slashed so rich people can have more money.

- An 11 percent reduction in Homeland Security funds available to state and local coordination efforts so rich people can have more money.

- $250 million cut from programs to train child-care doctors and other health-care professionals so rich people can have more money.

- Small Business Administration cut from $3.3 billion to $0.6 billion so rich people can have more money.

- Increase on charges for Veterans Health Care. Why? That's right. So rich people can have more money.

- Cutting Federal Foster Care Programs so rich people can have more money.

- Cutting Medicaid and Medicare benefits so rich people can have more money.

- Ending community services block grants, a $637 million program that helps pay for community action agencies founded more than 35 years ago as part of the fight against poverty, so rich people can have more money.

- Proposed cuts in aid to farmers, seniors, children, students, cops, veterans, the homeless, the hungry, the environment, Amtrak, *and* the Centers for Disease Control and Prevention so rich people can have more money.

- Gutting the low-income home energy assistance program, which is mostly used by the elderly. That's right, friends, he's cutting winter heating subsidies to the elderly so rich people can have more money. What are we now: The Gorgar People? Let's just cut to the chase. You hit 65, we ship you to the Aleutian Islands and place you on an ice floe with matches and a pointy stick. If you're a Republican, we take away the stick, because it's considered an entitlement.

Not So Almighty Dollar

Talk about how the almighty have fallen. The dollar is headed downhill faster than Bode Miller on a set of rocket skis. Think nose dive. Plummetville. Plunge City. Belly Floppo-Rama. "Recession" is such an ugly word. Try walking down a New York City street these days without getting knocked off the sidewalk by a gaggle of foreigners brandishing a circumference of high-end shopping bags like a cardboard armada. Can't be done.

I blame George Bush and his imbecilic economic chicanery

for subjecting us to these indignities. Spending $2 trillion on an unnecessary war. Silly boy. Lowering taxes during that same unnecessary war. Sillier boy. Policies that have prompted OPEC to make noises about following Brazilian supermodel Giselle Bündchen's lead, in asking to be paid in euros. Euros, hell, the lady should choose to be paid in clothes, because to look at her, she doesn't seem to own any. Somebody throw this girl a jacket. She must be cold.

The dollar has sunk lower than a strip-show flyer stuck to the undercarriage of a leased Lamborghini Murcielago. The pound is up to $2, levels not seen since the '50s. The euro is at its highest level against the dollar...ever. When? Ever! French President Sarkozy spent his summer vacation in New Hampshire. "Four hundred francs, and zat includes everything, including zee servants." Things have gotten so bad, Russian mob bosses are back to using 5,000-ruble bills to snort lines of cocaine off hookers' chests. It's like the October Revolution all over again.

That obnoxious sound coming from north of the border: the nonstop laughter of millions of Canadians playing a little game they call payback, mocking the play money we call moolah. "Oh, so I guess you would be talking aboot *American* dollars, eh? Oooh. I don't know, there, eh." Our economy isn't in the doldrums. Our economy can't even see the doldrums. Our economy *aspires* to the doldrums. Dubyah has turned us into a Third World banana republic. We're Costa Rica to the rest of the world. With lousier snorkeling.

Who can blame the hordes of Eurotrash from clogging the aisles of our Tiffany franchises like an extended family of hill-billies at a dollar store? Everything here is so incredibly cheap. We've turned into a discount playground for the world's trust-fund babies. High-end restaurants, the good hotels, VIP sec-tions of our most exclusive nightclubs, Saturday night movie tickets: pretty much off limits to anybody holding an American passport. We're the minimum wage security guards at a giant, high-end outlet mall known as America just one cut-rate Virgin flight away from true civilization.

And thank God that we, the general public, never fell for that whole "you got to save your money" B.S. and are still proud holders of the "Least Personal Savings of Any Country in the Industrialized World" award. Because you know what those dollars are worth now? Zero. Zip. Zilch. Nada. Nothing! Maybe kicking the greenback dollar under the couch is just the neocons' idea of how to squelch our looming Social Security crisis. Make the dollar worth so little that, in the future, any one of us will be able to cover the entire shortfall by digging into our own wallets. "$30 trillion? Is that all you're worried about? Why didn't you say so? Who here can break a quadrillion?"

America's Favorite Felon

If you ever needed proof of the extent of the culture gap between your New York television network news and your ordinary middle-class mortgage-paying mall walker, check out the reaction to the verdict in the Martha Stewart trial. For reasons as different as chocolate banana daiquiris are to Amish checkerboard quilts, normal ordinary civilians and big-time network reporters were both whacked into bewilderment upon hearing that the Queen Cream Dream was found guilty by a jury on four felony counts.

The media were astounded because Stewart had been a minor deity as long as they've been in the game, and a top five "get" on their career goal list has been an invitation to one of her parties. And they consider her actions less criminal than attempting to crash a velvet rope encumbered with uninvited guests from the Midwest wearing creased jeans. Insider information? It's the way of the world. Don't be naïve.

On the other hand, Midwestern mall walkers are incredulous that a bona fide celebrity actually got nailed for anything. The folks on the street are cognizant of what the suburban superstar was found guilty of. Not insider trading. Not lying to a federal agent. She was found guilty of being smug. Of being overly blonde. Of betraying the holy gospel of household perfection by cutting ethical corners. Of risking a $450 million fortune in a vain attempt to save a measly 50 grand.

She earned her chops as the domestic goddess for women from Connecticut. "Today we'll learn how to hacksaw walnuts into decorative napkin rings." Oh, for crum's sake, bite me, lady. You are the malignant knot on the arts-and-crafts knob. Your compass points due daft. We got families who need two incomes just to put food on the plate, and this socialite twit got famous for making housewives feel guilty because they can't find the time to carve a two-fifths cream cheese replica likeness of Mount Rushmore to honor Presidents Day? And at the end of every show, the reveal: "Look what *I* made." Oh, get real, you didn't make squat, Martha. Everybody knows you got 20 Vietnamese women backstage begging to go back to work for Nike. "She beats us when the camera lights go off."

But you know she'll be back: You can't keep a good girl down. And America loves redemption stories. I guarantee the domestic diva will be back. So she gets 18 months: 3 months before her release, Kmart will start promoting Martha Stewart's newest line of coordinates. Assorted shades of gray in muslin and burlap. Lots of vertical stripes. "Discover the confining beauty of slate and granite with the new Martha Stewart Solitary Collection: Busting Out for Spring."

FAQ: *The President's Social Security Reform*

Q. So what's going on with that whole privatization of Social Security thing these days?

A. Excuse me, but it's that whole *personalization* of Social Security thing, now.

Q. What's the difference?

A. Nothing, really. The second one tested better. Privatize—bad. Personalize—good. Liberate—gooder. Lottery win—goodest.

Q. Why does everyone have big beige banana bugs up their butt over the president's plans to finally fix Social Security?

A. A lot of baby boomers think of this fix as the same kind of fix a veterinarian performs on a dog.

Q. What do they think Bush is trying to turn Social Security into?

A. Something not very social and no longer secure.

Q. What about the Wall Street investment dealie part?

A. Dealie part?

Q. You know what I mean.

A. Since the Dow is down about 10 percent for the year, it's been sort of put on the back burner.

Q. How far back?

A. Way back next to the capture of Osama.

Q. Wow, that far? When was it, exactly, that the baby boomers decided to grow up and get old?

A. Don't know. I guess someone must have convinced them "old is the new black." Of course we are talking about free money here. Which could raise the blood pressure of anybody, much less a grandma wearing a "White Snake" T-shirt. You ever mistakenly take some blue hair's nickel slot seat?

Q. But don't these greedy geezers-to-be agree Social Security is in deep doo-doo and needs to be shored up?

A. Well, yeah, I guess, but you got to remember, Bush's Clear Skies Bill allows for more pollution and his Healthy Forests Initiative encourages logging, so you can understand how folks might tend to worry that the real goal of his Social Security Reform is fewer old people.

Q. What kind of ideas are being implemented in Bush's recently released reform package?

A. Mostly the plan is to forestall future cuts in benefits by cutting benefits in the future. Democrats call it a benefit cut. Republicans call it a cut in the growth rate of benefits. But I think there are maybe 80 other ways to throw "benefit" and "cuts" into the same sentence, so we're not done here. We might even see "bene cutifits," which probably means "above-average salami pants" in Italian.

Q. But doesn't the Administration maintain these benefit cuts are designed only to affect the wealthy?

A. Well, but according to the specifics of the plan, "wealthy" is defined as anybody making over 20 grand a year. Which means that a greeter at Wal-Mart or anybody asking "You want fries with that?" qualifies as a member of the financial elite in Bush's America.

Q. What happens if Social Security is allowed to fail?

A. Then we'll return to Bush's sepia-toned vision of an olden-timey America in which people lived before being enveloped into Roosevelt's Social Security straitjacket.

Q. Which means what?

A. Faith-based retirement.

4 | Blue
Red
Purple

*I think it was the election of '84 when NBC started
coloring Democratic states blue and Republican
states red. The night Walter Mondale valiantly
denied Ronald Reagan electoral unanimity by cap-
turing both Minnesota and the District of Columbia. And that was it. D.C. wasn't big enough to
register on the map so they encapsulated it, blew it
up, and positioned it in the middle of the Atlantic
Ocean. The visual effect was sad. One blue state
amid a sea of 49 red ones.*

*Sadder still are the false choices enforced on us by
having to choose one of those two hues. Because
even in the reddest of states, there's a blue city. And
in that blue city, there's a red neighborhood. And
you go to that neighborhood, there's a blue house.
And in the bedroom, you might find the* Weekly
Standard *on one bedstand and* Mother Jones *on
the other. What I'm saying is, we're all purple people
here. OK, violet.*

*Plum. Eggplant. Lavender. Merlot. That's it!—
we're all merlot people. Except those unfortunates
who are allergic to tannic acid.*

Intelligent Is as Intelligence Doesn't

Stealing valuable time from his busy schedule of clearing brush on what apparently is the most debris-infested ranch in the country, President Brush spoke to members of the press about his belief that both sides of the debate regarding the development of humanity should be taught in schools: evolution, the theory that humans descended from an infinite number of apes typing on an infinite number of typewriters, and Intelligent Design, the idea that an unseen force (not necessarily God, but not ungodlike either) nudged our genes with big, giant invisible fingers to the point where no child is left behind. Or something like that.

This is shocking to the same degree that goats eat shoes. Especially to anyone who's been semicognizant the last five years and watched Bush work his backward magic, personally disproving Darwin with a series of policies stripping workers and minorities and women and anyone who isn't an energy producer (and I ain't talking methane gas) of their rights. Not only does the president not believe in evolution but, ironically, he is his own best argument.

Not to mention that I.D. is just Creationism with a container load of shiny, brushed-aluminum siding tacked on. They try to dress it up as science but then the lab coat slips and the collar emerges whenever you ask just who this Intelligent

Designer behind the Intelligent Design is and in response you get: "I don't know, who do *you* think it is?" OK. Hasn't anybody figured out that all these Creationism adherents have never copped to the fact that over the years religion itself has adapted?

One of the logic wedges Intelligent Designers like to jump into with both semantic feet is Charles Darwin called his discovery "The Theory of Evolution." "See. It's just a theory!" Oh, grow up. What's next? You going to require the Principle of Atomic Force to attend PTA meetings? What about the Law of Gravity? Does an initiative for repeal lie in its immediate future? Apparently all we need do is to hire Denny Crane or petition one of those activist judges and voilà…broken vases and scraped knees—things of the past. Hey, it's just a law! And a bad one at that.

The theory of Intelligent Design maintains that life on Earth is too complex to have developed through evolution. Too complex? Oh, no! You mean there are things we don't know? Heaven forbid. No pun intended. Of *course* there are things we don't know. We have brains the size of peas. And I tell you, we keep dumbing down our schools, it won't be long before the concept of mint fudge confuses people. "Yes, it's chocolatey. But it's minty too. How does that work?" Wasn't too long ago people were dead-solid positive that a solar eclipse was evidence of a dragon eating the sun as it rode across the sky on the back of a giant turtle. I remember thinking that about five years ago, but that was just my Uncle Bud draining a six pack on his riding mower.

Now, don't get me wrong, the Bible is a great book, but it has as much to do with science as gummi bears have to do with aerospace navigation. As far as science goes, it makes a great paperweight to keep your lab reports from blowing away in the breeze. How soon before 2 + 2 equals…"whatever God wants it to be"? Back in the seventeenth century, Galileo proposed the Earth revolved around the sun, not the other way around, and was promptly convicted of heresy and imprisoned for the rest of his life at a time when home detention did not include half-way-decent satellite reception. In response to his pardon from the Catholic Church 400 years later, Galileo was conveniently unavailable for comment.

If these people are really seeking alternative theories as to how life originated, I got one. I got a doozy. Gisele the Mountain Sprite defeated the evil Martian overlords and flew us here from Pluto on Santa's sled. How about that? Hey, it's a theory! And I want to see it included on the blackboard of every science classroom as part of the new curriculum: Evolution, Intelligent Design and Santa's Sled. At least my Santa Sled Theory is flexible enough to explain the reason for the human appendix: the Martian mark of the insurgent.

This Little PETA Did Not Eat Roast Beef

Please only bounce the waffle iron off my forehead a couple of times as I tentatively mock and scoff and taunt one of the liberals' most sacred of all cows. Which is kind of a joke, although there's no reason you would know that yet. But before I launch into my superfluous onslaught, let me say that even though I don't agree with most of their missions or goals, I'm glad the People for the Ethical Treatment of Animals are there. Just like Michael Moore is the hefty lefty pendulum swing to Bill O'Reilly, PETA acts as a wacky counterbalance to the National Rifle Association in terms of embarrassing the two major parties on a fair and balanced basis.

All us commie pinko yellow rat bastards laugh, laugh, *laugh* during those silly legislative seasons when the NRA gets its knickers in a knot arguing how assault weapons can be used as legitimate hunting rifles. OK, sure, right, yeah—I can buy that

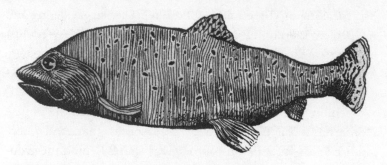

argument. I mean, you can also use a chain saw to cut butter. Just going to get a little messy around muffin time, is all I'm saying. If you think about it, a hand grenade will signal the end of recess. And they look like idiots. And it's good.

But then you read about a PETA program where they make field trips to elementary schools dressed in giant fish costumes encouraging kids not to eat fish because "fish have feelings too" and you just want to hide behind one of those giant Red Lobster menus and moan a little. Then, during the calamari appetizer, a small giggle escapes. But the moan returns. Because we look like idiots. And it's *not* good.

The worst part is imagining the hysterical laughter emanating from the far-right wing-nut flippo-units on their "anybody who doesn't agree with us hates America" radio talk shows. Using this brush of ridiculousness to paint all liberals. I always considered it a little cheap and easy to slam PETA. Like making fun of the long-haired blonde girl in the peasant skirt spinning and twirling out of time at the front of the stage while the jazz trio is on break. She ain't hurting nobody. Leave the poor kid alone.

But now, that girl is pointing at me, yelling "fish murderer!" Lady, we're talking fish! We can't eat fish, because we might hurt their feelings? For crum's sake, fish eat fish. The hell are we supposed to eat? Fruit? Vegetables? What's next: Be solicitous of the head of broccoli's self-esteem? I get the beef and veal deals (they can't move their little heads) and appreciate the meaning of "Free Range Chicken" (fancier packaging and 60 percent markup). But now I'm wondering if PETA isn't just trying to make up for the backsliding on the antifur campaign, which is losing ground fast due to the sheer numbers of ex-hippies getting rich and old and cold.

C'mon guys, they're fish. Have you ever heard the phrase "Smart as a fish"? No. Probably a reason for that. And where do fish sticks stack up on your feelings chart? Behind the grouper and ahead of the sea sponge? Even if you enlist Flipper or Nemo as spokesfish, you got a public relations vacuum here. As my lovely wife, Debi Ann, says when making out the bills while Annie the cat pads around on top of them: "There's helping and there's hindering." This is what you call your hindering.

Cyclops Pinkeye

President George Bush's nomination for U.S. Ambassador to the United Nations is John Bolton, and to say he's a critic of the UN might be an understatement on the order of saying the Swift Boat Veterans were not John Kerry's biggest fans. Bolton has gone so far as to declare that in his eyes the UN doesn't exist. Call me wacky, but shouldn't the guy who's going to represent us at least acknowledge the fact of the institution's existence? And does this skepticism extend to the structure itself? If so, how's he going to get to work? Is he destined to wander aimlessly around the East Side of Manhattan querying strangers as to the location of his own personal Brigadoon?

The 56-year-old State Department chief of arms control, a hard-liner with a suspicious view of U.S. arms control treaties, is also on record as having said that if you lopped off the top 10 floors of the UN, "It wouldn't make a difference." Oh yeah, let's have *him* run our diplomatic corps. Because who knows more about mending bridges than the guy planting the charges in an attempt to set fire to them? What does the Administration have in mind for future appointments? Howard Stern to head up the FCC? Michael Jackson as official envoy to UNICEF? Kenneth Lay as the new chairman of the Securities and Exchange Commission? Laugh at the first two, the last is not so funny.

Supporters describe Bolton as a blunt, straight-talking, tough-minded, tell-it-like-it-is, not afraid to ruffle foreign feathers while putting America's interests first, kind of guy. But we already got one of those kinds of guys in charge of the White House. And George Bush ain't too internationally minded, either. If the Ambassador Nominee's function is to be the designated rottweiler, I could understand, but we already got a kennel full of rottweilers, most of which appear to have missed the paper-training course in obedience school. I mean, "Tough Love" is one thing, but "Rabid Frothing at the Mouth with an Unattached Ear Hanging Out Between the Teeth" is another.

Detractors call Bolton an abrasive, confrontational, insensitive, kiss-ass, prudent as a flatulent porcupine, abusive with analysts who disagree with any of his views, kind of a guy. Obviously, politics, like beauty, is in the eye of the beholder, but in terms of ideologues, this Administration has developed a serious case of conjunctivitis. And in a bullying Cyclops, in charge of a bigger army than the rest of the world put together has, that kind of pinkeye can become diplomatically distracting.

Don't get me wrong, I'm not sure I totally disagree with all of Bolton's assessments of the UN. Such as it's as useless as cellophane underwear. And corrupt. And hopelessly entangled in red tape. And guilty of fostering anti-American attitudes while monopolizing the seafood stand at our all-you-can-eat buffet and discarding its used oyster shells on our nice clean carpeting. But whatever happened to good cop/bad cop? Bush plays bad cop/hothead brandishing a multipronged Taser in the dark cop. What part of the word "diplomacy" does the president not get?

White House Report Card

The bipartisan 9/11 Commission released a report card on the Administration's efforts in the wake of the attacks on September 11, and to say the news wasn't good is like saying abandoned minefields make for lousy hot-air-balloon staging grounds. George Bush ought to thank his lucky stars he doesn't have to take this report card home to Poppy and Babs, because I'm betting he'd be grounded for at least a semester and have the keys to his Porsche 944 turned over to Jeb. Needless to say, this is not the kind of report card that greases the skids for entrance into Yale, but that kind of thing never bothered a Bushie. Come to think of it, I'm sure this kind of thing has happened before. 1 A, 12 Bs, 9 Cs, 12 Ds, 5 Fs and 2 incompletes. C minus average. Half a grade below the C student Bush proudly calls himself. "I'm mediocre!" But this report was focused strictly on the Administration's response to 9/11. The Commission totally ignored other areas of the job. So, in the interest of a more informed nation, and a fully rebuked president, I'm here to do the rigorous work of finishing off the Bush Administration's Report Card.

Iraq. F

Got us a new strategy for victory. Apparently our old strategy for victory was defective. You know what? General Custer had a strategy for victory, too.

Oil Company Executive Economy. A

Everything's just ducky.

Not Oil Company Executive Economy. D–

Not as ducky.

Environment. D

One bright note: Defying conventional wisdom, the environment is still with us. One thing you can say about the Bush Administration is they've made outdoorsmen happy. The nature trails are wider and more plentiful, and the fishing is much more challenging.

Technology. C

Due to the diligence of our intrepid vice president, incredible strides continue to be made in the development of military craft and weaponry.

Immigration. C

A mixed bag. Thousands of Mexicans continue to stream north across the Rio Grande looking for decent-paying jobs, while at the same time thousands of Americans continue to stream north across the Canadian border looking for inexpensive pharmaceuticals and health care.

Torture. F

The Administration promotes the most torture-friendly atmosphere since William Shatner mercifully closed out his singing career.

Ethics. D

Grade would have been an F, but it's mostly Republicans who are caught taking bribes, mainly because nobody wants to bribe a Democrat. They can't get anything done. Besides, when you do give them money, they don't know what to do with it. They put it in the freezer, for crum's sake.

Emergency Response. F–

Wasn't aware New Orleans levees were at risk. My Aunt Hoogolah in Rhinelander, Wisconsin, knew. The administration didn't know refugees were huddled in the darkness of the New Orleans Convention Center. Anderson Cooper knew. Hell, he probably turned out the lights.

Cronyism. F

Like most Bush appointees, FEMA Director Michael Brown couldn't distinguish his ass from an Arabian thoroughbred's plantar fasciitis.

Uniting America. F

Because of Bush, this country is more polarized than a pawn in a poorly manufactured magnetic chess set. Inspired large groups of Christians to speak out against tolerance. He must be so proud.

Originality. D

President obviously copied directly from Dick Cheney's and Donald Rumsfeld's foreign policy homework.

Education. D

Encouraging continued Republican hold over Congress and White House by refusing to fund his education reforms.

Jobs. D

American job market is imploding. Major growth industry is bankruptcy lawyers.

Takes Responsibility For Own Actions. Unsatisfactory

So fond of allowing industry lobbyists to write legislation, construction should begin soon on a tasseled loafer repair shop in White House basement.

Penmanship. Satisfactory

Pleasant cursives in his autopen signature.

Works Well With Others. Unsatisfactory

Appoints John Bolton as U.S. Ambassador to the UN. A man who is to diplomacy what Oscar Wilde was to mixed-doubles bowling.

Gay Marriage en Mass.

Well, it started. The city of Cambridge was first to legally marry a gay couple in the State of Massachusetts, and the confused cacophony emanating from the various sanctified orifices of the Religious Right is enough to make you wonder who's in charge of running tape backward through speakers the size of Rush Limbaugh's ego. To say the vitriolic clamor is out of control is like suggesting that rotating sprinkler heads make for lousy drinking fountains.

One protester to the ceremony held up a sign reading: "God hates fags." Yeah, well, OK, but if you ascribe to that darling little slogan, you must also hold the converse opinion that God loves bigoted, intolerant idiots. And I must say, I don't know much about God, but I dare say he/she is a mite more charitable than that.

Of course, conservatives are seizing this opportunity to distract attention from the quagmire that is not a quagmire, by swiftly convening prayer meetings to hasten the shuffling off of Massachusetts' Supreme Judicial Court mortal coils responsible for this revolting turn of events. They have predictably trotted out their standard litany of godless commie pinko yellow rat bastard charges at the usual suspects like the ACLU and Teletubbies, but since this is an election year, John Kerry is understandably having his tail pilloried, as well, for the audacity of being elected to represent a state full of evildoers. And it is only with the greatest of restraint that I refrain from making a Texas joke here.

The arguments are numbingly familiar: "If this abomination is allowed, the fabric of America will be torn asunder." The exact same contention made about giving women the vote, and granting equality to African Americans. If you ask me, the fabric of America is pretty darn rent already. "Well, I don't believe people should marry someone of the same sex." OK, then. Don't. "Wait. My religion doesn't believe *anybody* should be able to marry someone of the same sex." But they don't belong to your religion. They belong to another religion, entirely altogether different. One that involves honey and mustard and lemon and you wouldn't like it.

Another specious argument you hear is "If this crime against nature persists and becomes accepted by society, you know what's next: bestiality." Let me think. *No!* There's still an age limit, isn't there? You ever seen an 18-year-old sheep? Not a pretty sight. No one marries mutton, my friend. Here's what I want to know: How does two people's happiness make these folks miserable? And why would men or women holding civil rights offend them?

You'd think these opponents to gay marriage have never met anyone even the slightest festive, much less gay. They sound like they're describing alien demons with pronged tails and scaly talons. For crum's sake, don't you get it? Gays are people. They're you and me. The only difference between gay and straight is which way your head faces during sex. That's it. Maybe the quality of wedding reception appetizers. Smoky cheddar salmon puffs on sun-dried tomato focaccia bread topped with sour cream and a puddle of caviar—that is not a straight ceremony. Anyway, I thought the whole idea was to keep gays from having sex. What better way than marriage do you know to accomplish that?

Crocodile Tears

The latest form of political theater premiering in D.C. is the ritual crying of crocodile tears. And this season's nominations for biggest mock drops are destined to be swept by Beltway players in their demonstration of their fake concern for South Dakota Senator Tim Johnson. Phony sanctimony has long been a staple of the American way of life. Each of us had an aunt whose major talent was feigning fawning sympathy. Usually she had a mole.

Mine was Aunt Hoogolah, who lived to talk up the distress of other family members in an attempt to lower her daughter's ranking on the screw-up chart indelibly chalked on the blackboard of every relative's mind. Sorry for the convoluted syntax there, but I'm trying to adhere to the embargo on use of the term "black sheep" till the Michael Richards onstage flip-out has been superseded by another celebrity meltdown. Once the Mel Gibson torch has been passed, all will be well with the dark ewes.

Right now our newspapers and televisions are witnessing such a flurry of fake solicitude that they should be handing out snowblowers. Mostly I'm talking about the excruciating sympathy leaking out of the mouths of political pundits everywhere, expressing commiseration for Tim Johnson's medical situation in their most grave and sincere voice. For 10 seconds. Then high-pitched squeals as they excitedly speculate for the rest of the show on possible ramifications resulting from his imminent demise.

"Our prayers go out to him and his family. [*Short pause; turn*

to center camera] But if, God forbid, he does die, we trust Governor Mike Rounds will do the right thing. And appoint a Republican to fill his seat, bringing the Senate back to dead even. No pun intended. Then when Vice President Dick Cheney breaks the 50–50 tie, the America-loving GOP will retain control of the senior branch of Congress and the sun will shine and birds will fly, but not a single George Bush–directed subpoena will."

Of course, short of dying, which Senator Johnson undoubtedly would prefer avoiding, it's unlikely he will abdicate his Senate seat. Historically, physical or mental incapacitation has never been a big handicap to the normal operating procedures of the Most Deliberative Body in the World. Let's not forget Senator Strom Thurmond, whose major accomplishment the last four years of his life was keeping the drool from pooling in his lap. C'mon, are you really serving the government when Willard Scott is wishing you happy birthday?

As to suspicions of some sort of hanky-panky going on with the sudden onset of Senator Johnson's malady, I'm of the opinion that Republicans will go to any length to hang on to power. Whatever it takes. And if similarities to the Vladimir Putin/ Alexander Litvenenko scene show up, with the whole radioactive sushi deal, I semiseriously propose that we zero in on a Republican Senator in a Democratic state and attempt to retrieve the status quo.

A twist on the old Sean Connery philosophy in *The Untouchables:* "If they pull polonium 210 on you, you pull americium 241 on them. If they put one of yours under the knife of a neurosurgeon, you put one of theirs under the wheels of a Peterbilt; that's the Democratic Way and that's how you get Trent Lott." This also applies to Independent Senators. From Connecticut. Who suddenly decide to become Republican. For any reason. At all. Mister Joementum.

The War on XMA$

Fox News is right. There *is* a war on XMA$. And one of the dastardly fiends behind the hostilities is me. I'm stuffed to the gills with incorrect holiday sentiments here, and I've only been to a mall a couple of times. The first holly-covered trigger that set me off was that the flacking for this shopping season began the week before Halloween. Red and green bumped orange and black. That's not right. Not to mention the whole turkey thing getting shunted behind a deluge of commercials featuring a car with a giant red bow on it. No, that's not going to stir up the vanishing middle class at all. Repeatedly imagining other people buying each other Lexuses as gifts. And now, *now,* the retail industry is not happy with the degree of greed by which we've been consumed, so before the Yule log has even been lit, much less embered down, they're already pushing AFTER-XMA$ SALES. Hey, settle down, people. We got a couple days to go here. OK, I've lost and XMA$ has won. The dark side has convinced me that if I don't do everything within my power to make certain that corporate America has a Merry XMA$, the terrorists will win. So, in the spirit of giving till it hurts, let me offer up to the least deserving of us my annual scathingly incisive, yet perennially trenchant, WILL DURST'S XMA$ GIFT WI$H LI$T.

- For former Speaker of the House Newt Gingrich, who says he's thinking of running for the presidency in 2008: second thoughts.

- For heiress Paris Hilton: a year-long sabbatical in Kazakhstan. Actually, that gift is for the rest of us.

- For Bill O'Reilly: a four-day, all-expenses-paid trip to the Folsom Street Fair in San Francisco.

- For Hillary Clinton: a new bestseller entitled *It Takes an Impeachment*.

- For the Democratic Senate: the gumption to continue the fight for the rights of minorities. Even if the main minority they're fighting for these days is themselves.

- For Secretary of State Condoleezza Rice: one blessedly quiet year in a Donald Rumsfeld–free zone.

- For the Democratic House of Representatives: a spine.

- For George W. Bush: an approval rating higher than his average test scores in college.

- For televangelist Pat Robertson: a Clue Train Fast Pass so he can ride for free for 30 days.

- For Supreme Court Justice Nominee Samuel Alito: a Harriet Miers Swimsuit Calendar.

- For Harriet Miers, who called George Bush the smartest man she ever met: a round-trip ticket to anywhere she wants as long as it's not Texas.

- For Vice President Dick Cheney: a five-gallon tub of sneer removal.

- For Barbara Bush: fewer photo-ops (and I only remember the one).

- For Alaska Senator Ted Stevens: permission to drill for oil in his own butt.

- For the King of Pop, Michael Jackson: enough sense to stay the hell in Bahrain.

- For the Iraqi people: an end to their civil war before the Bush Administration starts calling it that.

- For Rush Limbaugh: mint-flavored shoe laces to floss with the next time he puts his foot in mouth.

- For Mary Cheney's child: kindly faced, wise and sage grand-parents on the other side to neutralize Dick & Lynne.

- For Donald Trump and Rosie O'Donnell: matching muzzles.

- For George Bush, who said he was going to stay the course in Iraq even if only Barney and Laura were supporting him: some dog treats for Barney.

- For prospective Democratic presidential candidate Hillary Clinton: thicker skirts, so when's she's back-lit onstage you can't see her balls.

- For Princess Diana: on the tenth anniversary of her death, a moment's peace, for crum's sake.

- For O. J. Simpson: a one-way ticket to a deserted island populated predominantly by poisonous pampas grass.

- For Michael Richards, now that his career in Hollywood is on serious hold: a gubernatorial bid from the great state of Idaho.

- For Mel Gibson: a continuing series of Michael Richards–like incidents.

- For Britney Spears: some sort of reciprocal arrangement with Victoria's Secret.

- For Harry Whittington: trigger locks for all his friends.

- For Connecticut Senator Joe Lieberman: a scoop of Hillary Clinton's excess testosterone.

- For Jason Alexander and Julia Louis-Dreyfus: a good agent to say no to whatever scheme the *Seinfeld* team comes up with to promote the next release of DVDs after Michael Richards' exploits resulted in higher-than-expected sales.

- For Democratic New Orleans Congressional Representative William Jefferson: a home safe disguised as one of those minirefrigerators.

After the Beep

"Hello. You have reached the office of the president of the United States. Unfortunately he is either on another line or away from his desk. Please leave a message at the beep and Mr. Cheney will return your call at his earliest convenience. This call may be monitored to ensure quality service." [*Beep*]

"Hey, Dubyah. How ya doing? California here. You know; Golden State. Big long lanky plot of land hugging the left coast. Not as big as Texas, mind you, but fairly large. Vastish, even. Well, we like it. Remember us? We're the ones that sent you that nice fruit basket middle of December. Hope you enjoyed the grapes. A little nervous here. You can understand. Anyhow, thanks for agreeing to take this call. Hang on a sec, while I preheat the hot tub.

"There. Sorry. Just ground some beans and made myself a double decaf no-fat soy-milk latte. Starting to settle down a bit. OK. First of all, want to congratulate you on a most excellent inaugural. As the kids like to say, 'You rocked, dawg.' And what a lovely capper to the evening to see you and the beautifully gowned First Lady waltzing or whatever you call what you did at our ball, even if it was for about three nanoseconds, but we understand your schedule was more hectic than a Miami weatherman practicing bigamy during hurricane season. 'Scuze me while I pop this cup in the dishwasher.

"And speaking of Florida, could you believe what a mess they made down there? Again, kudos o'plenty definitely in order for your discreet handling of a very ticklish situation. You'd think former Vice President Gore (and I bet both you and your dad enjoy the sound of that), you'd think he could have mustered the simple common human decency to spare the country weeks of agonizing indecision by tactfully bowing out. But no. Perhaps the accumulation of eight years of close proximity to Clinton is not washed off by a simple series of showers. Need to steam clean that boy.

"Now, let me get right to the point here. Despite our surfer image, we're not totally dim. Obviously our 54 electoral votes could have come in handy, making the whole Florida thing moot. But it was one of those things. Not meant to be. However, just because we didn't vote for you doesn't mean we don't respect you as our true Commander-in-Chief. The time to put petty resentments aside is now. And the time to defrost the roast in the microwave is also now. Be right back. And I have to tell the kid to knock off the leaf blower, while I'm at it.

"We're back. Straight out? We have problems. To be honest, Mr. President, we're cold. Not Minnesota ears-break-off-from-frostbite cold, but shorts are not a viable indoors option anymore, which for us is tantamount to being sentenced to four consecutive winters in North Dakota. And we've got dark. Sudden dark. The worst kind of dark. Imagine how you'd feel if your mother were on an elevator when without warning a rolling blackout struck and she was penned in there with Hillary Clinton for a couple hours. That's really what we're talking about here...just plain folks. Kids are being stuck in those elevators too, you know. Mostly it's about the kids.

"We weren't the only state duped into selling our regulated utilities for some magic beans, so that your Administration could send a strong, compassionate, yet conservative message to the rest of the country were you to throw us a bone during this crisis. Imagine how this could also cement your position as a champion of bipartisanship. We're talking first 100 days here. Just think of us as a friendly new neighbor knocking on your door asking to borrow a couple of gigawatts of sugar.

"Maybe you could personally confab with Kenneth Lay, chairman of Enron, and is known as a family friend. God knows all it would take is a couple of kind words in his ear from you as a pal...and we could be back to wearing flip-flops and tank tops in no time. How 'bout it? You don't want to be known as the guy who roused America from its California dream and stuck it in a Yukon nightmare, do you? This isn't the Soviet Union, for crum's sake. What's next, bread lines?

"And we're not talking gratis, either. Perfectly willing and able to pay for whatever we get. We just need something now.

Whatever you got lying around. Diesel fuel. A couple of spare tanks of propane. Government-issued Ronson's lighter fluid. Anything. You want to raise exhaust emissions, no problem. Drop a derrick smack dab in the middle of Gray Davis's torso for all we care. Listen, man, all we need is a taste. C'mon, just something to get us through the winter. Otherwise the country is going to be treated to some weird candlelit shadows dancing across their Oscar ceremony.

"Well, that's enough yakking. Get back to me as soon as you can. Got to light the tiki torches around the pool and take the SUV in for its 500-mile checkup. Catch up with us on the cell. You got the number."

Skooter Skates

Who can tell what motivates the president these days? Maybe the commutation of Scooter Libby is meant to demonstrate his latent in-chargity. That he's relevant, dammit! That not only is he the decider, he's the commuter as well. With an approval rating lower than a drunk IRS agent wearing pinstripes behind the Red Sox dugout at Fenway, he probably wouldn't mind commuting, to and from the comfort of Crawford, Texas, four or seven days a week. Could become the First Telecommuting Chief Executive. "Really looking forward to Friday. That's 'No Pants Day.' " Bet Laura and the twins would prefer that. Dick too, just to clear the decks for some of the trickier bits.

Affirming his pertinence required George Bush to set a convicted partisan felon free as the proverbial bird. Although the identity of what kind of bird that phrase is intended to signify has been shrouded by the mists of time, it is safe to say it sure ain't no jailbird because, due to Dubyah's opportune intervention, Cheney's former chief of staff served less time than a spitballing junior-high study-hall miscreant sent to honors detention in the cafeteria.

Q. What's the difference between Paris Hilton and Scooter
   Libby?
A. 23 days.

The man whose defense was "I'm a busy man and can't be expected to keep track of all the lies I tell" didn't sing like a canary, either; as Paulie Walnuts might say, "You did good time, kid." So rest assured he has a bright future ahead of him on the *Forbes* magazine "Tired Old Leadership Axioms in Return for the Big Bucks" speaking tour, jointly sponsored by Homeland Security and the TV Guide Channel, now contemplating a mid-season replacement called *Skooter Skates*.

If Bush had explained that he wiped away the VP's right-hand man's sentence of 30 months for perjury in federal court, because you can't send a man named Scooter to prison, I would have understood. But the excuse used was that the sentence was "excessive." And we Americans, who are just 19 months shy of serving our full 96-month sentence living under the fear-mongering, torture-outsourcing and middle class eradicating efforts of this Administration, can totally relate.

"Excessive." That's what he called it. This is the same guy who when running for governor of Texas actually said out loud in front of people with microphones sticking out of their hands that he wanted to "stiffen the death penalty." Stiffen the death penalty? The hell does that mean? Was he going to apply it twice? Were doctors mandated not to rub alcohol on the point of insertion before lethal injections? Did he empanel a blue ribbon committee to figure out a way to dump the electric chair and wire up some bleachers?

But when it came to punishing his string puller's best friend, the president's compassion predictably welled up like a zit the morning of eighth-grade picture day. He did keep intact the other part of Libby's sentence, the $250,000 fine, but that didn't seem to pose much of a hardship, as the skedaddling scofflaw simply wrote a personal check for it. Don't feel too bad for him. I'm sure he'll be reimbursed by the Scooter Libby Defense Fund—or, as we are used to calling it, Halliburton.

Frog Soup

Ever since I was but a tadpole I've been hammered under the weight of this urban myth about putting a frog into a pot of water at room temperature, then slowly raising the flame. Supposedly, the frog continues to acclimate itself to the heat till it finally boils to death. I have questions. First off, who goes to the trouble of boiling one frog at a time? Smacks of wastefulness, not to mention the macabre. Do you need to keep hitting the frog in the head with a slotted wooden spoon to keep him submerged, or can he loll about with his little front arms over the edge of the pot like a pool patron in search of a towel boy?

For the true amphibian aficionado, a single frog must seem a cruel tease. A flashing torment of forbidden delights. What is the problem with bumping it up to a couple of frogs, or a veritable bevy of green? Or does crowding alter the experiment, turning it into some sort of weird, kinky, amphibious hot tub interlude? Also, it seems this whole frog soup arrangement hinges on an unspoken effortless conveyance of live frog into pot of room temperature water in the first place, which I suspect is an egregious oversimplification. Is our hoppy little friend anesthetized, and if so, isn't that cheating?

My point is, I need more information, but I do understand the allegory: We are destined to give up our rights one by one without a fight. Of that I have no doubt. If there were a Frog Soup Clock, his little webbed hands would be closing in on midnight. We're entering the dark part of Frog Soup Territory where scales are floating on top of fishy bouillon that has turned a bright shade of emerald, and two recent announcements from our fearless, lizard-loving leaders are contributing more than a soupçon to the soupiness of the situation.

Senator Ted Stevens (R-Alaska) has announced his intention to try to hold cable companies and satellite providers to the same primitive standards that the FCC currently holds broadcast networks to, which the House of Representatives has spinelessly decided should cost half a million dollars per infraction. This advance man for the American Taliban is trying to castrate the *Sopranos,* relocate *Deadwood* to outside Peoria and reapply the muzzle on the cantankerous mouth of Howard Stern.

For Senator Stevens, who is so concerned about the content of the cable channels he subscribes to, I have one thing to offer: You don't like something on your TV, *turn it off!* Most cable boxes come with a remote. *Use it.* Turn off *The Shield.* Watch Nick at Night. Unsubscribe to HBO. It ain't cheap. Use the

extra money to buy Disney DVDs or the best of *Sesame Street* and get your misplaced morality out of my TiVo.

In another part of town, as of April 15, the Transportation Safety Administration plans to ban all lighters on board all American flights in checked as well as carry-on luggage. Why? "Because if the shoe bomber had a lighter, he would have been successful." I thought that's why we take off our shoes before every flight. Now you want our fire? How 'bout pens? You could poke an eye out with one of those things. Why not outlaw the wheel in connection with luggage, and after we agree to that they'll want our thumbs. Only the guilty need thumbs. A truly innocent person doesn't require fire, pens or thumbs. Hey, what's that smell? I think it's time to start chopping up the garnish, because bowls full of hot scaly green broth are ready to be ladled out.

Empty Promises Are the New Black

It didn't matter how great the ovation that greeted the brooding Michael Chertoff as he expanded his line of carefully embroidered denials, or how detailed the chiseled John Roberts fashioned his impenetrable suit of murky conviction, or how dark were woven Donald Rumsfeld's comfortably reliable patchwork deceptions. It was abundantly obvious that everyone in the known universe (Washington) was waiting for the Big Pump to drop. To say that the balloons signaling the end of Fashion Week at the White House wouldn't fall till himself, the Dubyah, unveiled his Gulf Coast rhetoric onslaught, and to say that Karl Rove, the creative director at House of Bush, didn't disappoint, is akin to implying that Karl Lagerfeld has an impish sense of humor.

Commandeering an oppressively desolate Jackson Square as a backdrop, President Bush swaggered briskly to his podium, resplendent in a starched blue work shirt, echoing his watery theme in the middle of a breathtakingly beautiful Big Easy night. As a dramatically staged response to critics who had heaped derision on the House's slapdash and untailored response to Hurricane Katrina, the results were nothing less than stunning. The work shirt was a masterly touch, featuring sleeves impeccably rolled up, undoubtedly the result of one of the many master sleeve-rollers Rove reportedly has on call from the fabric slums of Milan.

Introducing a new line of fresh nonsense can be an exceedingly tricky business, but the Commander-in-Chief was up to the task as he deftly paid homage to the classic material and traditional patterns of past designers such as Johnson and Roosevelt, offering up the simple and timeless elegance of the promise of government help. He even playfully dipped into the trademarked "Emperor's New Clothes" Family line, doling out rustic (albeit purely ornamental) anecdotes and one-liners. From his first crooked smile to his halting farewell, this was an exercise in white space and a triumphant return to the well-constructed but empty suit we've come to know and love during times of crisis.

Liquid and pliable and fluid and inexact, the sludge coming out of his mouth cleverly matched the toxic moat surrounding the Ninth Ward. If one color stood out, it could be called ochre, auburn, burnt sienna or, as it is probably referred to in the House of Bush, good ol' brown. But not Brownie. You could see it in his speech, although his breeding and discretion kept him from describing the river of human feces that floated past former parade routes, his verbal weave was oddly reminiscent of it. Perhaps in an attempt to play off George's Wild West heritage, Messrs. Bush and Rove consciously manufactured audio reverberations of the litterings of a bull pen, and his target audience, a group of well-screened and thoroughly devoted fascistnistas, were simultaneously stunned and dazed by the audacity and humility of it all.

It was a night of fusion, a celebration of the sober alongside the frivolous, and if anybody could pull off this attempt at a return to business as usual by way of ridiculous theater, it was George W. Bush. Whether this season's line can catapult his fortunes back from his last disastrous attempt is of intense interest to the House of Bush's comrades and competitors. Has he reushered in a new era of nostalgic deficit spending, or is the runway smoke machine set on 11? Still your beating heart: Time will tell.

Apologies 'R' Us

Richard Clarke's mea culpa to the nation and the families of 9/11 confused many people. "Your government failed you. Those entrusted with protecting you failed you. I failed you." The hell was that? Encyclopedias were consulted. The Capital was all a-dither. Nobody could pinpoint exactly what happened. Residents of D.C. haven't witnessed anybody apologize for anything since O. G., Original George, of the Washington variety with that whole cherry tree deal and, even then, rumor has it, Dad had to pry it out of him with the business end of a blunderbuss. Nowadays, an apology is seen as a sign of weakness. The French apologize. In America, we find it much better to forge forward, ignoring all obvious mistakes, while trying to create enough noise and dust to cover our trail, which isn't all that hard here in the twenty-first century when the average attention span is close to that of a gnat blink. But now apologies are the rage and the fabric of our nation is at stakc.

This disastrous turn of events must be averted. Testifying in front of the 9/11 Commission, Condoleezza Rice may be forced to reverse her *60 Minutes* appearance in which she gamely resisted any urge to make amends. But little can be done to erase the image of Clarke as a folk hero, and don't think the word isn't getting out. Listen real close, you can almost hear the squeak of reluctant focus groups scrunching forward in their rented folding chairs. And I predict, unless this ghastly trend is nipped in the bud, big-time political consultants will be forced to report that when stuff goes bad, taxpayers actually prefer someone take responsibility and request forgiveness. If this gets out, it could lead to a veritable rampage of repentance. Folks will be knocking each other down running around the Capital apologizing willy-nilly into open microphones tying up conference rooms where important legislation could be stalled. Imagine the ugliness that could ensue.

- Former President Bill Clinton, for...well, you know.

- New York Senator Hillary Clinton, for not slapping Bill around a little when he deserved it.

- Senator Trent Lott, just for his hair.

- Governor Arnold Schwarzenegger, for smiling at inappropriate times.

- Vice President Dick Cheney, for running the country, not telling us and not doing a better job.

- Former President Jimmy Carter, for his brother Billy.

- Governor Jeb Bush, for his brothers Neil and George.

- Commerce Secretary Donald Evans, for criticizing John Kerry for "looking French." Yeah, right, and Evans smells like a tax-cut pardoner.

- Senator Edward Kennedy, for his behavior during the '70s.

- Condoleezza Rice, for her hair.

- Talk-show host Larry King, for those darn suspenders.

- Senator Edward Kennedy, for his behavior during the '80s.

- Senator Edward Kennedy, for his behavior...what the hell, for the whole thing.

- Former First Lady Barbara Bush, for not slapping George around when he was little.

- Democratic presidential candidate John Kerry, for inadvertently sharing a war with Jane Fonda.

5 | Yesterday Today Tomorrow

Past. Present. Future.

Flintstones. Simpsons. Jetsons.

Sepia. Color. HD.

The times they are a'changing. But they aren't a'changing fast enough. Or is it too fast? I always forget. All I know is, Yogi Berra was right: The future ain't what it used to be. For a while there, we defined what might be—with bad science-fiction movies and hokey exhibits inside Tomorrowland, which failed to set the bar terribly high. "In the future, you'll be able to open your garage door from inside your car!"

Hell, I remember as a kid, Walt Disney promised me a jet pack. Where's my jet pack? You and I should be chugging Tang in zero gravity right now. And are we?

Alas, no.

The End (Periodically)

Pointing out that the reading of newspapers and magazines these days no longer provides the ultimate in pacific leisure activities probably qualifies as breaking news, in the same manner that ashtrays in the arms of airplane seats seem superfluous. While Bush is busy threatening small Mideastern countries with healthy doses of democracy they don't want, Korea's Beloved Leader continues to kick demilitarized sand in our face, Osama bin Laden avoids capture while building a state-of-the-art television studio in a cave, and whenever our international back is turned Pakistan waggles its fingers in its ears and sticks its nuclear tongue out at India.

Meanwhile, we are treated to the disheartening spectacle of big-time government honchos tossing around phrases like "chemical throw weight," "tactical nukes" and "post-hostility squeegeeing." Which has set me to worrying. What if, suddenly, without warning (as sudden as it gets), a worldwide, five-alarm nuclear holocaust broke out? Wouldn't you be depressed as all get out because you missed seeing how your favorite periodical covered the end of civilization as we know it?

Well, yeah, I mean, sure, you'd be gloomy for a lot of other reasons too, like the slow, grisly demise of family, neighbors, friends and pets, not to mention *you*. I'm not sure that, even with a decent amount of advance notice, the debilitating fear of imminent annihilation would allow for much reading at all. And what little will get done would most likely be focused on weighty tomes like the Bible, *The Anarchist's Handbook* and *The Idiot's Guide to Sealing Yourselves Up with Plastic Sheeting and Duct Tape and Not Suffocating Like Dimestore Goldfish*. So, as a possible last act of extreme unction, I offer up this list of the last headlines we are destined never to read.

- *ABA's Barrister:* Looking for Loopholes: Pre-Redemptory Challenges.

- *American Rifleman:* Food—the New Weapon.

- *Architectural Digest:* Cave with a View: Lindsay Lohan's Former Personal Assistant's Brother's Personal Tour.

- *Better Homes & Gardens:* Rocks! The First Furniture.

- *Business Week:* Bear-ing Down!

- *Cosmopolitan:* 30 Seductive Ways to Gain Entry Into the Securest of Bunkers.

- *Field & Stream:* Are You Man Enough for the 6-Eyed, 320-lb. Perch?

- *Forbes:* The 50 Top Cemeteries in America for Gold Recoverings.

- *Golf Digest:* Don't Let a Containment Suit 'Nuke' Your Swing.

- *Gourmet:* A New Appreciation for…Water.

- *GQ:* Refugee Chic.

- *Guns & Ammo:* Who's Laughing Now, Monkey Boy?

- *Home Decorating:* Tossing Away Those Clumps of Hair? Big Mistake—Here's Why.

- *Inc.:* Chapters 7, 11, 13 or Revelations?

- *Life:* Parting Shots: The Collection.

- *MacWorld:* Windows Vista…Responsible?

- *Mad:* The Lighter Side of Bleeding Out.

- *Maxim:* Can You Imagine What Would Happen if Supermodel Giselle Bündchen Were Exposed to Massive Doses of Radiation, Mutated and Grew Another Rack? We Did.

- *Motor Trend:* Yabba Dabba Do-It-Yourself: The Flintstone Mobile Conversion Kit.

- *National Enquirer:* Angelina Falls Off Diet; Brad Missing.

- *National Geographic:* Fungi! The New Rulers.

- *New England Journal of Medicine:* Johns Hopkins Researcher Proves: Two Heads *Are* Better Than One.

- *New York Post:* Mideast Missing / Long Islanders Delayed / Mets Lose Again.

- *New York Times:* Billions Perish; Bush Calls for Caution.

- *Newsweek:* The Other Side: What Gives?

- *O Magazine:* Oprah Brightens Her Nuclear Winter with a Bountiful Banquet of Spam.

- *People:* History of the Species: Picks and Pans.

- *Playboy:* The Girls of Ground Zero.

- *Popular Mechanics:* New Tricks for the Trusty Stick.

- *Psychology Today:* Departuring Means Having to Say You're Sorry.

- *Reader's Digest:* 101 Key Bible Passages Your Family Needs to Know. Now.

- *Rolling Stone:* The Beatles: Together Again.

- *Seventeen:* Reincarnation: How Will Beyoncé Fare?

- *Ski:* Warren Miller Is…Gray Powder!

- *Soldier of Fortune:* So You Want to Start Your Own Country?
- *Sports Illustrated:* The Greatest Athlete EVER! A Reader's Poll.
- *Sunset:* Eye-Catching Arrangements in the Hue of Rubble.
- *Time:* Is Heaven Real?
- *TV Guide:* Armageddon: Cheers & Jeers.
- *USA Today:* How We'll Die: A Graph.
- *Variety:* Civilization Slumps / Harry Potter VII on Hold.
- *Vogue:* This Summer: Breakthrough in Burlap.
- *Weight Watchers:* Learning to Say YES!
- *Wired:* Downloading Redemption.
- *Yachting:* Tacking Into a Mushroom Cloud—A Partial Diary.

Partisan Witch Hunts on YouTube

Strap on your seat belts and nuke some popcorn because we got ourselves a battle royal between the two gnarliest branches of government that a tree has ever seen. In the left-hand corner, back from wandering in the wilderness, the Democrats are just itching to exercise some rediscovered clout. Over in the right-hand corner, after six years of unchallenged rule, the Executive Branch is not taking kindly to having to answer to mere mortals from across the aisle. It's Countdown to a Crisis! The stoppable force versus the movable object. The plot thins.

"Watch Executive Privilege do battle with the People's Right to Know! Thrill as Attorney General Alberto Gonzales takes on Senator Charles Schumer in a steel-cage match. Both in loincloths. Tremble as March Madness calls for a time-out from the hardwood floors and takes a spin on polished marble aisles. C-SPAN meets the WWE in a contest of Constitutional Chicken.

Who wins? The American people, that's who. And the lawyers, of course."

This holy mess stems from Congress's determination to talk to Harriet Miers and Karl Rove to ascertain possible political motivation in the firings of eight U.S. Attorneys. President Bush, however, is being steadfast, which is a nice way of saying stubborn as a Texas mule. He maintains that if his staff is compelled to testify, they might become reluctant to give him advice. Reviewing the advice they've been giving him lately, maybe that's not such a bad thing. Maybe he's the one who should be reluctant to accept it.

Reprising his award-winning East Wing talent show impression of Howie Mandel, the president issued Congress an ultimatum: You want talk, OK, they'll talk, but only off the record, in private, under a cone of silence, or not at all. Deal or no deal. The Democrats took about nine nanoseconds before putting the plastic cap on the big red "DEAL" button. Responding to their vow to uncover the wolf in the Administration, the president says that if subpoenas are issued he'll huff and he'll puff and he'll blow their House down.

The Justice Department did as the Justice Department does, exacerbating the situation by doling out more explanations than Will Ferrell has facial tics. Initially, the attorney layoffs were said to be performance related. Then the federal prosecutors were let go due to incompetence. Theirs, not the DOJ's. Other excuses started leaking out like melted Monterey Jack from an overstuffed quesadilla: low departmental morale. Insubordination. Pockets full of fishhooks. Double-knit pants. Substandard dinner table manners. Gray shoes. Cooties.

Why would anybody think the president's men would mislead us? Oh yeah, that's right—Enron. Middle-class tax cuts. Social Security. Stem cells. Prescription drug plan. WMDs. Valerie Plame. And what was Scooter Libby convicted of?

Why, it was perjury, wasn't it? I think the president is on the wrong track here, public relations wise, what with the whole behind-closed-doors, untranscripted nondeposition thing. This is America, George. We're not secret testimony people. We're out-in-the-open people. We're air-it-in-the-public-forum people. You should throw it up on YouTube. Besides, whenever our rights are being stripped from us to keep us free, aren't you the one who's always saying that the innocent have nothing to hide? Hmmm?

Deep-Throated Whining

"Speaking with us today is one of the men who spent some time at the eye of the Watergate storm. The man responsible for installing the electrical tape to cover the door latches during the break-in. Thanks for joining us. As you know, Washington, D.C., is mourning the loss of its favorite 30-year-old guessing game, as the whole country now knows the identity of Deep Throat. Being right there where it all began, what are your thoughts?"

"Disgust mostly. Call me an old-fashioned felon, but I'm revolted by how the liberal media machine is determined to convince a gullible public what a swell guy this Deep Throat character is. Trying to make him out to be a national hero, when he really was nothing but a lousy rat. Skulking around in darkened garages, not breaking into any cars. Deserves the mark of the squealer."

"So you disagree with the notion that Deep Throat provided a great service to the nation?"

"A monumental disservice, is more like it. This guy is nothing but a stone hypocrite. Claims he had evidence of corruption. Well, if he was so damned sure, he should have taken it straight to his superiors."

"But isn't it true that L. Patrick Gray, his immediate and

only superior at the FBI, was also indicted in the very same cover-up?"

"So what? W. Mark Felt was contemptible. Going to outside agencies is unethical. There are proper, Christian ways to go about this sort of thing, and at every juncture, the choice he made was shameful and dishonorable. Something a terrorist would do. Now, I'm not saying Felt was an advance scout for Al-Qaeda, but…"

"Say he had gone to the authorities with this information, what do you think would have happened?"

"That's easy. The focus would have shifted to him and the moral considerations of his whistle blowing, and Nixon would have scurried under a rock to wait for the glare to go away."

"Like what happened with Dan Rather, and with Bush's National Guard duty?"

"Exactly. Nobody bothered to find out if the information was correct or not, once it became clear the documents weren't. If Karl Rove were running things, Nixon might *still* be president."

"Weren't you convicted of burglary of the Watergate offices and subsequently charged with extortion, money laundering and illegal cattle insemination?"

"I acted under the direct orders of our Commander-in-Chief, for whom I considered it an honor to lie, cheat, steal and inseminate cattle."

"Illegal orders."

"I was a good soldier."

"So were the Nazis."

"And your point is…?"

"In a prepared statement, Mark Felt's grandson sees his grandfather's legacy as that of a Great American Hero. Do you take issue with that assessment?"

"Hero? The guy's a schmuck. He totally ruined his legacy. Instead of being known as a former deputy director of the FBI with the highest esteem of his colleagues, now he'll always be known as Deep Throat, the guy who ratted out a president."

"And you'll be known as a criminal sleazebag who broke the law, tried to cover it up and spent five years in federal prison."

"Yes, but I still have the esteem of my colleagues."

"Who are mostly career criminals."

"Touché."

"Well, thanks again for joining us. Next up, a Catholic priest gives us a stern talking-to on the Michael Jackson verdict."

2006 Predictions

It is the beginning of the New Year, and typically the time for us average ink-stained wretches to trot out ye olde tried-but-true Predictions Piece. The wretches who don't resort to trotting out ye olde trite-but-true Resolutions Piece, that is. Being the average traditionalist wretch with great respect for heritage that I am (especially when lacking any other fertile ideas whatsoever), I am proud to honor this revered journalistic practice. Hence, I got your predictions for the New Year right here. Resolutions will show up the next time I get stuck for other fresh and bright ideas. In other words, soon. Happy 2006, everybody.

In the Year 2006...

- I predict George W. Bush will continue to cut programs to the poor, the old and the infirm so that rich people can have more money. I also predict that through a series of tragic financial reversals, the 43rd president will die poor, old and infirm. Because that's the way God would want it.

- I predict Tom DeLay will lose his Houston Congressional race to conservative Democrat Nick Lampson, who lost his seat in '04 due to DeLay's redistricting scheme, because that's also the way God would want it.

- I predict this Administration will break more laws, then conduct investigations into who told the press about the broken laws, instead of investigating the crimes being committed. Like arresting Toto for revealing the Wizard of Oz's incompetence.

- I predict Paris Hilton will hold a press conference to which no one will show up and she will wither away like late-autumn leaves crushed by the tires of an 18-wheeler.

- I predict Dick Cheney's face will freeze like that.

- I predict technology will become so user-friendly that geeks will revert to being nerds.

- I predict air travel will become so much less user-friendly that certain discount tickets will require pedaling.

- I predict the San Francisco Giants will win the World Series, but in lieu of going to Disneyland afterward, Barry Bonds, the MVP, will instead be whisked straight away to a retirement village for a series of recuperative salt baths.

- I predict Bill Gates will develop a donor-recipient software program that makes himself obsolete.

- I predict that Iraq will have so many elections this year, voter turnout will drop to levels normally seen in North Dakota during blizzards.

- I predict Tom Cruise will lose another debate on the *Today Show*, this time to Katie Couric's assistant makeup artist.

- I predict that during a stump speech in upstate New York, gubernatorial candidate Donald Trump's hair will be wind whipped into the shape of a sail, whisking him airborne into a mall parking lot in suburban Vermont.

- I predict that lobbyist Jack Abramoff's squealings will bring down so many members of Congress, the 2007 Freshman Congressional House class will be known as "The Abramoff Babies."

- I predict Governor Arnold Schwarzenegger will move so far to the left in his attempt to mend fences with California voters that Fidel Castro will denounce him as a socialist tool.

- I predict that Secretary of Defense Donald Rumsfeld will engage in a bout of such verbal gymnastics he will confuse himself and inadvertently give a straight answer.

Leftover Top 100 Millennium Lists

A couple of years ago there were a spate, nay, even a plethora, of top 100 lists, where big-time professional wordsmiths made up lists of their versions of the top books, movies, sitcom episodes and mulch-based fertilizers ever. They seemed to be written mostly by competent hacks getting paid by the word, and you could always tell when boredom had set in, as the pieces kind of petered out near the end. Admittedly, these efforts took a lot of time to compile and involved a whole heap of impressive research, and, like everybody else, I vigorously read them and scoffed and screamed at the ceiling, "What about *Hot to Trot*? Where's *Hot to Trot* on the 100 best comedy films of all time?" Well, I channeled my frustration into creating my own version of these best-ever lists. But since all the really good subjects had been taken, I did the best I could with what was left and came up with these top 100s of the millennium.

Top 100 Foods of the Millennium

1. Gruel | 2. Potatoes | 3. Mud | 4. Rice | 5. Soup | 6. Stew |
7. Paella | 8. Gravy | 9. Chowder | 10. Mush | 11. Gumbo |
12. Cioppino | 13. Consommé | 14. Bouillon | 15. Yosenabe |
16. Gazpacho | 17. Bouillabaisse | 18. Poi | 19. Borscht | 20.
Shoes | 21. Grubs | 22. Algae | 23. Baba ganoush | 24. Grass |
25. Berries | 26. Seeds | 27. Nuts | 28. Roots | 29. Mush-
rooms, good | 30. Scum | 31. Eggs Benedict | 32. Turnips |
33. Bacon double cheeseburgers | 34. Rocks | 35. Boogers |
36. Squirrel | 37. Rocky Mountain oysters | 38. Carrots | 39.
Jerky | 40. Apples | 41. Bourbon balls | 42. Mushrooms, bad |
43. Bananas | 44. Corn | 45. Goulash | 46. Oats | 47. Wheat |
48. Couscous | 49. Polenta | 50. Crab bisque | 51. Chicken |
52. Cow | 53. Sheep | 54. Pig | 55. Frog | 56. Carp | 57. Clam
dip | 58. Butter-flavored microwave popcorn | 59. Ice cream |
60. Haggis | 61. Rumaki | 62. Kimchee | 63. Balut | 64. Fudge
brownies | 65. Coq au vin | 66. Nutria | 67. Beets | 68. Chow-
chow | 69. Meat-lovers' stuffed-crust pizza | 70. Cheese danish |
71. Kreplach | 72. Dumplings | 73. Matzo | 74. Gyoza | 75.
Garlic parmesan croutons | 76. Fritters | 77. Jujy Fruits | 78.
Sesame noodles | 79. Pigs in a blanket | 80. Cicerones | 81.
Fresh-Cook'd potato chips | 82. Rendezvous barbecue | 83.
Cousins' Special | 84. Almond windmill cookies | 85. Thasos
olives with red pepper flakes | 86. Wasabi, caramelized onions
and roasted garlic–mashed potatoes | 87. Fettuccine carbonara |
88. Thanksgiving dinner without the cranberries | 89. Broiled
oysters | 90. Diana's Meat Pie at Hunan on Sansome Street | 91.
Mr. Beef's Italian Beef sandwiches | 92. Crawfish étouffe | 93.
Stilton cheese | 94. Usinger's bratwurst | 95. Lobster thermidor |
96. PB&J | 97. Philly cheese steaks | 98. Horse | 99. Tinfoil |
100. Prunes.

Top 100 Years of the Millennium for the United States

No. 1. 1776 | No. 2. 1492 | No. 3. 1945 | No. 4. 1781 | No. 5. 1789 | No. 6. 1968 | No. 7. 1918 | No. 8. 1865 | No. 9. 1939 | No. 10. 1952 | No. 11. 1933 | No. 12. 1783 | No. 13. 1803 | No. 14. 1790 | No. 15. 1963 | No. 16. 1981 | No. 17. 1900 | No. 18. 1820 | No. 19. 1796 | No. 20. 1941 | No. 21. 1946 | No. 22. 1964 | No. 23. 1913 | No. 24. 1812 | No. 25. 1927 | No. 26. 1787 | No. 27. 1857 | No. 28. 1863 | No. 29. 1919 | No. 30. 1846 | No. 31. 1777 | No. 32. 1886 | No. 33. 1974 | No. 34. 1969 | No. 35. 1936 | No. 36. 1921 | No. 37. 1971 | No. 38. 1892 | No. 39. 1922 | No. 40. 1923 | No. 41. 1924 | No. 42. 1925 | No. 43. 1926 | No. 44. 1821 | No. 45. 1822 | No. 46. 1823 | No. 47. 1824 | No. 48. 1825 | No. 49. 1826 | No. 50. 1868 | No. 51. 1901 | No. 52. 1903 | No. 53. 1972 | No. 54. 1973 | No. 55. 1985 | No. 56. 1986 | No. 57. 1987 | No. 58. 1988 | No. 59. 1989 | No. 60. 1872 | No. 61. 1990 | No. 62. 1998 | No. 63. 1893 | No. 64. 1894 | No. 65. 1795 | No. 66. 1796 | No. 67. 1897 | No. 68. 1997 | No. 69. 1898 | No. 70. 1799 | No. 71. 2000 | No. 72. 1493 | No. 73. 1494 | No. 74. 1612 | No. 75. 1613 | No. 76. 1999 | No. 77. 1491 | No. 78. 1830 | No. 79. 1930 | No. 80. 1840 | No. 81. 1940 | No. 82. 1750 | No. 83. 1850 | No. 84. 1950 | No. 85. 1951 | No. 86. 1851 | No. 87. 1751 | No. 88. 1651 | No. 89. 1551 | No. 90. 1451 | No. 91. 1351 | No. 92. 1251 | No. 93. 1151 | No. 94. 1152 | No. 95. 1154 | No. 96. 1164 | No. 97. 1860 | No. 98. 1860 | No. 99. 1960 | No. 100. 1060.

The Top 100 Toys of the Millennium

1. Dolls | 2. Sticks | 3. Balls | 4. Mud | 5. Rocks | 6. Straw | 7. Water | 8. Boogers | 9. String | 10. Matches | 11. Logs | 12. Hair | 13. Knives | 14. Jacks | 15. Buttons | 16. Hoops | 17. Forks | 18. Glass | 19. Tops | 20. Spools | 21. Thimbles | 22. Ribbons | 23. Blocks | 24. Cardboard boxes | 25. Wooden boxes | 26. Wooden crates | 27. Steel crates | 28. Plastic milk cartons | 29. Upside-down buckets | 30. Jack-in-the-boxes | 31. Feces | 32. Magnifying

glasses | 33. Marbles | 34. Dead rodents | 35. Sock puppets | 36. Mousetraps | 37. Tinfoil | 38. Hammers | 39. Blasting caps | 40. Balloons | 41. Scissors | 42. Chutes and ladders. No, *real* chutes and real ladders | 43. Rattles | 44. Tiddlywinks | 45. Slinkys | 46. Cans | 47. Abandoned refrigerators | 48. Loose teeth | 49. Spoons | 50. Horseshoes | 51. Mars Polar Landers | 52. Straws | 53. Squirt guns | 54. Genuine Red Ryder Carbine Action Two-Hundred-Shot Lightning-Loader Range Model air rifles | 55. Cork guns | 56. Laser pointers | 57. Zip guns | 58. Tec-9s | 59. AK-47s | 60. Stinger surface-to-air missiles | 61. Darts | 62. Game Boys | 63. Suction cups | 64. Trains | 65. Trucks | 66. Big Wheels | 67. Sheep | 68. Beer kegs | 69. Checkers | 70. Pokemon | 71. Eleanor Roosevelt | 72. Pentagrams | 73. Dental floss | 74. Library paste | 75. Airplane glue | 76. Speedballs | 77. Wheelos | 78. Legos | 79. Tinkertoys | 80. Spoons | 81. Rotting fruit | 82. Fishing lures | 83. Close and Plays | 84. Cellophane | 85. Condoms | 86. Dad's lighter fluid | 87. Shellfish | 88. Other people's mail | 89. Paddle balls | 90. Colorforms | 91. Etch-A-Sketches | 92. Rubber bands | 93. Snow globes | 94. Skin | 95. Shaving cream | 96. Cows | 97. Birdnests | 98. Lug nuts | 99. Speculums | 100. Weebles.

All right. This is it. The last of those stupid top 100 lists you'll see. And when you get right down to it: the most important.

Top 100 Human Body Parts of the Millennium

1. Soul | 2. Heart | 3. Gut | 4. Pigment | 5. Female reproductive organ | 6. Male reproductive organ | 7. Thumb | 8. Spine | 9. Eyes | 10. Lips | 11. Thighs | 12. Ears | 13. Female nipples | 14. Teeth | 15. Washboard abs | 16. Hands | 17. Bowels | 18. Tongue | 19. Feet | 20. Artificially augmented mammary glands | 21. Nose |

22. Liver | 23. Mouth | 24. Hair | 25. Ring finger | 26. Muscles | 27. Knees | 28. Shoulders | 29. Skull | 30. Kidney | 31. Taste buds | 32. Pituitary gland | 33. Sinus | 34. Elbows | 35. Shins | 36. Forearms | 37. Neck | 38. Fontanel | 39. Temple | 40. Spleen | 41. Intestine (large) | 42. Brain | 43. Calves | 44. Larynx | 45. Lungs | 46. Ribs | 47. Forefinger | 48. Collarbone | 49. Coccyx | 50. Buns of steel | 51. Heel | 52. Big toe | 53. Stomach | 54. Upper palate | 55. Chin | 56. Hips | 57. Nostrils | 58. Groin | 59. Male reproductive organ's two best friends | 60. Cheeks (upper) | 61. Urethra | 62. Epidermis | 63. Fingernails | 64. Placenta | 65. Clavicle | 66. Back of knees | 67. Cheeks (lower) | 68. Fallopian tube | 69. Middle finger | 70. Mandible | 71. Forehead | 72. Pelvis | 73. Eyebrows | 74. Pancreas | 75. Freckles | 76. Vertebrae | 77. Trachea | 78. Inside of elbows | 79. Wrists | 80. Gums | 81. Achilles heels | 82. Veins | 83. Eyelids | 84. Capillaries | 85. Eyelashes | 86. Knuckles | 87. Belly | 88. Anterior cruciate ligaments | 89. Funny bones | 90. Side burns | 91. Palms | 92. Toenails | 93. Prostate | 94. Arches | 95. Duodenum | 96. Groove between nose and upper lip | 97. Tonsils | 98. Appendix | 99. Armpits | 100. Male nipples.

I lied, here's another list. But absolutely the last. Promise. Fingers crossed.

Top 100 Colors of the Millennium

1. Blue | 2. Red | 3. Yellow | 4. Green | 5. Black | 6. White | 7. Brown | 8. Grey | 9. Purple | 10. Pink | 11. Orange | 12. Violet | 13. Maroon | 14. Olive | 15. Tan | 16. Silver | 17. Gold | 18. Bronze | 19. Crimson | 20. Pine | 21. Royal blue | 22. Sky blue | 23. Midnight blue | 24. Navy blue | 25. Indigo | 26. Scarlet | 27. Lime | 28. Grape | 29. Pumpkin | 30. Eggplant | 31. Forest | 32. Blonde | 33. Peach | 34. Plum | 35. Day-Glo | 36. Gray | 37. Dark brown | 38. Khaki | 39. Light brown | 40. Baby-poop brown | 41. Chocolate |

42. Beige | 43. Mustard | 44. Burnt sienna | 45. Cream | 46. Sepia | 47. Butter | 48. Off white | 49. Near white | 50. White, only less than | 51. Ivory | 52. Bone | 53. Eggshell | 54. Sand | 55. Champagne | 56. Pearl | 57. Parchment | 58. Vanilla | 59. Taupe | 60. Desert stone | 61. Buff | 62. Mauve | 63. Ice | 64. Watermelon | 65. Hemp | 66. Turquoise | 67. Cinnamon | 68. Periwinkle | 69. Tortoise shell | 70. Charcoal | 71. Vermilion | 72. Rust | 73. Cayenne | 74. Cilantro | 75. Raspberry | 76. Lavender | 77. Persimmon | 78. Espresso | 79. Merlot | 80. Burgundy | 81. Rose | 82. Beaujolais | 83. Sage | 84. Blush | 85. Hyacinth | 86. Yellow green | 87. Green yellow | 88. Moss | 89. Brick | 90. Coral | 91. Aqua | 92. Chrome | 93. Jade | 94. Ruby | 95. Emerald | 96. Mahogany | 97. Licorice | 98. Puce | 99. Fuchsia | 100. Cerise.

9/11 Plus 5

Monday is the fifth anniversary of IX-XI, and President Bush has apparently decided to prepare us for our national day of mourning by delivering a weeklong series of seminars about the joys of fear mongering. OK, OK, maybe "fear mongering" is a bit much. Perhaps a better phrase would be "PR campaign of cheap political calculation," or "systematic exploitative pandering," or "a typical sleazy example from the Karl Rove electioneering handbook." Or, as we have to come know it during the last six years, "business as usual."

First, Dubyah played the Nazi card, calling Democratic plans for a phased withdrawal of our forces from Iraq an appeasement similar to Chamberlain's treatment of Hitler in 1939. I'm surprised he didn't unveil secret footage of Nancy Pelosi brandishing a rolled-up umbrella. Then he played the Red Menace card, invoking Lenin and intimating a hammer-and-sickle tattoo on Howard Dean's forehead (invisible only due to a thickly slapped-on layer of Dark Egyptian Number 4 makeup).

And if these two jackbooted images don't do the trick, expect to hear him summon up other, more ancient, scourges like the Huns and the Mongols and the Visigoths in his never-ending quest to keep Americans all aquiver so we run and hide behind his urban camouflaged pants right up till the clock strikes 8 p.m. PST, November 7, 2006. (Screw Hawaii.)

Uncharacteristically, Democrats refused to curl up in their customary flinching fetal position at the sound of the president's big bad wolf rhetoric, and ratcheted up their criticism of his war policies, calling for the institutionalized bitch-slapping of Donald Rumsfeld in a transparently futile attempt to get the Secretary of Defense to join 10,000 Intel workers in next month's unemployment line. Predictable as a papier-mâché roof in a category 3 hurricane? Yes. But, as they say about fire, it takes politics to fight politics.

White House spokesman Tony Snow knee-slapped and guffawed and scoffed that the Democrats' proposal portraying Rumsfeld as a bogeyman "may make for good politics but makes for lousy strategy." And one can't immediately discount that opine because, if anybody has experience with lousy strategies, it's this White House.

An Administration that strategized the best way to stem terrorist activity was to invade a country that had none. An Administration that strategized that applying car battery contacts to a prisoner's nipples was not torture because it wasn't life threatening. An Administration that strategized that causing the death of over 100,000 noncombatant Iraqis was going to win over the hearts and minds of their countryfolk. An Administration that considers the best strategist to be the one who carries the biggest stick. Do the names Dick Cheney, Donald Rumsfeld and John Bolton have any meaning here?

In just one of his series of deep-tissue massages of fear and loathing, Bush mentioned Osama bin Laden by name 18 times, conveniently neglecting to mention it was *he himself* who *disbanded* the CIA division devoted to finding the six-foot-seven-inch Arabian guy traipsing around the Kyhber Pass dragging behind him a solar-powered kidney dialysis machine from the Islamabad Sharper Image catalog.

A long, long time ago, in a galaxy far, far away, the president spoke to the country of bin Laden: "He can run but he can't hide." You know what, it's been five years. I think they're both hiding. One behind the billowing skirts of the other.

The 13th Annual Will Durst "Thank God for These Liquid Squeezebags Because I'm a Comic" Awards

As you have probably figured out by the alarming lack of hairspray, stretch limousines and $30,000 designer gowns available in your area, awards season is upon us. And, while we don't have any red carpets to roll out, we do promise that Joan Rivers will have as much to do with this column as Dick Cheney has to do with reality. Yes, it's that time of year again when vast groups of entertainment professionals pat themselves on the back to the point where they run the risk of spraining a delicate wrist or two. Millions of people ostensibly watch these oozing, moody egos toss cast-goldplated statuettes at each other, in order to live vicariously through them, but we all know it's really to ridicule fashion choices. And here at Durstco™ ("You Want the Best, So Do We"), having never spied a slow-moving bandwagon we weren't willing to jump on, it is with giddy self-congratulation that we settle in for the most serious and consequential of all the awards ceremonies: the Will Durst "THANK GOD FOR THESE LIQUID SQUEEZEBAGS BECAUSE I'M A COMIC" Awards. Sit yourself down in a comfortable chair and relax, folks. We got your back. And be assured, not a single *Brokeback Mountain* joke in the bunch.

The *"For Crum's Sake, Come On, Give Her The Money, She Slept with a 90-Year-Old Guy for a Year and a Half" Award:*
Anna Nicole Smith

The *"If They Were a Horse, We'd Have to Shoot 'em" Award:*
The Democratic Party

Best Makeup:
Harry Whittington

The *"Making a Bad Situation Worse" Award:*
In a crowded field, New Orleans Mayor Ray Nagin.

Best Performance by Strange Bedfellows:
George Herbert Walker Bush and William Jefferson Clinton. Together again.

Best Impression of a Sleepy Lizard in Search of a Warm Rock Award:
Once again, Dick Cheney, narrowly edging out Robert Novak and Sam Donaldson.

The *"Unclear on All the Words in Their Name" Award:*
The Federal Emergency Management Agency

The *"Skanky Ho Before My First Legal Drink" Award:*
It's a three-way tie! Paris and Nicky Hilton, and Nicole Ritchie.

The *"Most Important Man in America" Award:*
For the sixth year in a row, Supreme Court Justice John Paul Steven's doctor.

The *"Let's Settle All Global Disputes by Holding Hands and Singing 'Kumbaya'" Award:*
Perennial presidential candidate Dennis Kucinich wins handily.

The "Lurking Like a Ticking Time Bomb" Award:
Patrick Fitzgerald

The "Not as Dumb as His Hair Looks" Award:
It's a Tie! Reverend Al Sharpton and Donald
Trump split this honor.

The "Most Likely to Find God Real Soon" Award:
Scooter Libby

The "Unclear on the Concept" Award:
Former head of FEMA, Michael Brown, for
announcing he's opening a new crisis management consultancy.

The "Shut My Mouth" Award:
Another tie! Pat Robertson and Harriet Miers.

The Self-Control Award:
To George Bush, for visiting India and not asking
where all the teepees were.

Best Score:
Halliburton, for not just beating a gouging charge
but finagling a bonus out of it.

Best Makeover:
John Kerry, billionaire Boston Brahmin blueblood
who becomes an ordinary friend-of-the-mill-work-
er type guy in a pre-Iowa blink of an eye.

The "Oh My God, Not You Again!" Award:
Ralph Nader. Scarier than *Jason vs. Freddy III.*

Unsound Design Award:
George W. Bush and his privatization of Social
Security plan.

The "Losing His Grip" Award:
Karl Rove

Best Animation:
Howard Dean in his Iowa nonconcession speech

Misdirection Award:
Donald Rumsfeld. "Weapons of mass destruction? What weapons of mass destruction? We never said he had weapons of mass destruction. What we said was, he was a bad guy."

The "Why Won't Anyone Return My Calls?" Award:
Al Gore

Best Score:
$12 Million for Bill Clinton's memoirs and $8 million for Hillary's. That's $20 million for the recollections of two people who for eight years continually testified, under oath, they couldn't remember a single thing.

The "He Knows More Than He's Letting on and I Don't Think It's Good News" Award:
Alan Greenspan

Best Choreographer:
Karl Rove for managing to bury discussion of Bush's missing years in the Texas National Guard under drumbeat of necessity for a constitutional amendment banning gay marriages.

The "Most Deserving Disappearing Act" Award:
Joementum

The "Take Off the Blinders and He'll Still Run Right into an Eighteenth-Century Wall" Award:
John Ashcroft

Ring Around the Coercion

As we all know, *Newsweek* magazine recently rehashed an oft-repeated report involving American interrogators at Guantanamo Bay using religious coercion—in this case, flushing a copy of the Koran down a toilet. According to the magazine, the action was a way of trying to provoke detainees into talking. Love that word "detainees." Sounds so pastoral. "Uncle Achmed, you've missed seven of my birthday parties." "I was detained."

After hearing about the article, mobs in Pakistan and Afghanistan erupted into violent anti-American protests. And not your normal, average, everyday, regularly scheduled anti-American mob protests, either. At least 17 people died and many others were severely wounded. And no, I have no idea how they managed to get their hands on the latest *Newsweek*. My subscription issue usually doesn't show up till a couple of weeks later. For instance, did you know Pope John Paul II just died?

Now, even though it doth protest too much, the magazine is backing down like a badly beaten mule at cliff's edge. Mark Whitaker, *Newsweek*'s editor, said, "We're not retracting anything. We don't know for certain what we got wrong." Doesn't that also mean you don't know what you got right? Their purported source, a senior U.S. Government official, who for some unknown reason wants to remain nameless, is not sure whether his story is true. That's right. *He's* not sure if *his* story is true.

Whoa, whoa, whoa. Back up, here. This guy thinks maybe he made a mistake. Now, he thinks? Post-mob rioting, he thinks? I'm thinking, this guy wasn't thinking. Then of course the White House decides to throw their lily-white hands into the mix and starts blaming *Newsweek* for the deaths in Pakistan and Afghanistan. The White House. Blaming somebody for deaths because they got some facts wrong. These guys are bucking for poster boys for irony in the modern world.

Predictably, *Newsweek* retracted the article, citing the source's confusion, and some Muslims claim that pressure was applied to make this guy say he might have made a mistake. In fact, so much pressure was applied so fast, Bill Frist may want to make sure his "nuclear option" is in the same drawer where he left it.

The ludicrous part is the White House blaming *Newsweek*. First off, the magazine tried to vet the article with the Pentagon; second, it was just a tiny three-paragraph spread in the "Periscope" section; third, not to mention articles alleging similar activities by U.S. interrogators had been printed about a hundred zillion times since the war started. I guess Bush is worried this incident might harm U.S.–Islam relations. And just when things were going so well, too.

Neither is *Newsweek* blameless. How do you quote an anonymous source who may or may not have seen something about something else in a report somewhere or maybe it was jotted on the back of a grocery list or glimpsed behind the 24 Nautilus ad on a coffee shop bulletin board or perhaps it was all just a dream? Next time, before instigating worldwide riots, you might want to nail down some corroboration.

I'm sure you're blissfully unaware of this, but when it comes to the desecration of the Koran, you could say Muslims have a tendency to become a bit temperamental. You could also say a cooler full of blended margaritas makes an interesting driving companion, and muddy golf cleats are lousy crib mobiles. And most doubts could probably be cleared up with one quick trip to the grocery store with Salman Rushdie.

Plug Me In

At first I thought the only halfway nonghastly thing to come out of the Terry Schiavo tragedy was the delight in watching all those grandstanding politicians choke on their own bugles sounding retreat while rear ending each other on the way to the Tampa/St. Pete airport at speeds approaching mach VII. But I was wrong.

Another positive side effect was the vast legions of citizens who awakened to the realization that we are responsible for plotting our own demise. Newspapers are printing primitive but binding living wills next to the sudoku puzzle. Which is good. Facing up to our mortality might force a few of us to understand there are more important things to life than parties that somebody was or wasn't invited to and whose zirconium replica of Paris Hilton's dog's collar looks more real.

Right now, most of the concerned introspective meditations consist of chastened yuppies adamantly professing their refusal to end up a vegetable. "I guarantee that's not going to be me. I refuse to live like a rutabaga. If you love me at all, you'll pull my plug." To these well-meaning banana heads, I have one thing to say: "Not me, brother. Plug me in." I want to live. As man, as a vegetable or as a refreshing side order of fruit salad with a light dribble of strawberry yogurt sauce. Hell, I never thought I'd make it this far, to begin with. When I was a kid, anybody older than 30 was a withered ancient. A prehistoric geezer. A core sample of archaic decay. But, even then, I never bought into that whole "hope I die before I get old" crap. And now, I'm aiming for triple digits. A couple more years? If that's all you got, it'll do. A month. Part of a week. Cool. Cool. All I want is extra. I want more.

You see, now that I made it this far, I kind of like it. Puppies. Sunsets. Bases loaded, bottom of the ninths. New large-print James Lee Burke mysteries. Jalapeño-flavored potato chips. Turner Classic Movies. Life is good. And I plan to hang on to it, with the tips of my fingernails. If the only way to keep my respirator charged is by fluttering my eyelids 24 hours a day, I will flutter away. Who knows what tomorrow's scientists might come up with? Maybe they'll uncover a fountain of middle age. A perpetual eyelid flutterer. Why do you think they call it the "future"?

"So you're content to linger like a vegetable?" Yeah. Sure. Why not? What's the big deal? Call me Mr. Potato Head. Like I haven't been before. You think my soul will be indelibly soiled beyond repair because someone referred to me as Brussels Sprout Boy? Soil me. Isolate a webcam on my hospice bed and pay-per-view me as the Human Asparagus Video Blog. Water me from a sprinkling can. Use my open mouth as a pencil cup and call me Shorty. Test poisonous-toad cosmetics on my tongue. Lease me out as a large, prone, pincushion at a Tattoo Arts Convention. Fit me with scuba gear, bury me naked with my butt sticking out of the ground and use it as a bicycle rack. I don't care. Let me live. That's Will's Living Will. And if I do sink into a coma or become completely brain-dead, someone try and remember to hook me up to an IV drip of pure espresso, because I don't want to miss a thing.

The Bright Side of Global Warming

Oh, you're going to love this. It's the latest tripe being ground out of the ever-busy Bush Administration sausage factory of spin. Now that the evidence about global warming is pretty much nailed to the "real and actual" bulletin board, meaning every scientist on the face of the planet agrees that not only are so we neck deep in the middle of it the bottom of our earlobes are starting to tickle, it turns out—no worries. It's really good for us. Yes. "Glaciers are actually growing." Well, at least one is. In spots. Some scientists say this is also due to global warming, but hey, why work yourself into a lather? You can't deny shipping will profit due to the opening of the Northwest Passage. It's the fast-tracking of Armageddon. So what if other parts of the world are destined to suffer eternal droughts or total submersion or disappearing fauna and flora and coastline? That's merely what you call your collateral damage. Can't have an industrialized omelet without breaking a few hundred billion eggs. Just think of the future as the 12-ton boulder hovering over a hen house.

According to Al Gore's movie *An Inconvenient Truth,* we got a window of about 10 years before we hit the point of no return, and let's face it: Americans are the lead dog in this Iditarod to Hell. And we got less chance of altering our gas-guzzling ways in time than a pack of Chihuahuas has of pulling a sled carrying the entire 101st Airborne. Wouldn't you say it's just about time we weenie liberals accept the fate that God and ExxonMobil have mapped out for us, and search for the silver lining in living on a planet speedily replicating the atmosphere of Mercury? I would. It's the point of this column. So let us take a couple of moments to band together, spray ourselves down with SPF 450, stop whining and look at the upside of planetary overheating.

On Global Warming's Bright Side...

- Casual Friday becomes clothing-optional Friday.
- Not nearly as many frog species to catalog.
- MTV's Jose Cuervo Spring Break brought to you live from the world-famous beaches of Prince Edward Island.
- History Channel specials on picnics.
- Dive the ruins of Bangladesh.
- Extreme Siberian summers—in December.
- Fewer glaciers, more salt flats.
- Wyoming coconuts.
- Heated swimming pools: a given.
- Deteriorating ozone makes air travel too dangerous for politicians to make trips back to home districts.

- Knockoff Louis Vuitton full-body containment suits sold on streets.
- A flourishing alligator-sightseeing industry on Lake Michigan.
- Dune buggies everywhere, dude.
- Monkey wranglers: a North American growth industry.
- A perfect, all-over tan in less than 30 seconds.
- Aged Canadian coffee beans: Yukon Yuban.
- Worried about unprovoked polar bear attacks? Don't be, ever again.
- Oceanfront property in New Mexico.
- Antarctic pinot noir.
- Real black panthers in Oakland.
- Surfing + Sweden = nirvana.
- So many hurricanes, *your* name guaranteed to cycle through list much more often.
- Dwarf banana trees in every backyard.
- You won't have to retire to Arizona; Arizona will come to you.

E-Mail to the Cardinal

To: Cardinal Carmerlengo Eduardo Martinez Somalo
From: Rob Johnson, Mark Burnett Productions,
     VP in Charge of New Projects
Subject: POPE!

Dear Cardinal Chamberlain:

Thanks for getting back to me. I know how busy you are, what with 200 cardinals showing up, not to mention 4 million pilgrims. Must be total chaos. Like an Italian family reunion times infinity. Or is it eternity?

First, let me tell you how sorry I am for your loss. Never got to meet J2P2 personally, but I hear he was an absolutely terrific pontiff. Think we can assume someone is taking cuts in the line outside the Pearly Gates.

Still no face time with My Holy Father, Mr. Burnett (he's shepherding Martha Stewart through the eye of a needle right now), but his personal assistant's intern assures me all your concerns will be addressed.

Our goal is not just to make a lot of money on a successful reality series, but to throw a fresh spin on the best damn religion on the face of the planet. To make the Roman Catholic Church hip again. Islam is hot right now. Why? Been in the news recently. Publicity. That's all. Heat. Juice. Moxie.

The introduction of a new pope is the perfect window of opportunity for Catholicism to get a well-deserved Extreme Makeover.

Our show *Pope* plans to go behind the sacristy to reveal the intrigue and romance that goes into a new pope picking. But not reveal *too* much. We know you have secrets. We want to preserve and exploit them.

Just a couple of quick questions.

- The silver hammer. Did you really hit J2P2 in the forehead with it to make sure he wasn't sleeping? We need it. For use as a visual bumper along with a musical sting, à la *Law & Order*. Konk-Konk. Danny Elfman's working on it right now.

- Do the failed candidates get voted out of the conclave? Can they be? Are torches snuffed or staffs clipped? Can they be?

- The ballots. Wouldn't the show logo look great on them? Discreet, of course. I see a florid Latin script. Should research Michelangelo's old notebooks; find a proprietary font. You might be able to help out with that on your end.

- Do the cardinals compete in ritual trials, like endurance kneeling? Or who can hear the most confessions in an hour? Host tossing: judged on accuracy and distance? Is that part of the process? Can it be?

- Black & white doesn't read. Would you consider coloring the smoke coming out of the chimney? (FYI: Purple and pink tested off the charts.)
- Merchandising wants to know:

1. Before destroying the old dead pope's Fisherman's Ring, could we make a replica? Very, very, very limited edition. Great premium to hand out to critics before sweeps.

2. Do the cardinals drink Coke? Is there any rule against it?

3. Pick-A-Pope™ Trading Cards—totally out of bounds? The network is worried we're testosterone-heavy. Can we throw a nun or two into the mix?

- We need anecdotes. Any famous wacky conclave pranks? You'd think the cardinals must have punked one another during some unenlightened age.
- Understand J2P2 is to be buried beneath the crypt with 147 other popes. We would kill for that footage. Not literally. You know what I mean. But hey, everything is negotiable.
- Da Vinci Code. Understand your reservations, but they *did* inquire again about a tie-in, so let me broach this one more time: Spielberg *and* Hanks. Talk about infallibility. Still your call.

E-mail me back ASAP. We got ourselves a hook, and it's time to hit the lake fishing. And you're the fisher of men, right?

Casting off,

Sincerely yours,

Rob

Cry "Havoc" and Let Slip the Gods of War

You got to feel sorry for poor Pat Robertson. This guy has put his foot in his mouth so many times in the last week, he's probably this close to a shoe-glue addiction. First, he appears on his television show *The 700 Club* and calls for the assassination of Venezuelan President Hugo Chavez. And isn't it refreshing to finally see somebody speaking the truth about our foreign policy? This could be the start of a whole new trend. Next thing you know, President Bush will show up at a VFW rally and talk about how that punk Putin is just itching to be iced.

Of course, then the inevitable happened: A few near-sighted malcontents wondered aloud about Robertson's sanity and whether he should be herded off to a quiet place in the country and fed a steady diet of strained food, flavored just enough to hide the taste of the industrial-strength sedatives. Or shoe glue. Not to mention a few Venezuelans who took minor umbrage. So Pat reluctantly went back on TV, not to apologize, but to say he didn't really say what we all heard him say. "I didn't say 'assassination' [unh, yes you did]. I said our special forces should 'take him out.' 'Take him out' could be a number of things including kidnapping." Methinks either the Rev. Robertson is spending very little money on his public relations firm or he has made it his policy to plug his ears and hum "Sugar Sugar" while they speak.

Robertson went back on his television show and told his audience that maybe what he meant to say was that Chavez should only be kidnapped a little. Well, why didn't you say so in the first place? Kidnapping is so much more civilized than out-and-out assassination. Assassination is so final, what with the blood and the deadness and all. But kidnapping allows room for doubt, with the attendant missingness. Much more mysterious and romantic.

When you get right down to it, he's right; the phrase "take him out" could mean many things. It could mean place him upright next to the garage like a stack of old *National Geographic*s on garbage night. Or maybe take him out to dinner and then a movie followed by a long, slow drive to Inspiration Point with the top down and *The Best of Tony Orlando and Dawn* playing soft and low. He could have meant either of those, but I doubt it.

Asked to comment about Robertson's suggestion that our government "take out" Hugo Chavez, Donald Rumsfeld laughed it off as a ridiculous suggestion that would never happen because assassinations of foreign leaders are illegal. Nobody pointed out that so are the stealing of elections and the outing of CIA agents and the torture of foreign detainees. Sticky technicalities we've seemed to dodge in the past.

Of course, the Good Reverend is being portrayed by the radical right as a wacky uncle who likes his hot toddies a tad too much, but remember, this is the guy who once said feminism was responsible for women killing their children, practicing witchcraft and destroying capitalism. So obviously his hold on reality is about as tenuous as a room deposit for Courtney Love's fifth anniversary sobriety party. We can't expect him to lose his television show, but we can only hope his invitations to the Lincoln Bedroom have been assassinated. Or at least kidnapped.

Slogans: Good. Policy: Bad

President Bush tapped Karen Hughes this week to be his extra-special, supersecret advisor whose mission, should she choose to accept it, is to repair the image of the U.S. overseas, particularly in the Arab world. What are they code naming this mission: Sisyphus? Does the phrase "Finger in a dyke" have any meaning here? Perhaps a raffle or a bake sale is also in the works. As my daddy always said, "No matter how many ducky feathers you glue to a tank, you're still not going to get invited to swim in many inflated pools." Or something like that.

It'll be interesting to see what measures Hughes takes when she finds out the problem isn't so much our lousy public relations as our lousy foreign policies. You want to improve America's image? I'll tell you how to improve America's image. Put a leash on Rumsfeld and stop treating the rest of the world like it smells funny and made a doo-doo on the shag rug in front of Mother Teresa's more sanctimonious sister on Easter Sunday.

I got to say, creating the position of Spinmeister General does makes sense; at least we're playing to our strengths. As a country, we excel at selling the sizzle over the steak. Just last fall, this nation's veterans chose a borderline deserter over a decorated war hero. And the responsibility for that feat can be laid directly at the altar of advertising. There you go: Enlist the Swift Boat Veterans to launch an international campaign finally revealing the truth about Osama's chronic bed wetting. Which could prove to be ugly in a canted cave.

If Karen Hughes plans to craft a cuddlier image for us, she's going to need a little help. OK, she's going to need a *lot* of help. An aircraft carrier group of help. And I'm thinking some snappy slogans could come in handy. Quick. Simple. Buzz-worthy. So, in the interest of patriotism, I'm offering up a few. Gratis. No need to thank me, I'm here to help.

30 U.S. Foreign Policy Extreme Makeoverover Slogans. 30.

- Democracy: Just Do It.
- You're in Good Hands With Our State.
- You Keep the Sand, We'll Take the Oil.
- Sometimes You Feel Like a Crazed Tyrannical Despot, Sometimes You Don't.
- Freedom: Breakfast of Champions.

- When Democracy Reigns, It Pours.
- America: Just a Big Red, White and Blue Teddy Bear with a Whole Lot of Guns.
- Snap. Crackle. Pow. Thud.
- Be All We Think You Should Be.
- Tastes Great—Less Torture.
- They Don't Call Us the *Great* Satan for Nothing.
- America 2.0—Now with New, Improved Press Suppression.
- What's So Bad About Bread and Circuses Anyway?
- John Wayne: Not Just an Actor, a Way of Life.
- Don't Like Us? Get in Line.
- I'd Walk a Mile for a Camel.
- The U.S.: The Ultimate Lying Machine.
- Wouldn't You Really Rather Have a Republic?
- Badges? We Don't Need No Stinking Badges.
- Friendly Fire 'R' Us.
- We're Everywhere You Want to Be—Deal with It.
- The New, Improved Low-Carb, Atkins-Friendly America.
- Got Grenades?
- Don't Leave Home Without It—No, Really, Stay in Your Homes.
- I Can't Believe I Invaded the Whole Peninsula.
- Autonomy: It's the Real Thing.
- The Best Part of Waking Up Is No Dead Bodies on Your Doorstep.
- Aren't You Glad You Use a Free-Market Economy? Don't You Wish Everybody Did?
- Better Living Through Sovereignty.
- Nobody Doesn't Like Britney Spears.

6 You Me Us

We. And wheee! And wee-wee-wee all the way home. No roast beef for we. Not much for oui, either. But a surfeit of ennui. And a hell of a lot of us. And more everyday. The body politic is pregnant with quintuplets. But are we alone?

Hell, you've been out there. It's not all that hard to believe in a higher intelligence than humans. And what conceit, to imagine that we can envision the face of God. Like an ant at a town picnic contemplating a father/daughter three-legged race. Of course, I believe the proof there is intelligent life on other planets is the fact that they've obviously chosen not to contact us. "Stay away from the noisy blue planet. They pee in their water supply. Swear to God."

Giving Thanks

Aaah. Thanksgiving. The most bestest holiday of them all. Food, family, football: three of the four Fs. Not to mention four-story-tall helium balloons on rope tethers. What a grand day. Forty-foot cartoon characters, tryptophan overdosing, lime Jell-O with carrot shreds *and* a chance to see the Dallas Cowboys lose? Where's the bad? The good news is that right now it's not that difficult to come up with a list of what to be thankful for. You start with the old standbys: a wonderful family, good health, a roof and plenty to eat, odd friends and the fact that we're Americans and don't have to worry about the president of the United States calling in an air strike and bombing us...yet.

Then you move on to the obvious. Anchor Steam Christmas Ale and double cheeseburgers on a butter-grilled bun. But in these troubling times it's also important to look beyond our personal cubicles and find the universal threads that we weave together to make up the fabric of our lives. I have no idea what that meant, either. Mostly it's just a segue into a list of other things we should all be thankful for. "We," meaning that highly influential special-interest group encompassing, among others, political comedians and editorial cartoonists:

- China. For its status as a safe publicity haven for any politician sinking in the polls faster than a gravel truck with no brakes off a hairpin cliff turn into a mountain lake. Re: November trips for both California Governor Arnold Schwarzenegger and President George W. Bush.

- France. Because now the French are revolting. But that's redundant, isn't it?

- Robert Novak. For his inability to keep a low profile since leaking the name of CIA agent Valerie Plame. Does the term "hubris" have any meaning here?

- Our State Department. For invading a country based on the ramblings of a source nicknamed "Curveball."

- Corporate marketers. For their conspicuous, patriotic refusal to infringe on the sanctity of the Fourth of July by delaying the start of their Christmas campaigns till early August.

- The 22nd Amendment. For prohibiting this president from serving more than two terms, keeping the American public from making the same mistake more than twice.

- Vice President Cheney. For his epic condescension, from a man without whom we would never be cognizant of the subtle intricacies of the concept of "compassionate torture."

- President Bush. For his use of the tactic of "stonewalling," washing all us boomers in a nostalgic wave of a better time.

- The Administration. For wanting to have their turkey and eat it too. Swift Boating anybody who dares suggest we leave Iraq, then having generals leak plans to do the exact same thing.

- Karl Rove, Scott McClellan and Scooter Libby. For their unceasing and continuing efforts to stretch the bounds of human incredulity. And, oh yeah, let's not forget Tom DeLay and Bill Frist. And Pat Robertson. And the entire Executive Branch. And every Democrat breathing, save Congressman John Murtha. I salute each and every one of these oblivious reprobates for their part in making us rethink on a daily basis exactly how much crap we're willing to swallow to keep our SUVs full of gas.

- Congress. For the construction of a prescription Medicare plan just a wee bit murkier than the instructions for a wire mesh bookcase translated from the original Mandarin into Sanskrit before being printed on gray paper with insufficient toner in something almost resembling English. A little.

- Lobbyist Jack Abramoff for the pure chutzpa of convincing an Indian tribe to pay for his FedEx Stadium luxury suite to watch a team called the Redskins play.

FAQ: *Super Bowl and Janet Jackson's Boobie*

Frequently Asked Questions About the Super Bowl Halftime Show

Q. Do you seriously mean to tell me this country's entire radio, television and print media worlds went on a three-day saturation bender of berserk self-righteousness simply because we got to see Janet Jackson's boob for a split second in a long shot during the Super Bowl halftime show?

A. Well, to be fair to the press, not much else was happening this week—just a couple or seven primaries in not-so-important states and an admission by the president's chief arms uncoverer that there are no arms to uncover and the reasons we were forced to preemptively kill (I'm sorry: *liberate*) thousands of Iraqis never really existed. Oh yeah, and some suicide bombers. But we've gotten used to them by now.

Q. All this outrage was directed at the baring of one right breast, correct?

A. Yeah. What's your point? Boobies are evil. Ask John Ashcroft. Imagine the outcry if her left breast had been exposed.

Q. What *did* happen to her left breast?

A. Reportedly, it signed a development deal with Fox.

Q. Well, the whole halftime show was kind of raunchy, wasn't it?

A. Compared to *Touched by an Angel,* yeah. But actually, what America saw was an eight-minute truncated version of MTV, with indoor helicopter shots.

Q. What would you say to your kid after watching that?

A. I don't know. I'd probably be happy for the diversion so I didn't have to explain the side effect warning on the impotence drug commercial that advised anybody experiencing four-hour erections to call a doctor. Four hours? I'm calling a press conference.

Q. What does FCC Chairman Michael Powell mean by a "swift and thorough" investigation?

A. Just what he said. And you can bet it will be a lot swifter and thorougher than the Enron investigation or the Robert Novak leak investigation or the 9/11 investigation, or the CIA lack-of-intelligence investigation. This is about politics, not morality. I mean…the other way around.

Q. Who will ultimately bear the responsibility?

A. Right now, the blame wheel is set on permanent spin. Currently, the FCC's crosshairs are rotating between MTV, CBS, AOL, the PLO, the IRA, the KGB and NPR. Especially NPR.

Q. Not IBM or UPS?

A. No, and not AT&T or the IRS, either. They're not totally stupid, you know.

Q. Don't you think Powell's being a little disingenuous, especially considering what sound you make when attempting to pronounce the name of his commission?

A. That's not funny.

Q. My God, hasn't anybody ever seen a breast before?

A. That isn't the point.

Q. What *is* the point?

A. The point is, a lot of people were eating guacamole at the time, and dip flew off the chip when the "wardrobe malfunction" went down, and, well, you know how impossible it is to get avocado stains out of upholstery.

Q. Out, greased spot.

A. What?

Q. Nothing. Have you tried soda water?

A. You mean, like, Coke?

Q. No, tonic water, anything clear and carbonated.

A. No, that's a good idea, thanks. I'll give it a try.

Q. Dab at it, don't rub it.

A. Not a question.

Q. What was CBS's biggest regret?

A. This was not a reviewable call.

Q. What was MTV's official statement?

A. "Our goal with the Super Bowl halftime show was to produce an entertaining stage experience with a positive message about empowerment." And who's not empowered by seeing a mammary gland with a Christmas ornament hanging from it?

Q. Is Michael Powell going to have Janet Jackson spanked for this and, if so, will it be televised on MTV TRL?

A. Actually, with a new CD coming out in eight weeks, she might ride this puppy to the top of the charts, even if they ban her from the Grammies. The real losers are us, the American people, since CBS is bound to rebook its next turn of the Super Bowl Wheel with those three-time, veteran halftime performers Up With People.

Q. By the way, who won this year's Super Bowl?

A. Can't remember. I think the crotch-biting dog beat out the flatulent horse, but I'm not sure.

103 Jobs

That's right. 103 jobs. And yeah, yeah, yeah. I know. Trust me, I've heard it all before. At least a couple of times. It's not like I don't have parents, you know. A hundred and three jobs is way too many freakin' jobs. Like, 102 too many freakin' jobs. "Why, he's nothing but a reckless, disreputable hippie without a responsible bone in his body." Quit it, you sound like Richard, my stepfather. There you go, jumping to conclusions again. It's like that old Vietnam vet joke...

> *A. How many Vietnam veterans does it take to screw in a light bulb?*
>
> *B. I don't know. How many?*
>
> *A. You Don't Know Cuz You Weren't There, Man!*

First off, I always had, still have and probably forever and ever *will* have this eensy-weensy teeny-tiny itty-bitty problem with authority, which will be why you will see a lot of jobs listed as being held for one day or less. And, of course, I was always aiming for Big-Time Headlining Comedian Gig, for which there is no apprenticeship program, and it was necessary to keep my nights free. But enough excuses, here's the 103 jobs I've racked up thus far.

Actor, various cities, states and countries

Advertising copywriter, Cerveza Panama Campaign, San Francisco, California

Agricultural marketing agent, Indiana and Wisconsin

Assistant manager, Pizza Hut, Hwy. 100, West Allis, Wisconsin

Assistant manager, Radio Shack, downtown Waukesha, Wisconsin

Audience wrangler, Jerry Lewis Telethon, WTMJ Studios, Milwaukee, Wisconsin

Author, *The All-American Sport of Bipartisan Bashing: Common Sense Rantings from a Raging Moderate*

Baby management, New Berlin, Muskego, West Allis, and Waukesha, Wisconsin

Backstage manager, "Monkey," Cincinnati, Ohio

Bar back, Ellen's Supper Club, Hurley, Wisconsin

Bartender, Century Hall, Milwaukee, Wisconsin

Bellman, Milwaukee Athletic Club, Wisconsin

Beer Smuggler, Coors, Colorado and Wisconsin

Bicycle messenger, San Francisco, California (1 week)

Breakfast chef, Last Texas Cafe B & B, Amsterdam, Netherlands

Busboy, Dante's Sea Catch, Pier 39, San Francisco, California

Cab driver, Milwaukee, Wisconsin (1 day)

Camp counselor, Pelican Lake, Wisconsin

Cartoonist/illustrator, Peters-Bell Agency, Milwaukee, Wisconsin

Clerk at Administration Building, University of Wisconsin–Milwaukee

Clerk at B. Dalton's Book Store, Brookfield Square, Wisconsin

Clerk at Chess King, Southridge Mall, Greendale, Wisconsin

Clerk at Alexander's Stationery, Hollywood, California

Clerk in adult bookstore, Waukesha, Wisconsin (1 day)

Clown shill, Amsterdam, Netherlands (1 day)

Co-owner/general flunky, Crummies Sandwich Shoppe, Waukesha, Wisconsin

Co-producer, PBS documentary series, *Livelyhood*

Coffee boy, All You Can Eat Pancake Stand, Wisconsin State Fair

Comedian, various cities, states and countries

Comedy club owner, Holy City Zoo, San Francisco, California

Corn roaster, Wisconsin State Fair

Delivery boy, Simon's Drugs, Waukesha, Wisconsin

Desk clerk, Milwaukee Athletic Club, Milwaukee, Wisconsin

Dishwasher, Bright Angel Lodge, Grand Canyon, Arizona

Dishwasher, Smiths Bakery, Seattle, Washington

Ditch digger, Waukesha, Wisconsin

Disk jockey, WUWW, Waukesha, Wisconsin

Dock attendant, Johnson Controls, Milwaukee, Wisconsin

Door-to-door soap salesman, Milwaukee, Wisconsin (1 day)

Dorm cafeteria subassistant, University of Wisconsin–Milwaukee

Electronics wirer, Can't Remember the Company, Waukesha, Wisconsin

Electrician's assistant, Bessemer, Michigan

File clerk, Western Steamship, San Francisco, California

Foam factory, Can't Remember the Company, Waukesha, Wisconsin (3 days)

Forklift driver, Aqua Chem, Milwaukee, Wisconsin

Hay-baler, Burlington, Wisconsin

House painter, Bessemer, Upper Michigan

Humor columnist, *Bugle American, National Lampoon, San Francisco Examiner* and others

Ice cream van driver, Waukesha, Wisconsin
Janitor, employee dorms, Grand Canyon, Arizona
Lemonade stand worker, Westward Ho Subdivision,
    New Berlin, Wisconsin
Line cook, Burger Chef, Waukesha, Wisconsin
Lunch cart ("roach coach") driver, Waukesha,
    Wisconsin
Liquor store stockman, Oakland Liquors, Milwaukee,
    Wisconsin
Magazine editor, *Mans*Laughter,* San Francisco,
    California
Mall maintenance guy, Brookfield Square, Wisconsin
Margarine smuggler, Illinois and Wisconsin
Mold cracker, Grede Foundry, Waukesha, Wisconsin
Movie reviewer, University of Wisconsin–Milwaukee *Post*
Mover, Starving Artists Movers, San Francisco,
    California (1 week)
NASTAR race starter, Indianhead Resort, Upper
    Michigan (1 winter)
Newspaper bundler, Richland Center, Wisconsin
Oyster shucker, San Francisco, California (1 day)
Parade tomato, Winterfest, Milwaukee, Wisconsin
    (3 hours)
Parking lot attendant, West Allis, Wisconsin
Pedicab driver, Fisherman's Wharf, San Francisco,
    California
Pinsetter, Capitol Lanes Bowling Alley, West Allis,
    Wisconsin (1 day)
Pirate, Long John Silver's, Prospect Mall, Milwaukee,
    Wisconsin (1 day)
Playwright, *Nasty Norman Saves Xmas,* Gimbel's,
    Milwaukee, Wisconsin
Postal clerk, Waukesha, Wisconsin

Poster maker, Milwaukee, Wisconsin

Powdered graphite sprayer, Milwaukee Tool & Die, Wisconsin

Prop master, *Second Greatest Entertainer in the World*, Milwaukee, Wisconsin

Publicist, *Better than a Sharp Stick in the Eye*, Milwaukee, Wisconsin

Quality control technician, Sony, San Diego, California (2 days)

Radio talk-show host, *Will & Willie Show*, KQKE, San Francisco, California

Receptionist, Butterfly Temporary Services, San Francisco, California

Recording artist, *You Can't Make Stuff Up Like This*, laugh.com

Rock singer, Ornjj, New Berlin, Wisconsin (5 paid gigs)

Ronald McDonald, Fox River Valley, Wisconsin (twice)

Roofer, Abbey Ski Lodge, Bessemer, Michigan

Santa Claus in a ghost mall, Southtown, South Milwaukee, Wisconsin

Shipping-receiving clerk, Allis-Chalmers Warehouse, West Allis, Wisconsin

Shoe salesman, JC Penneys, Downtown Waukesha, Wisconsin

Singer-dancer, Kids From Wisconsin, various states (mostly Wisconsin)

Sod farm mower, New Berlin, Wisconsin

Sound technician, CETA video documentaries, Doojie Aces, Milwaukee, Wisconsin

Squeeze molder, International Harvester, Waukesha, Wisconsin

Stable boy, Eagle Cave, Richland Center, Wisconsin

Stamping machine operator, Aqua Chem, Milwaukee,
Wisconsin

Teacher, drama, seventh grade, Martin Luther King Jr.
High School, Milwaukee, Wisconsin

Technical writer, San Diego, California (1 day)

Telephone solicitor, Milwaukee, Wisconsin (1 day)

Theater director, *The Effect of Gamma Rays upon Man in
the Moon Marigolds*, Bessemer, Michigan

Theatrical producer, *Big Fat Year-End Kiss-Off Comedy
Show*, Bay Area, California

Tour guide, Eagle Cave, Richland Center, Wisconsin

Truck driver, Plaster of Paris Molds, Milwaukee,
Chicago, and points east and south

Usher, Oriental Theater, Milwaukee, Wisconsin

Valet, Milwaukee Athletic Club, Wisconsin

Warehouseman, JC Penneys, West Allis, Wisconsin

Will the Cosmic Waiter, Century Hall, Milwaukee,
Wisconsin

Wisconsin State Highway Construction G-29,
Waukesha County, Wisconsin

Yardwork, New Berlin, Muskego, West Allis, and
Waukesha, Wisconsin

Whom I Don't Trust

I don't trust lawyers who call losing "a moral victory."

I don't trust subliminal tapes. I'm always afraid the subliminal message is "Buy more tapes."

I don't trust people who clothe their pets. Bandanas, sweaters, pants, culottes. Nothing. They creep me out.

I don't trust any covering over an underground opening. Especially metal mesh where you can see the bottom and there's a lot of stinky, pointy stuff down there.

I don't trust blond weathermen.

I don't trust spokespersons.

I don't trust *People Magazine. National Enquirer,* yes. *USA Today,* occasionally.

I don't trust sushi east of the Rockies and west of the Mississippi. Especially Montana. Sushi in Montana is like ballet in Upper Michigan.

I don't trust evangelists who need to make a comeback.

I don't trust people who wear all black.

I don't trust people who wear sunglasses indoors.

I don't trust radicchio. Or that frisée stuff. Arugula, yeah.

I don't trust therapists with bruises. No, scratch that, I don't trust therapists.

I don't trust satin sheets.

I don't trust sincere antidrug public service announcements by aged rock 'n' roll singers.

I don't trust mourners.

I don't trust moaners.

I don't trust movie reviews from papers or magazines I never heard of. What is *60 Second Preview,* anyway?

I don't trust late-night radio talk-show hosts whose major advertiser is Gold Bond Medicated Foot Powder.

I don't trust afternoon radio talk-show hosts whose major advertiser is Gold Bond Medicated Foot Powder.

I don't trust guys who fill hotel rooms with flowers.

I don't trust people to whom rent is no concern.

I don't trust authors rediscovering their connection to America on their book tour.

I don't trust new jeans that are supposed to look old.

I don't trust three out of four doctors.

I don't trust 4 a.m.

I don't trust people who make sweeping generalizations.

I don't trust any espresso drink topped with whipped cream. Or chocolate sprinkles.

I don't trust financial projections by Bush Administration economists.

I don't trust second-show Friday night audiences.

I don't trust anyone with a hyphen in their name.

Whom I Do Trust

I trust third-graders.

I trust the U.S. post office: 41¢ to send a piece of paper anywhere in the country. Are you kidding me? Besides the styptic pencil, that's the best value for money we got going today.

I trust Regis, but not that Kelly person.

I trust tugboat pilots.

I trust one-armed security guards, but not if they wear a gun.

I trust bartenders in dives.

I trust gospel singers.

I trust sports reporters. Even if they're blond.

I trust Jerry Brown, but I wouldn't want to sit next to him on a bus ride to New York.

I trust burger joints that grind their own meat.

I trust *60 Minutes,* and any CBS correspondent named Charles.

I trust PBS's *The News Hour,* but remain convinced it makes a better radio show than it does a TV show.

I trust flannel sheets.

I trust any pair of blue jeans older than Hannah Montana.

I trust vests.

I trust midnight.

I trust slobbering dogs.

I trust willow trees.

I trust people who admit that, every once in a while, they don't know.

I trust old men who wear black socks with sandals.

I trust black coffee. Fancy, aged, Indonesian black coffee and 10-hour-old gas station black coffee. Black coffee.

I trust single red roses.

I trust farmers for directions, but for the life of me I can never understand them.

I trust the American flag but not most of the people who wave it.

I trust the crucifix but not all the people who wear it.

I trust living rooms with lace doilies on the arms of the chairs and couches.

I trust first-show Saturday night audiences.

What They Say/What They Mean

Justice. We all know about justice. It will prevail. It's blind and its wheels turn slowly. There are many different kinds of justice: frontier, instant, karma. There's even David Justice, who got divorced from Halle Berry, which doesn't sound very just to me. But what we say about justice and what we do about it are two different things.

WHAT THEY SAY: You have the right to remain silent.
WHAT THEY MEAN: Although you might find yourself saying "ow" on occasion.

WHAT THEY SAY: In America, you are innocent till proven guilty.
WHAT THEY MEAN: In America, you are innocent till proven broke.

WHAT THEY SAY: All men are created equal.
WHAT THEY MEAN: Then, most of them end up with public defenders.

WHAT THEY SAY: The law has always been color blind.
WHAT THEY MEAN: Unless that color is green.

WHAT THEY SAY: You have the right to a speedy trial.
WHAT THEY MEAN: Before we hang you.

WHAT THEY SAY: Justice delayed is justice denied.
WHAT THEY MEAN: Take a number and bring a pillow.

WHAT THEY SAY: All men are created equal.
WHAT THEY MEAN: With Viagra they are.

WHAT THEY SAY: You have a choice.
WHAT THEY MEAN: Your wallet or your life.

WHAT THEY SAY: Anything you say will be used against you.
WHAT THEY MEAN: You might not want to say "steel-toed boots."

WHAT THEY SAY: Americans don't torture.
WHAT THEY MEAN: As long as we get to define "torture."

FAQ: *Cheney Shooting a Guy in the Face with a Gun*

Frequently Asked Questions About Vice President Dick Cheney Shooting a Guy in the Face

Q. Harry Whittingon, the man the vice president accidentally shot, suffered a minor heart attack. What exactly is a minor heart attack?

A. One where the patient (who isn't you) doesn't die.

Q. Did the official statement explain that the 17-hour delay before anybody told anybody anything was because they wanted to make sure the statement released to the media was accurate?

A. He shot the guy. In the face. With a gun. How many more facts were needed? The barometric pressure at the time wasn't all that necessary.

Q. Isn't this event illustrative of why they invented the word "accident"?

A. This and the Bush presidency, yes. Besides, who hasn't mistaken a 78-year-old lawyer for a 6-foot-tall quail in an orange vest?

Q. How many pellets of bird shot did Whittington get hit with?

A. Doctors estimated between 5 and 200. Nice margin of error there. That's 102, plus or minus 97.

Q. Didn't Cheney call the day of the shooting "one of the worst days of my life"?

A. Yes, he did, although we're pretty sure it's not way up there on Whittington's list, either.

Q. Let's straighten this out: Did Cheney drink a beer at lunch or didn't he drink a beer?

A. According to different reports: yes. And no.

Q. Didn't he also say, "You never go hunting with someone who drinks"?

A. Apparently he's never been deer hunting in Wisconsin.

Q. Isn't it true he retired to the Armstrong lodge and ate a "somber roast beef dinner"?

A. Still probably tastier than the hospital food Whittington got during an equally solemn face-pellet picking.

Q. Why did the vice president choose Fox News to give his interview to?

A. A simple desire for the interview to be fair and balanced. And to pay off Brit Hume on a Super Bowl bet.

Q. Who was to blame for the accident?

A. Both Vice President Cheney and Mr. Whittington agreed there was no blame. And that Whittington could just as easily have damaged Cheney's gun with his face.

Q. What are some of the more popular conspiracy theories attached to all this?

A. That Cheney was sending a message to the terrorists, and the message is: "Look what we do to our *friends*."

Q. Anything else?

A. That these guys are really, really serious about tort reform.

Q. If the lawyer happens to die because of the wounds inflicted by the VP, he could be charged with involuntary manslaughter, right?

A. That's true, but because it is Texas, we're most likely looking at a $10 fine for shooting a lawyer out of season.

Q. Where's the upside?

A. Our veterans win. The people most thankful that Cheney

received five deferments to Vietnam are our troops, especially considering his penchant for shooting his own men.

Q. Any other ramifications?

A. Outside of George Bush's noticeably wearing more Kevlar, no.

Q. Don't you think it's time for the liberals to lay off this and move on to more important affairs of state?

A. Point well taken. They should promise not to give Dick Cheney's lack of moral judgment a single second more attention than was given to Bill Clinton's.

The Victims of 9/12

Now that Labor Day is over, it took stores about 14 seconds to get rid of their back-to-school displays and replace them with shelves of Halloween regalia. And, never missing a beat, Karl Rove had George W. Bush take advantage of his Secret Service Platinum Card to get an early start on the pagan celebration by donning the most frightening disguise available and heading out to spook the countryside in a weeklong variation on the old "trick or treat" trek. This "fear and smear" tour featured the president digging deep into the pockets of his Pumpkin King costume, tossing seeds of dread and horror to all in the crosshairs of the media deluge of mourning in America on the fifth anniversary of 9/11.

I know *I* cowered. But can't figure out if it was a reflex recoil at the sight of the superserious mask Bush uses to hide his condescending smirk, the sheer gall of his distorted reasoning, or the threat that Cheney was going to detach his jaw and swallow Tim Russert whole. Maybe these guys really do believe the B.S. that oozes out of their mouths. Or maybe they're just testing the limits of the whole Joseph Goebbels Big Lie Theory. Wouldn't that explain a lot, if this were all only a failed senior thesis? Just take the incomplete and get it over with.

"The lessons of 9/11." "The horrors of 9/11." "The victims of 9/11." It's all become… "The dial tone of 9/11." They chanted it like an airplane hangar full of Buddhist initiates. Mr. Solemn and Mr. Sober. Pouring their hearts out for the families of the victims of 9/11. Yeah, right. Apparently, Messrs. Bush and Cheney have so much respect for the victims of 9/11 that they formed their ashes into the shape of a football and kicked it around the country for a week of electioneering photo-ops. "The hardest part of my job is linking Iraq with the war on terror." He said that. Out loud. In front of Katie Couric and everyone. And Rumpelstiltskin's hardest job was spinning gold out of straw.

You aren't honoring the victims of September 11th. You're dishonoring them by kicking their remains around for petty partisan purposes. Why don't you honor the survivors of 9/11 by telling the truth for once? Iraq was a mistake. And when I say "survivors of 9/11," I mean us. The victims of 9/12. This is an election year, and we know your scary overture was just the beginning of a five-act opera. It's time to get out our B.S. umbrellas. And keep them upraised for seven more weeks. Hopefully, enough time for us victims of 9/12 to band together and kick you heartless, greedy, sanctimonious thugs out of office. Nothing personal, I mean that in a good way.

I hope the point of diminishing returns has been reached. That these liquid squeezebags have gone to the well one too many times and there's a hole at the bottom of their bucket. That the boys who cried "Wolfowitz" will finally get their come-uppance and the 110th Congress will wreak holy, nonsecular havoc. Because the people have had it with their load of Iraq B.S. and they ain't buying it no more. That the message we will

hear rain down from the purple mountain's majesty is... "Stop it, Mr. Bush, and get thee away from us now. And take that hideous Cheney thing with you."

The Scourge of Mockolate

I never thought I'd be talking smack about the Hershey Company. It makes me feel like I'm wiping my oily hands on America's sweetheart's prom dress. We all know Hershey. We all love Hershey. For crum's sakes, they're the chocolate people. Got a whole town named after them. The sugar-rush dealers of our youth: Almond Joy, Mounds, Kit Kat, Reese's Pieces and, of course, the ubiquitous Hershey Bar. Which, if you believe all the fairy tales of the Greatest Generation, were used in WW II to acquire the overnight company of comely, foreign-born ladies. What could be more American?

But now this Pennsylvania champ of snacks seems to be allergic to its own concoction and itching to get out of the chocolate business and into the imitation-chocolate business. They recently petitioned the Food and Drug Administration to legally redefine the term "chocolate" so that it includes artificial sweeteners, milk substitutes and trans fats. That's right. They're about to become the foremost manufacturers of something destined to be known as Mockolate.

They claim the broader labels are necessary to keep up with changing consumer tastes. Yeah, right. Unbeknownst to us, phantom consumers have stormed the placid town of Hershey, rallying and protesting the disgusting flavor of actual chocolate and crying out for something just as fattening, and worse for our health, that tastes like cardboard dipped in stagnant runoff. Reminds me of those mock apple pies the Ritz Cracker people tried to pawn off on us back in the '60s. Mmm, mushy crackers instead of baked apples. Now, that's good eating.

I don't understand this whole "close, but no cigar" business. Like decaffeinated coffee. You schmuck. That's why I drink it. You take the caffeine out of it, this stuff is useless to me. It's hot, bitter, dirty water. Without the kick. "I like the wiry buzz, it's the rich flavor I could do without." Wine without alcohol. Why? I thought Welch's had that gig sewed up. And the kids and their juice sticks. Juice Sticks? Whose major connection to juice is, what? The fact that their color is often not totally dissimilar to the fruit they're named after?

A spokesperson for Hershey says this is about modernizing food standards, increasing flexibility and accommodating changes in technology, but the real answer lies right where you expect it, melting down there on the bottom line. Cocoa butter costs $2.30 a pound. Vegetable oils? Less than a third of that. You know who I blame for this whole propagation of bogasity? George Bush. He's earned his position as poster boy for this national avalanche of hollow charade through a fraudulent masquerade as leader.

His Healthy Forests Initiative attacked trees like a steroided pulp beetle. His Clear Skies Bill was a sop to big contributors. His Patriot Act stripped ordinary citizens of civil liberties to spread democracy across the globe by scooping up the excess we have here. Success and acceptance these days has nothing to do with what you do. It's how you sell what it is that you do. Or don't do. And what you do (or don't) call what it is that you do do. And it won't be long before our candy bars will soon be, just like George Bush already is…full of doo-doo.

Passenger Bill of Rights

Due to a spate of recent negative publicity, the airline industry has embarked on a public relations blitz aimed at reversing the public's perception that modern flight travel has sunk to winged-Greyhound-with-holes-in-the-floorboards levels. Good luck. I can't believe it took this long for people to finally flip out, because over the last couple of years we frequent flyers have become so accustomed to being treated like fleshy baggage that some of us have spontaneously sprouted handles.

JetBlue blamed its meltdowns on weather and overtaxed computers, but its problems are endemic in an industry that routinely treats its customers like mushrooms, keeping them in the dark and feeding them an especially fertile form of compost (in lieu of in-flight meals). And it takes a threat by Congress to pass a legislated passenger bill of rights, to goose the industry into running around promoting a series of noncompulsory and voluntary programs whose implementation will last about as long as an igloo concession in the Gobi Desert. They've pulled this penitentiary wool over our eyes before and will continue to do so just as long as they can.

You know the dance. An in-house publicist strides purposefully to a podium and solemnly announces the airline is "really, really, really sorry and promises to try harder and will do everything in our power to make sure something like this or that or whatever happened never happens again. Ever. Honest. Scout's honor." And if something like this does happen again, tough. Just stay out of their face, mister, and don't try whining to a gate agent or they'll summon security so fast it'll make your head swim like a school of goldfish in a blender. Shockingly, they're a bit vague about specifics, but of this I can assure you: The changes will be strictly cosmetic and about as effective as a rope handle on a shovel or a colander constructed out of 2 by 4s or a parka quilted with an insulation of pudding. Here's a few of the rumored service improvements we members of the 7-Mile-High Club can expect to see coming to a jetway near you:

- After a plane is stranded for a minimum of six hours of tarmac delay, First Class male passengers allowed to use Coach Class bulkheads as urinals.

- From this day on, corporate policy mandates gate personnel will respond to questions about departure delays with an indecisive shrug instead of a condescending sneer.

- Flight attendants will no longer shriek at passengers "Suck sand and die!" without first flashing a trademark friendly-sky smile.

- Gravel used to fill headrests to be pounded into pea-sized fragments instead of marble-sized fragments.

- Once departure delay passes four-hour mark, liquor to be poured directly into passengers' mouths at a 10 percent discount.

- Airsick bags now double lined and minty fresh.

- Emergency exit information cards soon to feature four-color illustrations of Cajun artist Rodrigue's lovable Blue Dog.

- Seatbacks to recline a full 13/16 inch instead of previous 3/4 inch.

- Crying children under age of 4 to be sequestered in overhead compartments.

- Luggage certified to no longer arrive late and at a destination other than yours. Now you're guaranteed one or the other.

- Reading lamps will be repositioned to focus on your seat partner's knees rather than your seat partner's feet.

Our Offspring Fontanel

Oooh. He's clever. And obviously knows exactly what he's doing. This is all a setup, people. Has to be. Yes, I'm talking about George Bush's veto of the State Children's Health Insurance Program, or S-CHIP. Who but a total stoned horned ogre would do that? Maybe an ogre with something up his sleeve, eh? Has anyone thought of that? I'm just waiting for him to drop the other shoe. Or throw it at a crippled puppy. Either way, there's a hidden agenda in there somewhere.

To intimate that it didn't seem like his finest hour is akin to saying that sinking your IRA into tying live vampire bats to a horizontal stick and trying to sell them to the Fisher Price people as above-crib mobiles is probably not your best retirement strategy. As public relations go, this was on the order of handing out celebratory exploding cigars near the oxygen tents of an intensive-care ward.

Does Bush seriously want us to believe he has no problem asking for another $190 billion for his oil war, but can't find $7 billion a year for children's health care? Are you kidding me? "No child left behind." More like "no child left standing." The man has opened himself up to charges of criminal child neglect. An Amber Alert featuring Air Force One should be triggered.

Crazy? Like a fox. He scuttled the S-CHIP, hush-hush style. Like a cat burglar at night, in a closet, with the lights off, under a raincoat, wearing a ski mask and a fake ZZ Top beard. The legislation was intended to reduce the number of children without health insurance and extend coverage to several million more poor children. But the threat that some wrong kids might inadvertently receive coverage makes that totally unacceptable? Who believes that?

Oh, we know the president's public stance: He doesn't want to slide down the slippery slope toward socialized medicine by expanding the program to higher-income families. But he's not as dumb as he looks. Surely he knows that when it comes to kids, America's got a collective soft spot right at the top of our heads. Call it our offspring fontanel.

That's why this has to be a ruse. Accusing Democrats of authoring a plan that would hurt children…that doesn't even make sense. Here's the deal: Since the Prez is not up for reelection ever again, he's in league with party leadership and they're using this dodge in a drastic attempt for the GOP to hang on to the White House. Painting the Bush Administration as so malevolent that, in comparison, all the '08 Republican candidates look like Latter-day Saints of Jesus Christ. You know what I mean.

And we better hope this works, or the next public event is bound to be even more provocative. I can see it now: Bush emceeing an apple pie poisoning exhibition, right after a quick round of mom-slapping, held on the South Lawn by the light of a massive teddy bear bonfire with refreshments of barbecued pet parakeet skewers and goldfish shakes.

The vote to override the S-CHIP veto comes in a week or so, and it will be interesting to see if the Democrats can stir any movement from across the aisle, using this issue as a crowbar the size of Idaho. Or if they'll just roll over on their bellies and dare the president to keep throwing shoes at them. The gray matter beneath the soft spot in my head makes me suspect the latter.

Nuclear Two-Step

This might be a good time to try to explain George Bush's Middle East nuclear policy, which to the untrained eye must seem trickier than doing calculus on a solar-powered calculator in the front seat of a high-speed roller coaster while wearing gloves at night. As leader of the free world, he's taken a monumental task upon himself, to divide the world into two distinct and separate groups: those countries sober and sensible enough to handle the whole nuclear thing in the mature manner of a good democratic nation like the United States, and then all those other fourth-rate, scorpion-infested hellholes that still allow barnyard animals to board airplanes.

And what of the borderline calls? You know, countries with a couple of low-rent knockoff fast-food franchises whose streetcars still allow live chickens in the overhead compartment? Easy. The nations we like can have nuclear weapons. And the ones we don't like can't. It's that simple. And don't give us any lip, either. Or we'll talk to some buddies of Warren Buffett and get your Burger Imam licenses revoked.

Being the sole member of the "We Made a Big Badda-Boom" club burdens us with the authority to write the admissions policy for all guild applicants. Not a pretty job, but someone has to do it. And the more like us you are, the more likely we'll let you have what you want. As long as what you want is what we want you to want. The *less* like us you are, the more likely your topographical features will become a vast expanse of smooth green glass.

Although we've had the bomb for over 60 years, we have proven ourselves to be totally reliable and trustworthy, having only used it on actual people twice. Sure, we've waved it around a couple of times, but if you can't menace somebody with a nuclear bomb, what's the use of squandering your children's future to build it? George Bush is going the extra mile to make sure that every nuclear wannabe is as determined to pursue diplomatic answers to complex international problems as he is. And those who don't like it might want to start sleeping in lead-lined pajamas.

Israel, Pakistan, India...sure; no problem, boys; load up. *You* can go thermonuclear. Because not only are you like us, you're our friends. You invite us to your birthday parties. And give us ice cream. Your leaders wear suits, which makes us feel comfortable. Syria, Iraq and Iran? No, I'm sorry. You wear funny clothes and you're mean to us and never had us over to the house for cookies and milk, so no nukes for you. What it boils down to is: It's not enough to *be* like us, you also have to actually...like us.

Besides, everybody knows the only reason people who refuse to see the world the way that we see the world want nuclear weapons, in the first place, is to destroy the delicate balance of peace that exists today in the Middle East. That delicate balance of peace we've been so instrumental in fostering. Hence, George Bush's job. To keep bad people from accomplishing their stated goal of destabilizing the Middle East. In a way that is different than the Middle East is being destabilized now. Which is why he has to work so hard that it makes his head hurt. Mine too, come to think of it.

The Do's and Don'ts of Asking Your Boss for a Raise

Smack dab in the middle of the catalog of scary traumatic events in the course of an everyday normal life, only a few are guaranteed to raise one's blood pressure like the prospect of asking your boss for a raise. Informing a spouse you are skipping off to Belize with a massage therapist two years from voting age, or telling your children they were adopted from a family of Albanian fish merchants: yeah, maybe those. Requesting a biker to kindly remove his big fat furry white butt from your bumper, un-hunh, I could see that. The seeming hours of uncomfortable silence at Thanksgiving dinner after your mother-in-law asks how you like the oyster raisin walnut dressing and before you formulate an answer you hope will result in neither tears nor stabbing. OK, so perhaps there are a couple of things more traumatic than asking your boss for a raise, but for ordinary humans facing the long, lonely walk into the corner office, it'll do.

The first item on the agenda is psyching yourself into believing you're worth it, because, face it, you are. Repeat after me: "I deserve this. I so deserve this. Much more than that cretinous kiss-ass in Accounting." The biggest obstacle in this assignment is the fear of the unknown. To nip that in the bud, let's assume it all does go straight to Hell—what's the worst that could happen? Rejection, recrimination, resentment, unemployment, bodily harm, hunger and sharp objects to the eye socket. Forget about that. It's the anticipation of the deed that causes us to freak out, resulting in severe cottonmouth and various unsightly facial rashes. Not the actual groveling.

It is important to understand that anxiety is normal. Breathe regularly. Most of our jobs are sad little fiefdoms of idiosyncratic hierarchies run by mad and pitiable despotic demagogues. No, I'm sorry, that's government service. The private sector is much better. The pitiable despotic demagogues are usually noticeably less mad. It is, however, imperative that each approach be individualized according to which kind of boss you work under: whether he's a bean counter who commissions computer programs to plot individual paper clip consumption, or she's the kind who screams so loud and often that the safety glass replacement team is on speed dial, or they're one of those intense sorts whose deodorant shows signs of failing around 10 a.m.

Asking for a raise is something everyone needs to do at least once. And if you haven't done it yet, maybe it's about time you finally attempt to fulfill that fantasy which lives in us all. You know the one: storming into the boss's office, chin held high, dropping dark hints of squirreled-away illicit negatives. The thing you must remember is there's no script. No right way and no wrong way to do it. But guidelines, yeah, sure, there's a few. So let us examine a couple of things you might want to remember of what to do and what not to do when asking for a raise.

Do's of Asking for a Raise

Do keep your voice low enough so that employees on upper floors aren't forced to pound on the ceiling with broken-off furniture legs.

Do look your boss in the eye, but avoid staring contests. Just in case, bring Visine.

Do be punctual, but refrain from smashing all clocks with the incorrect time, crying out at the sound of each crash, "See, there's your whole problem!"

Do make sure food is not sticking from between your teeth or visibly hanging out of your pockets.

Do smile, but learn to differentiate between a smile and a grimace that makes small children cower and weep.

Do restrain yourself from spray painting LOSER in Day-Glo orange on the driver's side of your boss's car till *after* you've thrown his desk out the window and quit in disgust.

Do stand your ground, but no one will blame you if you acquiesce after being hogtied by security personnel brandishing Taser weapons.

Do maintain a modicum of integrity, but realize your modicum may vary from your boss's modicum.

Do bring examples of your work. Not the ones resulting in restraining orders.

Do tend toward dressing in conservative colors, and leave the paisley corduroy in the trunk with the free oil-change coupons.

Don'ts of Asking for a Raise

Don't drip melted black wax in the shape of a pentagram on the carpet.

Don't use your right hand to rhythmically whack a 10-inch section of pipe into your left hand as soon as you get in the door. Wait a while.

Don't come into the office wearing a radiation containment suit.

Don't frantically slap at imaginary insects. Especially ones that land on your boss's forehead and neck.

Don't spray the seat of the chair you're about to sit in with lemon-scented Lysol or wipe your hand with a wet nap after shaking hers.

Don't wear a tie-dyed T-shirt and rhythmically chant, "I need a miracle here."

Don't fall to your knees, begging the boss not to pin you with his evil eye.

Don't giggle whenever your boss mentions what an "asset" you are.

Don't pick your teeth with one of your boss's business cards.

Don't lean over on the desk and shout in your boss's face, "Do you have any idea of what I'm worth to this company?"

Don't skip over to the window, run into it and cry, "I'm a birdy and my wing is broken."

What They Said/What They Meant: Katrina

Who: President George Bush, two days before Hurricane Katrina made landfall.

What He Said: "A State of Emergency exists in Louisiana, beginning yesterday."

What He Meant: "But since I'm still on vacation, I first need to stage a few photo-ops strumming a guitar and playing golf."

Who: Speaker of the House Dennis Hastert.

What He Said: "I don't know about that [rebuilding New Orleans]. That doesn't make sense to me."

What He Meant: "It's just poor people, right?"

Who: President Bush.

What He Said: "We want to make sure that we can respond properly if there's a WMD attack or another major storm."

What He Meant: "It was Al-Qaeda again."

Who: Barbara Bush at the Houston Astrodome.

What She Said: "So many of the people in the arena here, you know, were underprivileged anyway, so this is working very well for them."

What She Meant: "It's just poor people, right?"

Who: President Bush in Alabama, four days after the hurricane.

What He Said: "Out of the rubbles of Trent Lott's house—he's lost his entire house—there's going to be a fantastic house. And I'm looking forward to sitting on the porch."

What He Meant: "If you expect help, you better move to a state run by Republicans. Even better, a state run by my brother."

Who: Homeland Secretary Michael Chertoff.

What He Said: "The conditions at the New Orleans Super Dome were nowhere near as bad as the TV images suggested."

What He Meant: "Lying next to dead people in toxic waste without food and water while terrorized by thugs ain't so bad."

Who: President Bush, September 1, 2005.

What He Said: "I don't think anyone anticipated the breach of the levees."

What He Meant: "I don't think anyone imagined people would fly airplanes into buildings."

Who: Senator Rick Santorum.

What He Said: "You have people who don't heed those warnings and then put people at risk. There may be a need to look at tougher penalties on those who decide to ride it out."

What He Meant: "And when I say 'tough penalties,' I mean worse than drowning in your attic."

Who: President Bush speaking about FEMA Director Michael Brown.

What He Said: "Brownie, you're doing a heck of a job."

What He Meant: "For a former head of the Arabian Horse Association."

Who: Barbara Bush, at the Houston Astrodome.

What She Said: "What I am hearing, which is sort of scary, is they all want to stay here in Texas."

What She Meant: "For crum's sake, I *live* in Texas."

Who: President Bush.

What He Said: "What I intend to do is to lead an investigation to find out what went right and what went wrong."

What He Meant: "We will track down these evildoing hurricanes. They can run but they can't hide. We will liberate the brave, freedom-loving hurricanians."

Who: President Bush.

What He Said: "I remember New Orleans as a great town where I used to enjoy myself occasionally too much."

What He Meant: "I could use a drink."

Who: President Bush.

What He Said: "If things went wrong, we'll correct them, and when things went right, we'll duplicate them."

What He Meant: "One list is going to be longer than the other."

7 | Executive Legislative Judicial

The three branches of the American tree of democracy. The newly formed Cheneystative Branch not included.

However, a couple of the former branches have contracted a slight case of Texas dwarf blister rot.

The system of checks and balances seems to have been reconfigured into one that writes many more checks while ignoring any semblance of balancing the accounts.

The Department of Just Us

For those of you who enjoyed the devastation the Bush Administration unloaded on America through the Federal Emergency Management Agency and the K Street Project, you're going to love the *Extreme Makeover* going on over at your new Department of Justice. Where justice stems from the eye of The Decider.

You might think that, dragging around an approval rating lower than that of a flatulent weasel crashing a preschool prophylactic pageant, President Bush would be handicapped in accumulating another stash of clueless roommates, obscure toadies and party hacks to fill important government posts, but you, my friend, would have another think coming. Even in his position as the lamest of ducks, the Prez remains steadfast in his two-term mission to replace experienced professionals with the wretched excesses of party flackery, or, more precisely, a reflection of him.

The story so far: Say you're a good Republican afflicted with a problem U.S. Attorney who has not demonstrated proper exuberance while prosecuting Democrats near election time, or one who refuses to apologize for stepping on a few big contributor toes. Well, don't you worry your pretty little head, because a single call to the Attorney Weasel, Alberto Gonzales, and you got yourself a slack-jawed partisan lackey waiting to fill the offending prosecutor's shoes. With Kleenex.

Eight U.S. Attorneys have been fired without explanation despite positive internal performance reviews. And most have been or are on track to be replaced with candidates whose major qualification is knowing that the correct response to the Republican Party's "Jump!" command is to inquire "How high?" Head Toady Karl Rove undoubtedly has a basement assembly line stamping out a series of clones practicing his sinister brand of myopic kowtowing, even as we speak.

Apparently the fact that these guys have less experience with the law than your average IHOP early-bird shift manager is a good thing. Can't teach an old dog new suck-ups. Although many potential replacements must have gained valuable experience from being called as character witnesses for the defense in Scooter Libby's recent trial.

Some of those fired—I'm sorry, "let go," or rather, "victims of partisan duty management"—were warned not to talk to the press or risk retaliation such as the further trashing of their reputation. Who knows what diabolical measures these fiendish minds might conceive? Possible links to Joe Biden? Or having Robert Novak disclose connections to such anti-American movements as law school?

In the old days, before the threat of terrorism loomed over everything in this country like a rain gutter over an ant farm during monsoon season, the Administration needed Senate approval for appointing new U.S. Attorneys, but snuck a provision into the Patriot Act allowing the Attorney General to appoint new federal prosecutors at his discretion. "Checks and balances? We don't need no stinking checks and balances."

You'd think that, if anybody, the Department of Justice would be immune from politics. You know…justice-moral integrity. Rightness. I'm thinking someone became fixated on the left-hand part of that last word. Totally forgot about the people's Justice. By, for and of the people. But these are the new days. When even an Easter egg hunt can be politicized. And the Department of Justice can become the Department of Just Us. And that *us* don't include you or me.

Reefer Absurdity

In its finite wisdom, the U.S. Supreme Court upheld the federal government's ban on medical marijuana. Screwing all 10 states that legalized it and leaving a lot of folks in those 10 states with superfluous glaucoma diagnoses. Now, first off, let me clarify: I don't smoke pot. I don't. It makes me paranoid. No, I'm serious. I am the author of the paranoid trilogy titled *What Is It? Who Are They?* and *Why Me?* I get the munchies, go in a restaurant, the waitress says, "Hi" and I go, "Yes, I am. I'm sorry. Don't tell my Aunt Mary." But you know what, I don't drink Wild Turkey anymore and yet harbor no desire for that vile liquid to be made illegal, either.

Justice John Paul Stevens said plaintiffs suffering chronic pain should turn to "the democratic process" for comfort. He addressed this opinion to the two plaintiffs, who suffer, respectively, from a brain tumor and a degenerative spinal disease. I'm a'thinking the 85-year-old liberal Justice needs to bone up on his bedside manner a bit. "Take two democratic processes and call me in the morning." Wonder if this guy has consulted for any HMOs lately? Going to have to revise the new edition of the *Physician's Desk Reference* by inserting "Activist Judges" next to "Cottonmouth" under possible side effects.

Besides, how can they cite an interstate commerce jurisdiction over homegrown, which, according to Justice Clarence Thomas, "has never been bought or sold, that has never crossed state lines, and that has had no demonstrable effect on the national market for marijuana"? That's right, I'm quoting

Clarence Thomas. Which means tomorrow, all the residents of Hell might want to break out the sleds and earmuffs. Who knows? Maybe it was a stem of Maui Wowie and not a pubic hair on that Coke can.

That roar from the red states you hear is the orchestrated shout-out that conservatives normally toss whenever we godless heathens have been defeated. And one of the ironies can be found in the accompanying sound of millions of brewskies being popped in celebration. What is *wrong* with these people? Don't they realize that marijuana grows in the ground? They don't call it "weed" for nothing, you know.

Think of all the different, complicated operations you need to perform in order to make liquor. It's not like you can walk into your backyard and pluck a piña colada off the cocktail tree. Pot—you pick it, dry it and smoke it. Hope you're not saying that God screwed up here, are you? It's pot. It's not heroin. It's not acid. It's not even Marlboro Lights. For crum's sake, you can bake it into brownies. Brownies! What's more American than that?

And another thing, why do politicians always insist on lumping all drugs together? Even a fourth-grader can tell you that crack is to pot like an Uzi is to a banana. Crack: kills. Pot: giggles. Say you do run into a crazed pothead. What's the worst thing that's going to happen to you? OK, you might get fleas, but that's about it. So there's Twinkie cream on your shirt, wipe it off. Can't get the song "Stairway to Heaven" out of your head, deal with it. Potheads don't mug, they hug. The same cannot be said about the Supreme Court.

Libby on the Label

"When it says Libby Libby Libby on the label label label, it means that evidence given, is mostly fable fable fable."

The team in charge of Scooter Libby's defense has already

tipped its hand as to the vice presidential Chief of Staff's legal strategy in the Valerie Plame case. Apparently he's going to stick with the "I'm a busy guy" defense. We've all seen it before. They trot out a stack of papers as big as a phone book, and call his phone logs "Defense Exhibit A." "We're talking about a busy person here, people. How could this man possibly be expected to remember at what precise time he betrayed one of our secret agents as revenge on her husband for criticizing our government's motivations for going to war? This is the Chief of Staff of the most powerful man in the free world. 'Payback' is his job description. Exacting vengeance on perceived enemies is a 24/7 job. For him, the skirting of the boundaries of treason is like you and me going to the copy machine. You want the truth, America? Let me tell you something, *you can't handle the truth!*"

In the interest of avoiding this boring, tiresome and clichéd charade while at the same time fulfilling my duties as a consultant to *Court TV,* I've provided a couple of other possible defense strategies the vice president's team might want to check out.

- Too preoccupied with the grave responsibility of preserving the safety of our great nation from evildoers to recall exact sequence of events over 26 months ago.

- Perjury! Since when is perjury a crime? What are you guys, liberals?

- Playing Scrabble in the presidential suite of the Mayflower Hotel with Dick Cheney, Bill Frist, Karl Rove and Tom DeLay at the time. What time? Any time you want.

- Indictment is simply the desperate death rattle of a partisan prosecutor determined to advance the empty agenda of a hollow opposition party by exploiting extreme legal technicalities.

- Come on. His accusers are jailed journalists. Who you going to believe? The people committed to protecting us from terrorists or a bunch of Geraldo wannabes?

- Fixing broken crutches of crippled children at an orphan hospital at the time of reputed phone calls. And why weren't you?

- Russian Embassy microwave interference distorted his space–time continuum.

- You just can't send a guy named Scooter to prison.

- Couldn't have made calls in question, as he was consulting with evangelist Pat Robertson in a one-on-one seminar about how better to spread the message of our Savior and Lord Jesus Christ across the globe.

- If the glove doesn't fit, you must acquit.

- Inner-ear infection caught while rescuing drowning puppies in the Potomac River had him all discombobulated. But he's much better now.

- Recently diagnosed with an 18 1/2 minute gap in his memory.

- In the middle of obsessing over the cancellation of *Buffy the Vampire Killer,* subsequently went on a two-week ecstasy bender and can't recall anything from that time period except a Portuguese seamstress named Eva and a three-legged llama.

- He was on Twinkies at the time.

- Unable to process precise memories due to lead poisoning contracted while growing up as a poor black child in Queens.

- Before single-handedly stymieing a hitherto unpublicized terrorist attack in the cookbook section of a Borders bookstore in the Crystal City Mall, he took a direct hit from a radioactive Al-Qaeda bicycle pump hose, causing him to suffer from debilitating headaches and occasional blackouts.

Mad Politician Disease

Federal authorities said on Friday that it could take weeks or months to trace the exact spot where a Congressman in Washington, D.C., who contracted the nation's first case of Mad Politician Disease, was contaminated with bad advice. The task may prove to be too difficult, and investigators refuse to offer any assurance of success.

Uncovering the partisan committee that counseled the diseased member of Congress, who was humanely slaughtered on December 9, is thought to be crucial to determine how many other civil servants may also have contracted MPD and how far it has spread. The disease, a degenerative debilitating ailment known as conscientious spongiform encephalopathy, causes politicians to accept any money thrown their way, forgoing any and all ethical considerations. It is believed to take at least two full two-year terms to incubate and can usually be traced back to a single unwholesome contribution.

Since the questionable legislator was found to be tainted late in his second term, investigators believe he was probably infected by accepting suspect contributions at an early state in his career, contributions that could have also been accepted by other naïve bureaucrats or facilitated by aides who may have moved on to other staffs.

A delay or failure to find the source of the poisoned contribution would probably intensify the already-growing number of calls for a national system to track political funding. But, as a practical matter, regardless of whether the dubious money's source is ever found, federal officials are destined to come under heavy pressure to increase further regulations and testing, possibly including ear tagging, as early as at the initial announcement of the formation of exploratory committees.

Regulators already face calls to eliminate all oil and tobacco moneys from the political food supply, and insurance and pharmaceuticals are sure to be next. Other demands might include mandatory testing of brain cells from slaughtered Representatives who show any signs of a nervous condition when questioned at citizen forums or, as was the case with the "Downer" politician in Washington, an inability to stand for anything other than the National Anthem.

"If we're lucky, we could know something within a matter of a day or two," said Dr. Depak Phillips, dean of the University of Virginia's School of Politics, in a conference call with reporters on Friday. "Hopefully, this will speed the momentum for a national identification system, enabling us to isolate the corrupted campaign consultants so we can eliminate them without further contamination of the various components of our government."

This optimistic view of the Mad Politician scare was not shared by all. Bradley Ogden, chair of the Ethics in Government Panel of Bethesda, Maryland, cautioned: "If not stemmed immediately, this epidemic could reach all the way to the top," repeatedly winking and nodding toward a television set airing a presidential press conference. He went on to say, "Even if the dirty dollars of 'Consultant One' can be found, it is not necessarily going to be possible to figure out who bought the lunch that led to its infection. Imagine yourself a politician and trying to remember what money you accepted four years ago. That's not really the kind of thing these people keep accurate records on."

Asked to comment, the White House claimed the Mad

Politician scare is an isolated incident inflated for political purposes by the enemies of freedom, and indicated that the source will eventually be traced to a batch of bad PAC money originating from nonprofit animal rights groups based in Northern California.

The Shameless and the Spineless

This...Is...CNN.

We now return to the Supreme Court Justice confirmation hearings live from the Senate. While we were away, Judge Samuel Alito's wife was placed on a stretcher and whisked out of the committee room after bursting into tears during the questioning of her husband. She will also be tested for rabies after accidentally brushing the arm of Democratic Senator Joe Biden. The Republican chairman of the Judicial Committee is about to reconvene the proceedings by asking a question of the nominee.

"Order. Order! First off, Judge Alito, let me just say that I've already made up my mind that you're a fine, fine man and will make an exemplary Justice, and nothing you say is going to change my mind, outside of calling for the overthrow of the country by Michael Moore. And even that is just a maybe. [*Laughter*] I also want to say I think you've handled yourself with an aplomb that any reasonable person would expect of a judge of your extreme moderate temperament, even in the face of mean, rotten, radical, out-of-the-mainstream liberal questions. Biased partisan questions from extremist jackals who have sunk to the level of trying to take you to task for belonging to a harmless fraternity group in college, which you don't even remember joining, not to mention making your wife cry, for which, I assure you, they will burn in the fires of Hell. Now, I will try to elicit some answers out of you that I'm sure the American people want to hear. And I warn you, sir, these will not be softballs. I intend to ask some tough ones. Are you ready?"

"Yes, sir, I think I am. Ask away."

"All right, then. Judge Alito, do you think the American justice system is a good system?"

"Why yes, Senator, I think it is a very good system. The best system in the world."

"And are you basically a good person?"

"Well, Senator, I certainly hope so."

"And the flag?"

"It's a grand old flag."

"You're not a bigot, are you, Judge Alito?"

"No sir, I'm not."

"No, you certainly aren't, and if you had to describe yourself, would you say you are predominantly pro-good and anti-bad, or pro-bad and anti-good?"

"Well, sir, I would describe myself as mostly being pro-bad and anti-good."

[*Pause*]

"Excuse me?"

"I'm sorry, I mean the other way around. I'm just a little nervous here."

"Totally understandable. I think we all would be a little nervous in your position. Especially with so many partisan jackals lined up to nip at your distinguished heels. Well, I must say, you've answered all my questions with deference and clarity. I haven't heard anything here that's going to change my mind. And may I say, sir, I'm sure I speak not just for myself but for all the people of my great state that many prayers will be said for your wife to recover from her tragic experience."

"Thank you, Senator."

"This meeting is adjourned."

[*CNN announcer continues*]

Well, there's a surprise. It seems the Democrats have given up their right to ask Judge Alito any questions and are now all lying slumped, willy-nilly, over the committee table as if their spines have been literally torn from their bodies. Hmm.

Well, that's it from here. Let's go back to the studio where Anderson Cooper will interview Angelina Jolie's exhousekeeper and discover what Brad Pitt likes to put on his cornflakes, and it's not what you think.

This...Is...CNN.

He's the Leakingest

This is in-leaking-credible. According to leaked grand jury testimony, it turns out Scooter Libby was instructed to leak classified information about pre–Iraq War intelligence by the Oval Office. Can't wait for them to play "Hail to the Leaker," as he enters the Capitol next January for his State of the Union Leakage. "Ladies and gentlemen, please welcome the First Leaker of the United States of America, George Leaky Bush." I always suspected the president was a leaker. And now it turns out, he's the Chief Leaker. The Chief Executive Officer of Leakwell Incorporated. Chicken Leaker.

Let's welcome today's guest, the headliner of the third annual Leakapalooza: lead singer Leaky Leakman of Leaky Leakman and the Leakers. That crafty veteran manager of the five-time defending champions, the Texas Leakers. And because news of his leakage has leaked, the Leaker-in-Chief is seriously involved in heavy-duty leakage control. Trusted in that old adage "Leak and Learn," so he leaked his ass off. Fortunately, they have adult garments for that now. I think they're called "Leakenders" or "Leakaways." "Wear Leakaways and you won't leak a ways."

"Leak" is such an ugly word, isn't it? "Leaker" is even worse. Like a loser with the dribbles. Leak leak bo beak, banana fana fo feak. Fee fie fo feak. LEAKY! When the going gets tough; the tough leak like a colander. Leakers unite! And form a trickle. Voted least leakly to succeed. Through the leaking glass. Going to have to face it: He's addicted to leaks. He's going to leak, leak, leak around the clock. And this ain't the first time. Ever since college there have been rumors he had a leaky beak. The man is positively leakalicious.

He doesn't have to answer to us. He's the leaker of the free world. From the party of Lincoln to the party of Leakin'. A lesson learned from Nixon: Stonewall and you stonewall alone; leak and the world leaks with you. Leaking like the confidence of the forward shooters in a Dick Cheney hunting party. As leaky as the roof on the last duplex standing in the Ninth Ward. Leakier than a condom on the 50-yard line after a Green Bay Packers double-overtime playoff victory. The human personification of a rusted rain gutter in Seattle during January. Leaky. As the vice president told Senator Patrick Leahy on the floor of the Senate: "Go leak yourself!" Leak me? Leak you! This leaking leaker's leaked.

Who knows why he leaked. Plausible leakability, perhaps. Might have been an involuntary muscle spasm, or maybe it's just the leak of love. One explanation is that he didn't mean to leak, he was just being leaksadaisical. Morphed into Dr. Kevorkaleaker before our very eyes. Just wanted to assure himself of a major role in the newest production of *Around the Truth in Eighty Leaks*. Filmed in Leak-O-Rama. Wasn't really his fault, he and Captain Hazelwood of the Exxon Valdez were playing a quick game of "Leak, leak, splash," when all hell broke loose and his pie hole began to leak partisan ooze. Reminiscing about his days as star point guard for the Los Angeles Leakers. Or maybe it's a simple case of living out his childhood dream of finally becoming one of the lesser-known Knights of the Round Table: Sir Leaksalot.

Changing of the Guard

As Phase One of President Bush's long-awaited second term midseason staff purge-athon, Scott McClellan abandoned his plum position as White House Press Secretary. The rumor is he wants to follow in his predecessor Ari Fleischer's footsteps and spend more personal time lying to his family. This follows Chief of Staff Andrew Card's resignation and signals a desperate attempt by the Bush Administration to give the perception of a change of direction that could most accurately be presently described as sub-basement directed. Does the term "rearranging deck chairs on the Titanic" have any meaning here? Even Karl Rove has seen his role diminished. I imagine he needs more personal time to file the scuff marks off his cloven hooves. That's right. Bush's brain has been laid off. And yes, that is redundant.

In an attempt to reverse poll numbers that are falling faster than an Acme Company cartoon anvil catapulted off the top of the Empire State Building with a confused coyote clinging to it, the president is looking to a changing of the guard as his approval-rating equivalent of an animated trampoline. Reportedly, nobody's position is safe, which means even the twins are worried about being supplanted by a couple of good Mormon girls. And although Dick Cheney's head is reputedly on the chopping block, the conventional wisdom inside the Beltway is whoever actually acts as pink-slip messenger to the vice president had better be wearing a full-body containment suit that is impervious to both birdshot and political fallout of the nuclear variety.

Unfortunately, the person the president refuses to replace is the one whose head everyone keeps calling for: Secretary of Defense Donald Rumsfeld. If this were *White House Survivor,* Jeff Probst would be snuffing out Rummy's torch while fellow castaways snickered on wooden benches, huddling together for warmth. The dapper and verbally flatulent Secretary, however, remains a man who doesn't know the meaning of the word "quit." As it turns out, he seems unfamiliar with a few other words as well: like "strategy," "consensus" and "diplomacy." The recent call by between six and eight hundred generals for his Dumpstering has met with stubborn resistance from the boss. When asked, the president said, yes, he hears the voices that call for Rumsfeld to be returned horizontally to the private sector, but it would be *he* who decided, because *he* is the Chief Decider. He's not a divider but a uniter, and a decider. Who hears the voices. Hmmmmm.

Speaking of Rumsfeld's prize quagmire, Iraq, President Bush said, "Failure is not an option." No, with these guys, it comes factory installed as standard equipment. Thank the maker. Not sure the tentative, low-level alterations Dubyah instituted are quite the infusion of new blood his election-bound Republican brethren were calling for. Not even sure these guys qualify as old blood. More like sickle cell anemia blood from badger roadkill. Apparently, for the GOP, a changing of the guard is similar to a game of political volleyball. Every two years, someone yells "Rotate!" and the players switch positions. I'll be honest, I can't wait for the photo-op of this entire corrupt, cursed, imperial ruling class standing in line at the unemployment office or, better yet, shuffling off into the sunset chained together wearing orange jumpsuits. After all, doesn't real regime change start at home?

The Fratlomat

It was quite a performance the president put on at the G-8 Summit in Saint Petersburg, Russia, this year. If you, like me, understand the phrase "quite a performance" to mean "whoa, dude, chill." Maybe a switch to decaffeinated is in order. "Yo,

Blair." That's how he hailed the prime minister of Great Britain at a photo-op at the closing of the conference. "Yo, Blair!" Sounds like how I might greet one of my friends, but you know what, I'm not the president of the United States of America at a major world summit. Which, as Martha Stewart is wont to say, is a good thing.

Bush then proceeded to mumble some spurious advice to Tony Blair with a mouth full of partially masticated roll, answering once and for all why his staff goes to such lengths to keep him corralled like a roping calf in Crawford, Texas, where chewing with your mouth open is considered an art form as well as a compliment to the chef. We got some spoiled fruit running the country and he's loose and playing frat-boy diplomat with the big kids and everything is going horribly awry, people!

As bored with the whole concept of diplomacy as a five-year-old stuck in the quantum physics section of a Jamaican library, and obviously distressed at not finding Premier Putin to gaze soul-searchingly into the eyes of, Bush wandered around the big conference table, finally lighting upon German Chancellor Angela Merkel. Distractedly, he began to give her a back rub, prompting a typical Teutonic reaction, in which Merkel tensed up tighter than a retaining wire on the mast of a sailing ship in a Force 5 gale. She hunched her shoulders, grimaced and threw her hands up in an apparent plea for the World Court to augment Bush's future war crimes trial with a sexual harassment charge.

What did he expect? For her to turn around and whisper seductively, "I'll give you a week to cut that out"? She's not just German, she's East German. Everyone knows the East Germans are as cuddly as a bone splinter. I imagine we should consider ourselves lucky he didn't grab her butt and make "honk-honk" noises. Or pull a "gotcha" where he pokes her in the chest and then tweaks her nose after she looks down.

And you *know* the cupped hand under the armpit maneuver is definitely in his arsenal.

We haven't even talked about the word that rhymes with "spit" and would cost me $325,000 if I accidentally blurted it out during my day job on the radio. The hypocrisy of his signing that sanctimonious bill is so thick you can scrape the excess mendacity off the top like froth off a cappuccino. *Then,* without missing a beat, he asks President Hu of China, "How long does it take you to get home? Eight hours? Wow. Russia's a big country. So is China, isn't it?" Yes, George, China is a big country. Got a lot of people in it, too. Mexico, too. Great Mexican food. And full of Mexicans. But you already know that, because you speak Mexican, don't you?

Can you imagine Roosevelt giving the Reich's Führer a back rub? Well, actually, I guess Neville Chamberlain kind of did, but that's not the point. Instead of grandstanding for its election-year base, it is incumbent upon Congress to save our nation further embarrassments by passing a law immediately prohibiting all the members of the Bush family from any televised meeting with a foreign leader where food is being served. And mittens: They should be required to wear mittens.

Dennis Hastert's Crow Plate Special

HUBRIS (pronounced *HYOO-bris*)—noun. Excessive pride or self-confidence. Arrogance.

That's the dry, dictionary definition. But if you want to see hubris in all its gooey partisan glory, check out the machinations that Speaker of the House Dennis Hastert is going through as he twists and turns like a Chinese acrobat in zero gravity reacting to the Congressional page scandal. His first vault into the Olympics of sleaze was picking up the phone. Why? To express his outrage at Florida Republican Mark Foley's inappropriate overtures to young boys? Unh, no. OK, to console the families of the children ensnared in these lurid imprecations? Well, no, not precisely that, either. Then, to demand an investigation into why the report on Foley's behavior was buried by his office? Well, unh, no, no, not really, no. Wait! Wait! Let me think. Unh, no. Nope. 'Fraid not.

He called to demand an investigation into who leaked the report. In the face of overwhelmingly lurid evidence, his major priority was to cover his ass. This guy is so transparent I'm surprised he hasn't leased himself out during winter recess to one of his suburban Chicago constituents as a storm window. By refusing to investigate, he allowed a sexual predator to remain chairman of the House Caucus on Missing and Exploited Children, which would be funny in a sad and degrading way if only it weren't. But it does give a whole new meaning to "No Child Left Behind."

After receiving a quick pep talk from Team Bush about the best defense being a ludicrous offense, Hastert next began to lash out at the liberal press and claimed the scandal was a plot engineered by Democrats. His proof: With just a month before the election, the timing is perfect, *and* it's a genius political strategy. Let me see. Timing, strategy. Naw, doesn't sound like the Democrats to me. This charge is especially amusing when you realize what he's saying is, "Hey, it's what *we* would have done."

The sticky questions facing the Speaker now are threefold: What did he know, when did he know it and has he ever eaten a meal with less than a pound of red meat covered in béarnaise sauce on the plate? Denny, you're the Speaker, you're supposed to distribute the pork, not consume it all. I'm not saying he's guilty simply because he bloated up like a poisoned toad, but dude, have you ever heard of vegetables? Carrots: supposed to be good for the eyes and might help you see that the story you've been peddling is slipperier than the sweat on a wire-wearing lobbyist's palm. First, your office knew about Foley's hinky e-mails a few weeks ago. Then it was earlier this year. Or was it last spring? Early 2005? Just answer this: first or second season of *Lost*?

Now a former aide to the Prince of Pages himself says he warned the Speaker's Office three years ago that odd behavior was afoot. Did the House office supply clerk deliver defective calendars? We all know why Foley got a pass. Hard to rally the base when the Family Values Party morphs into the North American Man–Boy Love Association Party. Especially during an election year. And since the Speaker is destined to spend an inordinate amount of time in front of cameras explaining his calenderic malfunctions, I'd suggest he try a salad with that hubris pie and side of crow he's about to get stuffed down his throat. Maybe a raw spinach salad.

The Stealth Judge

Can someone please have the simple, common, human decency to help me understand why all the usual suspects on both sides of the aisle are on such a high twitch concerning the Harriet Miers nomination to the Supreme Court? As a liberal hearing that Charles Krauthammer has contempt for her appointment, my first reaction would be "Hey, sign her on, she's my kind of woman."

Besides, isn't it kind of "neat" the president picked someone who thought he was "cool"? That's what Miers called the president. She also said, "He is the smartest man I've ever met," which is, admittedly, a bit disquieting. Makes you wonder just how many men the lady has actually met in her life. I'm guessing a number in the low double digits; 30, tops. A majority of whom must have been encountered at bus shelters on the way to Dewey Decimal System restocking competitions.

Defending the selection of his longtime personal consultant, President Bush said, "I picked the best person I could find," which raises the question of how hard he was looking. Perhaps it was part of his famous multitasking philosophy and he went with the best person he could find while still hanging on to the leash walking his dog in the Rose Garden. Or maybe it was one of his charming, country-boy practical joke searches and she was the best person he could find blindfolded on his hands and knees in 20 minutes. Or it was a test of the Emergency Justice Network and at the sound of Dick Cheney making "whoop whoop" noises, he went with the best person within range of the Oval Office cordless phone. Who knows, maybe she won a spot check of the cleanest tray in the White House Mess and a Supreme Court appointment was first place.

White House Spokesperson Scott McClellan acknowledged a few candidates pulled their names from consideration due to the nature of the confirmation process. This is a shame because one of them apparently was a better "best person" than Miers, if not the bestest "best person" Bush could find. But their demurral is totally understandable, since all D.C. confirmations these days are akin to throwing raw meat between the bars of cranky-lion cages. McClellan said, "It was just a couple of people" who asked that their names be withdrawn, but Scott has been known to be a bit unreliable concerning his grasp of figures, so some people question whether his "couple" might actually mean 142. OK, the "some people" are me, but still.

Slapping at the Dobermans nipping at his far-right flank, the president got conservative broadcaster James C. Dobson to announce he supported Miers, based on "things that I know, that I probably shouldn't know." Ooh, that's good. Supersecret double-cryptic wisdom. Unimpeachable confidentiality. From Bush or God himself, doesn't matter, since one channels the other these days. Which way the direction flows is a subject still up for debate.

Harriet Miers's major qualifications seem to be loyalty and friendship, which sounds more like a background check for First Terrier, but he's the president. He gets to pick. Since she describes herself as a born-again Christian evangelical, I'm sure he considers her stealth stance on *Roe v. Wade* to be a slam dunk, but the wearing of the robes does funny things to a person. Although she claims not to have an opinion on abortion rights. Unh-hunh. Yeah, I believe that. The same way I believe that lions lack an opinion on meat.

The Wireless Cable Man

Speaking of his new appointment to head up the Central Intelligence Agency, President George Bush called four-star General Michael Hayden "the right man to lead the CIA at this critical moment in our nation's history." Let's hope Hayden isn't too much of a student of history. Otherwise, he might read the president's statements about Porter Goss, the man whose position he is filling, when Goss was appointed to head the CIA, 18 months ago. "He's the right man to lead the CIA at this critical moment in our nation's history." Or perhaps Hayden has been assured that, of all the right men, he's the rightest man for the job. And you can take that any which way you want.

Uncanny how Bush was able to find these two right men for the CIA at these various critical moments in our nation's history. Have you noticed that every point in time is a critical moment in our nation's history for this guy? He even claims to have special powers because of this critical moment in our nation's history. Apparently mixing up the script is not one of them. But I'll tell you why every point in time in his Administration is a critical moment in our nation's history: It's not the terrorists, it's not the price of gas, it's not the illegal immigrants or the domestic spying, *it's because he's the president. That's why.*

George W. Bush possesses the unique ability of turning nap time at a preschool into a critical moment in our nation's history. Because even attention-deficit 5-year-olds are bright enough to toss and turn on pins and needles dreading whatever blunder President Fossil Fuels has up his sleeve for the future. Have you ever smelled a classroom full of interiorly stained GrrAnimals? Ooooh. Not a good thing. Neither is Sponge Bob Squarepants getting the contact shakes. And let's get real here: Turning the CIA over to Pentagon authority is not the lullaby to lay these kids down to sleep. As far as soundtracks go, this is more Bernard Hermann than Randy Newman.

You want an example of putting the military in charge of intelligence? How 'bout the SS or the KGB? Besides the fact that the term "military intelligence" takes us deep into the heart of Oxymoronia, that mythical land in the Middle West where the Bush presidency first sprouted its logic-defying, genetically modified seeds. Saying "military intelligence" is like requesting wireless cable. Or a Donald Rumsfeld mix tape. Or *The Wall Street Journal Presents Dick Cheney's Executive Guide to Getting Along by Going Along.*

Then again, with Bush's poll numbers descending into Nixonian if not Stalinistic sublevels, we can only surmise that, each and every day, more and more Americans are able to acknowledge that piercing wake-up call telling them George Bush is the wrong man to lead the country in this critical moment in our nation's history. And I predict our nationwide insomnia will reach its peak in November of '07, when a Democratically controlled Congress convenes the first of a series of impeachment trials. Maybe we should embark on a national project to erect huge statues of the president all over the country, just for the cathartic release that will consume us when we attach wireless cables to tear him down.

The Curious Case of the Amnesiac Attorney General

I'm afraid it is my duty to impart some bad news, people, and I advise you all to sit down before you fall down. The Attorney General of the United States apparently has been infected with a horrible disease. Best-case scenario is a tertiary attack of situational amnesia, here. And for a lawyer, that can't be good. In his recent appearance before the Senate Judiciary Committee, Alberto Gonzales was unable to recall something...45 times. Before lunch. Maybe it's simply a case of hypoglycemia, since after lunch he couldn't recollect only 29 times. I don't mean to minimize the critical nature of this crisis, but the solution seems obvious to me: between-meal snacks.

The scary part is, as head of the Justice Department, Gonzales is ostensibly the country's top lawyer. After this performance, I doubt if he'll be the top lawyer on the Greyhound back to Texas. Hey, he's the guy who said, "The moment I believe I can no longer be effective, I will resign as Attorney General." Right about now, even his staunchest supporters are ordering Mylar balloons delivered to the D of J with DON'T LET THE DOOR KNOB HIT YOU IN THE BUTT ON THE WAY OUT stenciled on them.

When asked about the decision to fire eight federal prosecutors, Gonzales insisted he wasn't involved. Then, after e-mails about meetings he attended were released: OK, maybe then he was involved. But just a little. Microscopically. An eensy-teensy teeny wee bit of a tad. Suddenly he did admit to making the decision to fire the U.S. Attorneys—he just couldn't remember when. It's a perennial theme with this Administration. "Had absolutely nothing to do with it. Oh, you have evidence? Nope. Sorry. Can't remember. It's all a blur."

At the hearing, Senators accused Bush's torture champion of being dishonest, deceitful, incompetent, evasive, inept, underhanded, misleading, smelling like rancid olive loaf and looking like he's wearing his father's burial suit. Not to mention scaring small children with a high, squeaky voice that, when broadcast over airwaves, has been known to activate smoke alarms, lawn sprinklers and TiVo recordings of gladiator movies. And those were the Republicans. With friends like these, who needs Democrats?

In a show of solidarity, the president assured the country that the Attorney General had his full confidence. "Doing a heckuva job, Alberto." Bush actually talked about how pleased he was with Gonzales's performance, even though a staffer conceded Bush had not seen any of the testimony. I'm thinking the main reason he's supporting him is that "Attorney General" and "Alberto Gonzales" have the same initials, and it's the only way he can remember who's filling the position. It's a mnemonic device.

The low point may have come when Gonzales attempted to explain away the personnel changes as "not the right people at the right time." South Carolina Republican Senator Lindsey Graham asked, "If I applied that standard to you, what would you say?" and the entire room erupted into laughter. You know what? That can't be good, either. For him or for us.

You Got to Love Dick

You got to love Dick. Vice President Cheney, that is. He made another unannounced visit to Iraq in his unofficial capacity as heavy-schtarker foreign-policy hit man for that Halliburton subsidy, the Bush White House. "So, Mr. Iraqi Prime Minister Nouri al-Maliki, you're planning on letting the Iraqi Parliament go on vacation for two months while our troops keep on protecting your sorry asses. Well, perhaps a few minutes alone with the *Enforcer* will set you straight." [*Cue* Darth Vader *theme*]

To me, the biggest shocker is he entered a battle zone under his own free will. Must have burned through all his deferments back in the '60s. Then again, maybe wars, just like kids, are different when they're your own. Yes, they are! They're special. A gift from God. Landing at an undisclosed base near Baghdad, he descended the airplane steps wearing a flak jacket under his suit coat, which seems to indicate his bullet-repelling powers are diminishing.

But his powers of polarization remain intact. When Hugo Chavez called President Bush the devil at the UN, he was way out of line. Everybody knows Bush isn't the devil. Cheney is. Bush is just one of his little helper-monkeys. I can prove Cheney is the devil. Who else could shoot a guy in the face with a gun and get the victim to apologize? "I wish to beg forgiveness for placing my bulbous head between the gun and the bird, thereby ruining the shot of my Dark Lord."

I got to say, there is something about Dick Cheney that I admire. His single-mindedness, for instance. The man will say or do whatever it takes to get what he wants. Probably explains why he's so dismissive of Democrats. He legitimately does not understand them. He will do anything: lie, cheat, steal, eat bugs, subvert the Constitution, sell out his daughter; whatever he deems necessary to achieve his goal. While with Democrats, well, like Robert Frost said 100 years ago, "Sometimes it's hard to get a liberal to take their own side in an argument." And not much has changed. With the vice president, there's no artifice. I'm not saying he doesn't lie. He does. Often. Without regard to any facts. He just doesn't give a good rat's ass whether you know he's lying.

Who else can look evil wearing a short-sleeved shirt? Who else can get laughs by drinking a glass of water while George Bush talks? Who else could sell the country on the concept of compassionate torture? He's a shark with glasses. Which might be the basis of his heart problems. His native species is not totally familiar with the function of that particular organ. What's he have, a cardiovascular event every three weeks? Got a pacemaker the size of a garage door opener. And I'm going to miss him when he totters away from the public eye. Too bad he can't run for president, but the Secret Service would never abide a Chief Executive susceptible to assassination by microwave oven.

The Little Boys Who Cried "The Other Side Is Nothing but a Bunch of Big Fat Liars"

One thing you got to say about the Bushies. They sure are consistent. But every one else lies. Al Gore? Lying liar. Campaigned with his pants afire. Riddled with standard falsifying disease endemic to the Democratic Party, most prominently exemplified by his mentors, Slick Willie and Hillary "the Human Serpent" Clinton.

Department of the Treasury Secretary Paul O'Neill, who had the audacity to criticize the Administration in these tenuous times? Obviously lying. A dastardly turncoat Democratic mole who betrayed the good people of this country for purely political reasons. *Which* purely political reasons, we're not sure. Probably purely political reasons being dictated to him from a secret Clinton agenda-bunker originating deep in the Harlem underground.

Richard S. Foster, the accountant who claimed he was threatened with firing or worse if he ever breathed a word of the true cost of the Medicare bill ($100 million more than the bill sent to Congress?)—lying dupe or lying traitor? We may never know. What we *do* know is he's only making stuff up. Brainwashed, hypnotized or just a venal little weasel with a Napoleonic complex feebly trying to take down the most compassionate Administration in the nation's history with a tapestry of falsehoods, prevarications and perjurious distortions.

Former antiterrorism czar Richard Clarke? The lyingest of all the lying liars. An evildoer whose testimony before the 9/11 Commission was nothing but a grandstanding load of transparent lies in a pitiable attempt to hype sales of his libelous collection of untruths published by a subsidiary of Viacom, which also owns CBS (wink-wink). Can't seem to keep his whoppers straight; changes stories like a librarian's Rolodex in a wind tunnel. In league with liberal media, the Clintons, Osama bin Laden and Al Franken. Not to mention, beady little eyes.

Our brave, stalwart president and his loyal band of altruistic acolytes, who ignored the weak, doddering and senile protestations of the entire commie pinko yellow rat bastard world by taking this country into a preemptive war based on charges of weapons of mass destruction that mysteriously never materialized: pure innocents. Misled newborn duckies whose only mistake was to trust the mean old info wizards at the CIA, most of whom are treacherous flunkies of Al-Qaeda sympathizers, i.e., contributors to John Kerry's campaign, like Jane Fonda. It sure is easy when you live in a world of good and bad, black and white, and, as we all pretty much know but are loathe to admit, it's even easier when you're the white.

Roving Target

"Hello, this is the president of the United States. Yeah, I find it hard to believe too, but go ahead and leave a message and either Dick or Karl or my Dad or Laura will get back to you. BEEP!"

"Yeah, boss? This is me, Scott. McClellan. You know, your press secretary? You remember. Kind of balding? The one who always falls for your finger on my chest, then I look down and you hit me on the nose trick? Listen, I got a problem here. Um, this thing is getting weird. I mean, the reporters won't get off the Karl Rove–Valerie Plame story. They're like rabid wolverines and I'm the wounded bunny. I did the whole 'can't comment on an ongoing criminal investigation' deal like we agreed. And kept doing it. Christ, I must have said it maybe 80 times and they wouldn't stop. The hell is that? I thought we had a deal with these guys. Even Carl Cameron from Fox News! You should have seen him: 'Does the president still have confidence in Rove?' I wanted to slap that weasel smile right off his smug mug. Some dame even asked, 'Who is Karl Rove?' and I totally blanked and launched back into 'ongoing criminal investigation,' looking like a complete idiot, which I know is what you pay me to do, but holy crap, they just wouldn't lay off. Where's Jeff Gannon when we need him?

"Anyhow, boss, please please please tell me we're not going to run that stupid 'he never mentioned her name' defense. I mean, c'mon. He did say Joe Wilson's *wife* worked for the CIA. Which, unless the guy is the King of Bahrain or an Elder in the Mormon Church or an Eskimo or something, sounds pretty definitive even to me. And unh, if you do talk to Mr. Rove about this, could you leave my name out of it? To be honest, the guy kind of gives me the heebie-jeebies. Remember that time I spilled coffee on his lap, and everyone laughed? Later on he pushed me into my office and started screaming and all the doors and windows shut on their own and the air got dense and I swear his eyes turned all red and stuff and a bunch of papers on a chair burst into flames. They were just a pile of old *Post*s so it was no big deal, but still! And I've been asking around and I'm not the only one he creeps out. Cheney's Chief of Staff's head intern told my intern that she walked in on the vice president and Mr. Rove in that big marble bathroom upstairs dancing around waving dead chicken carcasses and using the decapitated heads as finger puppets. And now she's got warts on her eyes, and I know you don't want to know anything unless you need to know, but this is stuff I think you need to know.

"If you ask me, I think we ought to go right back to good old Plan A where we criticize the criticizers. Get McConnell or one of the boys to express their patriotic outrage and say how picking on Karl Rove is endangering our troops and, well, you know the routine. That's it, I guess. You know me, I'll do whatever's good for the team. Except for that hot tub thing with Robert Novak. But you were just kidding around, right? Ulp, here comes Matt Cooper. Got to run."

The Rare Double-Pronged Red-Footed Bushie

There are a lot of things President Bush would rather do than give a speech to the nation. Play golf with his dad. Fall off a mountain bike. I even think clearing brush wearing nothing but boots at high noon in the middle of an August scorpion migration would win hands down over the speech thing. But this week, America was treated to a rare double-dose of the president talking out of both sides of his mouth. Happy and sad, that is.

The early part of the week we were presented with his sad, serious side. The one without the Texas accent. Where "having learned the lessons of 9/11, our mission is clear, we must stay the course, and advance freedom in what has become a terrorist's paradise." A situation for which neither we nor the people of Iraq have ever properly thanked him, and, being the simple, humble man he is, for which he takes little if any of the credit, when truth be told, it is a single-handed accomplishment that he need not share with anyone. Bravo, Mr. President! Bravo!

In less than 25 minutes, Dubyah managed to slip in five references to 9/11, at a time when over 50 percent of the country believes he misled us into Iraq. Does the term "stop beating that horse, he ain't breathing, and is starting to smell funny already" have any meaning here? Recognizing the fact that national recruitment is so low that the slogan "An Army of One" is destined to soon become a reality, he also threw in: "There is no higher calling than service in our armed forces." Which apparently is a plea for the privileged sons of politicians to join the Alabama National Guard.

That was the tough one. He only gave it because his poll numbers are skewing lower than snake-belly futures. And he gave it in front of 750 soldiers who could only work up enough enthusiasm to interrupt the speech with applause once, and that was for the joke applause that always comes when a politician says "in conclusion." You think we're frustrated with a policy in search of a mission, imagine having to defend it against desperate zealots who think you're the devil.

But then, on Friday, it was another story altogether. We got to see the very same George W. Bush squeal with girlish delight as he broke into daytime television soap operas to deliver the news that Swing Vote Sandy was retiring from the Supreme Court and now he finally, *finally,* gets to make an appointment, and his Texas accent was so thick I half expected the word "hornswoggle" to slip out at any minute.

And, oh yeah, the nation thanks what's-her-name for her long-time valuable service and blah blah blah and hee hee hee. The excitement shone in his eyes, with an interior dialog clearer than branch water poured over distilled ice. "Watch out, you Senate Dems, because here comes the wrath of Rove. And he is going to smite righteously down on you liberal pantywaists who only want to give the terrorists back rubs." Bush seems determined to announce an appointment in time for Advise and Consent to finish up before the Supreme Court reconvenes in October, so you might want to replace the filter in your air conditioner, because this looks to be one of those long, hot summers.

George Bush: *President of Workaholics Anonymous*

A great many things can be said about George W. Bush. Here's just a few.

- He has the speaking skills of a former left tackle who played three seasons of Big 10 football without a helmet.

- His head is so far up the butt of the Christian Right, the back-and-forth movement of his shoulders puts a shine on the rear of Pat Robertson's pants.

- Every Memorial Day you expect him to lay a wreath at the tomb of the Unknown Service Record, then sign an Executive Order extending its military commitment.

But one thing you can't say about the 43rd president of the United States is that the man needs some sleep. He looks well rested, and I'm thinking for good reason. Even his wife makes jokes about his penchant for hitting the hay around 8 p.m., which is about an hour before I even start work. For crum's sake, who goes to bed at 8? I don't care what time you get up, that's four hours of sleep before midnight. As a small child, was he frightened by the moon?

This is a total 180-degree turnaround from Bill Clinton, who used to stay up till 3 in the morning talking policy with staff and visitors. And yeah, yeah, yeah, I know: With Clinton, the emphasis in "policy wonk" was definitely on the wonking. Coed wonking. But to say George Bush is not a workaholic is to say Nebraska is not known for its suspension bridges.

It's not just his early-bird-eats-worms lifestyle, but also his work habits, that have me as confused as a hyperactive chameleon on a plaid kilt. When, exactly, does he work? Whenever news breaks, we always hear he was notified while working out in the gym or falling off his mountain bike or clearing brush on his ranch. Sure seems to be a lot of brush there. Is that what he grows on that ranch: brush?

Mountain biking in Maryland is where he supposedly was during the airspace incursion and partial evacuation of Washington, D.C., last month that the Secret Service neglected to tell him about. I guess his people thought it prudent to wait till he was back safely playing in the sandbox. (Who knew Maryland had mountains?)

Later this summer, Bush is scheduled once again to go on his customary 35-day vacation to his Crawford, Texas, ranch. People, five weeks is not a vacation: It's a retreat, a leave of absence, a sabbatical. Must be why everybody wants to be president. Nice gig. The only people who get five weeks' vacation are German trade unionists, Parisian waiters and Santa Claus, and arguments can be made that the last two are fictitious.

Not to mention that five weeks of dead-solid summer in West Texas has to be as enchanting as a herd of gut-shot armadillos tied to your ankle with molted snakeskins. The dew point down there is normally shaking hands with triple digits, not to mention winged insects the size of footstools. So we may be talking cumulative brain-fry here, which could explain a lot.

So you figure, 8 to 10 yearly trips to Crawford, every other weekend at Camp David, he goes to bed at 8, and that means, in the average year, he's actually at work, what, about a week? George W. is truly the first slacker president. "Dude, the job doesn't pay much, but the perks are egregiously righteous." He's President Keanu. That must be what the W stands for: "Whooaaa!"

8 | Iraq
Iran
Irat

*OK, it's just Iraq & Iran. Threw the "Irat" in there
mostly for scan. This is the Year of the Rat, though,
if that makes any difference. Didn't think so.*

*Oh, wait: Could be the title of Donald Rumsfeld's
autobiography after President Bush leaves office:*
I, Rat. *Not your paradigm of bipartisanship, perhaps, but you have to understand, the Administration thwarted my every effort to mock and scoff and
taunt the Democrats equally by relentlessly filling
the newspapers with ludicrously satiric fodder on a
daily basis.*

*Such as: Turns out it wasn't Iraq with the weapons
of mass destruction. It wasn't Iraq with the ties to
Al-Qaeda. It was Iran.*

*Man, we were so close. Probably just a clerical error.
You see my dilemma.*

Iraqi Good Stuff

On the third anniversary of his misadventure into Iraq, President George Bush strove to sell his invasion and occupancy policy by holding a press conference and announced that getting U.S. troops out of Iraq is not his problem. Instead it's going to be the problem of future U.S. presidents and Iraqi governments. In other words, there's no light at the end of this tunnel, just a secular guerilla holding a flashlight, and we're backing out as fast as our little cowboy boots can carry us. Civil war: the gift that keeps on giving.

To say he was a bit testy is like saying freshly laid asphalt is not as nutritious as it looks. He even snapped at Helen Thomas. For crum's sake, who snaps at Helen Thomas? It's like biting the head off a Smurf. He also proceeded to duck questions asked of him and to answer unasked questions his handlers had prepared him for and, overall, had the look of a guy who was trying to fake his way through not having done his homework... for the last 13 semesters. He did his best to reassure America that it's not as bad as it looks over there. Which is good 'cuz, to be honest, it looks pretty freaking bad over there.

He was adamant that progress is being made but, when asked to explain where and how, ran into a couple of minor roadblocks. Like examples of where and how we're making progress. But if you believe Dubyah, which I'm not even sure Laura and the twins do anymore, except for the prison assaults and the assassinations and the suicide bombings and the boots on the ground getting buried, things are actually pretty good. It's that darn media that's screwing everything up. By showing stuff. Bad stuff. If only that rascally American press could report some of the Good Stuff coming out of the Middle East, everyone would settle down and birds would sing and gay people would drink beer and have babies and all would be right with the world. So, being the patriot that I am, I've gone out—not far—and done the research and collected a bunch of the Good Stuff coming out of Iraq in a little something I like to call...

Will Durst Finds the Bright Side to Xenophobic Genocide

- Baghdad University fraternity hazings way down.

- $6 billion a month we won't be wasting on pork-barrel politics.

- Advances in battlefield medical procedures destined to benefit all mankind.

- Due to their renewed dedication to killing each other, Sunnis and Shiites seem much less interested in targeting Americans these days.

- VFW membership rolls are headed for a bull market.

- Grisly footage of dead in Iraq diverting attention from that whole ugly Jack Abramoff thing.

- Marked increase in downtown Baghdad available parking.

- Every single car-bomb explosion means another opportunity for Detroit fleet sales.

- Where tomorrow's stars of the Cadaver Dog World get first-class training today.

- Senseless secular violence has obviously intensified the truce in Northern Ireland.

- There's a Burning Man Festival every day of the week.

- When you're thinking organ donor heaven, we're talking Iraq.

- Hey, it could be worse. There could be leeches.

- And the final piece of good news coming out of the Iraq... spring has sprung.

Scoundrel City

"Patriotism is the last refuge of a scoundrel."

—Samuel Johnson

OK, get this and get this straight. Criticizing our government is not the same as criticizing our armed forces. OK? Just as criticizing our government is not the same as criticizing our postal workers. Or criticizing our zookeepers or our ceramic mosaic tile grout installers. And let me make this clear, I am not in any way suggesting that any of these groups be criticized. Especially the postal workers.

Furthermore, telling the press that you are disgusted by reports of torture does not endanger our troops. You're all so fired-up desperate to know what endangers our troops; I'll tell you what endangers our troops. Greedy cretinous toad leaders sending them 12,000 miles away to a desert to fight a war based on lies. Lies about an imminent threat and lies about a phantom desire to negotiate. That's who put our troops in harm's way. The idiots who sent them into this...and yes, it's time to say it out loud...this quagmire.

"Quagmire," as in bottomless morass. "Quagmire," as in Vietnam. A minor conflict that tore our country apart about three decades ago. Perhaps some of you patriotic Republicans remember? I know none of you bothered to serve over there, but you must have seen a History Channel special on it. Does the movie *Apocalypse Now* ring a bell?

Democratic Leader Nancy Pelosi called the Iraq War a "grotesque mistake," and House Speaker Dennis Hastert reacted like she funded secret poisonous kimchee research in North Korea. "Leader Pelosi and the Democratic leadership should support our troops instead of spreading inflammatory statements." Hey, Hastert! Pay attention. The lady said nothing about our troops. She was talking about you, you moron, and the rest of the majority leadership. And trust me, I use the term "leadership" extremely loosely. For crum's sake, you pay enough for your polling, put the donut down and read some of it. America agrees with Pelosi. Big fat enormous monstrous grotesque mistake. Repeat after me: "War: bad. Troops: good." See, it's possible to say and to mean, as well.

Then you scream at Senator Dick Durbin, the anti-torture dude, instead of the idiots who keep sending our troops over there without the proper equipment. Why aren't you screaming at the dimwits taking away benefits from those very same troops you're so protective of when they come home? It's like teaching the 9/11 terrorists a lesson by invading a country that had absolutely nothing to do with it. Oh, OK, I see. It's a pattern.

Are you saying it's treasonous to denounce torture? Or do you mean to imply that torture comes with codicils? "Torture is bad. Unless it's us doing the torturing. In which case it is not torture, but rather 'results-oriented questioning.' " Samuel Johnson was a piker. With these scoundrels, patriotism is not the last but the first, second and every *other* refuge. The Republicans need to learn: More strident does not make you more correct. If it did, Joan Rivers would be running things.

Son of the Scoundrel: The Sequel

Oh no, you didn't. Don't you tell me that you did. Not again. Because only a gutless swine would trot out that weak, tired line of crap. Again. Dividing America. *Again.* You didn't really say it, did you? That anyone who criticizes you is endangering the troops? Not again! Can I just ask, where the hell do you get the cojones, after everything we've gone through the last three years, to let that pathetic argument ooooze out of your pie hole one more time? Must come from your mother's side.

Please tell me I'm wrong. Please tell me you didn't give a speech on *Veterans Day* accusing your critics of being the ones who are dividing this country. That all that's necessary to comfort the enemy is to possess the temerity to question your bogus transparent motives for going to war against a nation with absolutely *no connection* to 9/11. A war you have since claimed to have gotten the permission of God to execute. You know something? You got a mean God. Probably likes giving spina bifida to babies.

And don't tell me, either, that you made this declaration while employing members of our armed forces as a backdrop to give you the cover of credibility. Hiding behind the very people you put in harm's way. Again. I take it back. To call you a gutless swine is to disparage the contribution that male pigs with empty intestinal cavities have given to this great country of ours. Spineless jellyfish is more like it. Something to be scraped off the bottom of a shoe.

Yeah, sure, fine. Lots of people agreed that Saddam had weapons of mass destruction in 2002. Teddy Kennedy, Bill Clinton, Saddam's neighbors, France, Denmark, your wife. Lots of people. Who cares? They were wrong, too. What difference does that make? Since it's been proved beyond a reasonable doubt (which excludes Limbaugh and Hannity) that your Administration jobbed the figures these people were able to review. For crum's sake, I *knew* Saddam didn't have any WMD. Why? Because he didn't use them.

"Then why did he claim to have them?" Who the hell knows? I work in bars. And you know what I see all the time? People taking swings at cops. All the time. Why the hell would anybody do that? Best-case scenario of swinging at a cop is you miss while his head is turned and he doesn't see it. Makes no sense at all. And yet it happens all the time.

You also claimed Saddam had a mess of mushroom clouds waiting for us, 45 minutes away. No he didn't. You can't tell a bunch of people lies, have them repeat what you told them and then claim that you were influenced by the people you convinced. Besides, you have never listened to a single word Ted Kennedy has said in his entire life. Why would you start now? What are you going to pull out of your butt next: his brother's Domino Theory?

Sir, you are a failure of monumental proportions. A blanched husk of an empty shell. If they had an opposite of Mount Rushmore, your face and Millard Fillmore's would anchor it with whichever Harrison gave the three-hour speech in the rain, caught pneumonia and died. And like the bumper sticker says, I wish someone would be willing to take a bullet for this country and commit fellatio on you so we could impeach your lying ass.

Good News/Bad News

It's almost dead-solid meteorological summer and the crossing of the solstice seems to have inaugurated a season of good news/bad news for George W. Bush, the Democrats, Iraq, you, me, pretty much everybody. Allow me to illustrate.

The GOOD NEWS is that George W. Bush pulled off a secret mission and flew to Baghdad in the dead of night.

The BAD NEWS is he only stayed five hours and then came right home.

The GOOD NEWS is Ben Roethlisberger is going to be OK.

The BAD NEWS is that diagnosis is based on the Gary Busey scale.

The GOOD NEWS is oil prices are going down.

The BAD NEWS is they're taking stock prices with them.

The GOOD NEWS is Iraq's future is in its own hands.

The BAD NEWS is Iraq's future is in its own hands.

The GOOD NEWS is Karl Rove is not going to be indicted in the Valerie Plame case.

The BAD NEWS is Joe Wilson got his hands on some curare.

The GOOD NEWS is the Republican Party won the special election for Duke Cunningham's 50th Congressional District in San Diego.

The BAD NEWS is they had to spend the GNP of Estonia to do it.

The GOOD NEWS is Bill Frist's gay marriage amendment went down in flames.

The BAD NEWS is the flames are being put out by the drool dripping out of his mouth just thinking of the flag-burning amendment in his back pocket.

The GOOD NEWS is we've uncovered a new tactic of Al-Qaeda: asymmetrical warfare.

The BAD NEWS is that the three guys at Guantanamo Bay who introduced it aren't able to tell us where to send the royalty checks.

The GOOD NEWS is Abu Musab al-Zarqawi is dead.

The BAD NEWS is 72 virgins in Heaven just filed a restraining order.

The GOOD NEWS is Senate Democrats have scuttled a Republican attempt to eliminate the estate tax.

The BAD NEWS is their kids are really pissed off.

The GOOD NEWS is Michael Chertoff has determined New York City is without any national monuments and therefore safe from terrorism.

The BAD NEWS is Michael Chertoff gets to determine anything.

The GOOD NEWS is U.S. President Bush has resolved to stop taunting the world at large with his tough-guy he-man posturing.

The BAD NEWS is Iranian President Ahmadincjad is taunting the world at large with his tough-guy he-man posturing.

The GOOD NEWS is the president got an Al-Zarqawi bounce.

The BAD NEWS is it's not as high as Al-Zarqawi's body actually bounced.

The GOOD NEWS is President Bush got to look Nouri al-Maliki eye to eye.

The BAD NEWS is al-Maliki has to sleep with a chicken foot under his pillow to counter the curse of the evil eye.

The GOOD NEWS is Tiger Woods is back on the PGA Tour.

The BAD NEWS is he's playing like me. (This was a while ago.)

The GOOD NEWS is U.S. air carriers are expected to be more crowded this summer than any time since 9/11.

The BAD NEWS is one more cut in service and they'll have to tear out the seats.

The Terrorists Follow Us Home

A lot of trees died in vain wasting valuable newsprint this week, reporting details of President Bush's desperate attempt to float a new trial balloon in his tortured, six-year war against logic, reason, gravity and physics. Apparently he's in need of a new sack of gas to tie his failed Iraq War plan to. Due to the fact that his most recent verbal bag of helium, "Stay the course," has been tossed onto the same discarded pile of shriveled rubber as "Dead or alive," "Smoking gun as a mushroom cloud" and "Welcomed with flowers and candy."

He held an hour-long press conference in an elastic attempt to sound reasonable, having about as much success as a rabid jackalope trying to hide in a half-empty spinach fettuccine bin at Whole Foods. Trotting out a series of empty mantras, the president courted the opinion of average Americans, who, recent polls say, still retain their admiration for the man for his stick-to-it-ive-ness, although they remain a bit skeptical of his synaptic activity. Much like a man intent on breaking through a brick wall using only his forehead. While you got to admire his persistence, you probably don't want him doing much math.

Experimenting with the calibrated residue of Karl Rove's extensive hot-air polling of focus groups, Dubyah introduced the new official buzz phrase of the Iraqi occupation: the word "wrong." Cutting and running is "wrong." The Democrats are patriotic but "wrong." Spandex on NFL linemen? Screw Kappa Napa. It's all just "wrong." He went on to say if we don't finish the job in Iraq, the world will see us as quitters, and you know what they say about quitters. "Quitters bruise their shins and winners never evacuate and are destined to bloat up like a beach ball inflated by a big-rig-tire air hose," or something like that. He wasn't really clear. As usual.

"There's a lot of people—good, decent people—saying, 'Withdraw now.' They're wrong," Bush said. "There are a lot of people in the Democrat Party who believe that the best course of action is to leave Iraq before the job is done, period. And they're wrong." Unfortunately he steadfastly refuses to tell us exactly what job he is talking about. I'm thinking it has to do with developing a falafel-based oil substitute.

He further explained that if we leave, the terrorists will follow us home. And if they follow us home, we'll have to walk them twice a day and feed them and brush them and they'll need shots and let me tell you right now, they're sleeping outside, mister. Oh sure, they're cute when they're young, but when terrorists grow up, they're just like animals. Constantly begging for scraps and whimpering because they're afraid to be left alone. "Allah is watching." Chewing shoes. Peeing on their prayer rug.

At the end, he mixed up a strange cocktail of the weirdly poetic and the loopy. "Sometimes I'm frustrated. Rarely surprised. Sometimes I'm happy, you know. But war is not a time of joy. These aren't joyous times. These are challenging times... and they're straining the psyche of our country." And as one who's had my psyche strained, I got to admit, he's right. "We're not leaving so long as I'm the president." OK, Mr. President, whatever it takes.

The Sissy Box

What a surprise. Republicans feverishly exploiting their echo chamber to pound out the familiar percussive drumbeat that Democrats are weenie girlie-men who can't be trusted to keep their frilly underwear unsoiled, much less protect this country from terrorists. GOP mole Joseph Lieberman parroted the same crass, cross-party line when he nasally whined that Ned Lamont's win over him in the Senate race was a victory for the kind of people involved in the British Pakistani airline bomb plot. One news anchor on Fox News called Democrats "the Al-Qaeda Party." And in response, Democrats have vowed to mount a vigorous defense. Soon. Maybe. Once they rinse out their underwear.

What is *wrong* with these guys? They got to get out there. Now. No, now is too late. They got to build a time machine. Go back to Friday the 11th. Issue pre-dated press releases. And drag everyone along with them. Dig up a couple or three initialed dead Dems like JFK and FDR and LBJ and send them out on tour. Do whatever it takes to keep the GOP from locking them into the sissy box. Again. Get Al Gore to put together a PowerPoint presentation to display exactly which party is at fault for America's being less safe now. And convince him to regrow his beard.

It's time to fight back. Time to start slamming Bush and his toadies for diverting the money for research to screen for liquid bombs to fight a war against the wrong people. We got to remember that 60 percent of us aren't happy about *invading the wrong country*. And it's time to lambaste the whole do-nothing Beltway crowd for not implementing the 9/11 Commission's recommendations on airport security. Not to mention the futility of busting passengers for possession of toothpaste.

With only 12 weeks left before the midterms, they got to trot out their history of proposing security legislation that the Congressional majority routinely scuttled. They should have every single Democratic Congressman go out and tell those same silly people who still believe Iraq possessed weapons of mass destruction that the reason we don't have bomb-detection technology for this sort of thing is Bush wasted all our money on his rich buddies. Is Paris Hilton going to buy D.C.'s Dulles Airport a liquid bomb scanner? I don't think so. I doubt if she can spell "D.C." Point out that Bush has created more terrorists than he's killed. And point out how odd it is that nobody in this Mickey Mouse Administration is familiar with *The Sorcerer's Apprentice*.

And then have our bravest, most charismatic Congressman (from the safest district in the country) reel off all the Democratic plans to secure our borders that have been trashed by Bush's Congress, and hoist these squeezebags on their own petard by warning Americans that "Every vote for a Republican is a vote for another 9/11." And when they come at him with teeth bared waving sharpened flagpoles, and they will, just blow up the paragraph from the *Washington Times* where Tony Snow and Dick Cheney and Joe Lieberman said the same damn thing in reverse. And brace yourselves for an October ad campaign featuring Nancy Pelosi in a burka.

Compassionate Torturer

I always tremble like a hamster duct-taped to a Rototiller when George Bush struts into the spotlight on the world stage, as he did this week addressing the UN. The same feeling I get when San Francisco Giants closer Armando Benitez takes the mound in a save situation. It's a cover-your-eyes-and-peek-through-your-fingers sort of deal. A breath-holding, whispered-prayers kind of time. Exciting, but not in what you call your good way. What you call your sweaty way.

Especially now, after six years of being reluctant members of the studio audience laugh track for his sitcom: We've seen his work, we know too much. So many things could screw up. What if the TelePrompter goes awry and he tries to exercise his ad lib skills? Could he drag us into a war by mistake? Again? Suppose the first ADHD POTUS succumbs to the urge to wander around the General Assembly and begins to apply unrequested back rubs to female heads of state? Can we as a country be prosecuted for sexual harassment?

What if an accidental Red Bull overdose encourages him to attempt to pronounce Iranian President Ahmadinejad's name? In front of people? And what about his safety: Aren't we exposing him to unnecessary risk? Say he gets the munchies, pops some pretzels and starts choking. Again. Mightn't the United Nation's EMTs conveniently recall previously forgotten appointments, once they discover the identity of their prone, blue patient?

Or, God forbid, he'll start to lecture the international community on the subtle intricacies of the "moral high ground," which apparently means speaking from the taller pile of dead enemy bodies. Or even worse, fleshes out his" compassionate torture" concept. Explains how America would never torture people. We just don't want to rule it out. How we don't torture, we utilize something called "enhanced interrogation techniques," which is totally different because it has seven more syllables.

It's obvious the president assumed that his retroactive military tribunal reform bill was going to be as easy as a slam dunk from a step ladder, but he was confounded, not by his familiar foes, those darn obstructionist Democrats, but by three Republican Senators, who claim that if this bill passes—hold for it—our troops will be endangered.

You got to love the irony of the president having that phrase batted back into his face. And waving an oversized racquet is John McCain himself, whose graduate degree on the torture subject trumps the president's skimming of the course description in the syllabus. We're talking about someone who has lived through five years of hell. And no, I'm not talking about the Republican primary in South Carolina. Mr. President, please leave the torture business to people who have some experience with it. Karl Rove, Howie Mandel and the poor beleaguered translators of Hugo Chavez's speeches.

Bring Back Saddam

"Democracy is the worst form of government except all the others that have been tried."

—Winston Churchill

I don't know if you've got your head screwed on tight right now, but if not, you might want to pull out some eight-penny nails and a claw hammer and place them in the ready position. Because chances are, after you hear this, you're going to want to nail your skull onto your spine before it spins off into the ether like a runaway flesh-colored helium balloon. A bipartisan commission, headed by James Baker, is investigating options to George Bush's strategy of "staying the course" in Iraq. And it seems pretty apparent that, as soon as possible (i.e., hours after the midterm election), wholesale changes are in store. Although it has yet to be determined whether any of the strategic plans call for the president to step down and accept the position of greeter/shoveler at the official stables of the Arabian Horse Association, as is my suggestion.

One of the options being bandied about is the slow withdrawal of our armed forces, known as "cut and run" when proposed by Democrats, but I'm sure Baker will trot out something a bit more circumspect, like "shave and split," "slice and sprint" or "sever and saunter." Another possibility includes what is being referred to as "alternatives to our effort to establish a democracy." Let me repeat that; alternatives to democracy. Let's see, which alternatives to democracy are available for consideration? Communism? Unh, probably not. A theocracy? No, we tend to spend a lot of money to avoid that very sort of thing. Fascism? Doubt it. Can't impose an impossible burden on the nascent infrastructure by demanding that the trains run on time.

They might want to give a ruling monarchy a try. We seem to like it. Another possibility is tyrannical despotism. Or, as it would be known to the Iraqis, "the good old days." When you think about it, an oppressive dictatorship holds the benefit of both being familiar to the citizens and having recently been demonstrably successful in the area. Oh sure, a benevolent dictator would be preferable, but it's never been a real deal-breaker to our foreign policy. And I know this may sound a bit wacky, but instead of holding another big round of purple-fingered elections where candidates and their relatives get knocked off at a frequency that would make the folks in Deadwood blanch, why not Saddam?

He's tan. He's rested. He knows the territory. Not doing much right now. Still has huge name recognition. Wouldn't have to reintroduce him to the populace. And be honest, how much worse could his re-reign be than what's going on right now? Hell, we don't need some big-time fancy commission to tell us what to do. Henry Kissinger is on board; ask him. Just resurrect his 32-year-old plan for Nixon: We declare victory and leave. Reinstall a chastened, reformed Saddam Hussein and appoint someone to watch over him. How 'bout Dick Cheney? Kills three birds with one stone. Gets the vice president and his approval rating (now lower than anchovy milkshakes) out of Washington *and* in place to provide hands-on control over his Halliburton operation, *and* Bush gets to appoint a successor for 2008. Besides, if Cheney can't instill the fear of Allah in Hussein, nobody can. And most importantly, it gives us someone to blame. Two someones. Two Dicks.

Don't Not Stay the Course

If you need more proof that President George Bush is as clueless as a goldfish on a leash in a space shuttle, you obviously didn't see him in all his counterintuitive glory this week adamantly refuting the slogan of "staying the course" while keeping its policy *exactly the same*. That's right, George Bush is cutting and running from "stay the course." This doesn't mean he's a Defeatlican, though. Because "We are winning in Iraq and will continue to win." And you'd better hope we do, because if this is winning, you really, *really* don't want to see what losing looks like.

He went on to speak of the differences between "a timetable" and "benchmarks," declaring one to be the way of the winner and the other the path to Loserville City. Now, as to which is which, your guess is as good as anybody's. And that probably includes his own staff. It definitely includes Iraqi Prime Minister Nouri al-Maliki, who either has or hasn't agreed to benchmarks

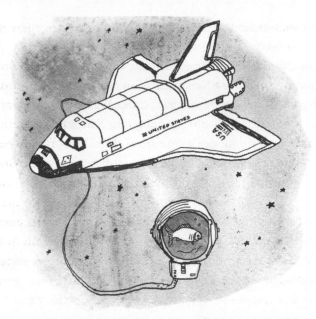

or timetables or touchstones or yardsticks, although a Donald Rumsfeld yard sign looks to be entirely out of the question.

Straight lines. Stark choices. Bold differences. Say what you will about Bush, that's what he's always stood for. "Us versus them." "Good versus evil." "Black versus white." Now, that may be a great worldview…for an eighth-grader, but hey, in the last six years of fighting for the hearts and minds of American voters, it's worked. Nuance is for sissies. Shades of gray: the way of the testosterone-challenged. The White House is a place where the "b" in *subtlety* is not necessarily silent.

Of course, now that polls reflect us midterm electors evidencing a wee bit of reluctance to continue in the president's lemming footsteps marching lockstep over the Iraqi cliff of doom, Bush is determined to prove himself…flexible. Yes, the giant clanking Oval Office robot is intent on demonstrating he has morphed into one of those pliable 14-year-old female Olympic gymnasts with that rubberizing agent still in their bones. President Iron Giant is no more. Long live President Olga Korbut.

The president did admit that he may be dissatisfied, but he's not disillusioned. He's patient, but his patience is not unlimited. Springy but not spongy. A little bit country. And a little bit rock 'n' roll. You say goodbye, I say hello. The war is going according to plan, but it's a limber plan. Not a stay-the-concrete-course plan, but an elastic sort of course plan that we're either staying or not. Kind of like one of those road races where you can cut across to the other side between the bales of hay.

So even the president has agreed that the phrase "stay the course" is a dirty word. Bunch of words. And to all the Republican candidates whom he seduced into repeating that phrase often enough to be used for opposition election ads, it won't be long before the phrase "George Bush" is also a dirty word. And I envision a day not too far in the future when just mentioning the president's name on the radio will result in getting hit by the FCC with a $350,000 fine...for obscenity.

Reading Isn't Fundamental

Right about now is when it could come in real handy to have a president who reads. A book-learning kind of wonk. A guy not allergic to the printed word. George W. Bush even admitted it himself. I think his exact quote was: "I don't read." And you know what, I believe him.

Then this summer, something happened. I think it was part of that midterm campaign thing, when the president claimed his beach reading list included Camus' *The Stranger* and what he referred to as "three Shakespeares." Three Shakespeares? Sounds like a customer at Baskin-Robbins ordering up a triple scoop of smart. And very suspicious, coming from a man famous for struggling through the same page of *My Pet Goat* for seven minutes.

The whole reading deal is important here because he should have been tempted to give the Iraq Study Group Report a brief scan before repeating "The Study Group agrees with me." Unh. No. They don't. He said this during a joint press conference with Tony Blair that could have been a TiVo of any of his previous 80 gazillion press conferences with Tony Blair. Tony looks and sounds like a statesman and George like an eighth-grader trying to fake his way through a book report on *A Tale of Two Cities,* which he didn't bother to pick up. Does the term *Cliffs-Notes* have any meaning here?

At the risk of switching milieus, we're stuck in *Groundhog Day.* Doesn't matter what happens, we wake up the next morning and instead of hearing Sonny and Cher singing "I Got You, Babe" we get the president playing the same lame game he has for three years: "It's a tough time. Going to take some hard work. We're working hard." His supporters say he's resolute. Resolute? What does that mean? You know what, so is butt cancer.

We won't even get into the ironic nature of his "hard work" mantra. How odd to be coming from a guy who, pre-president, was the poster child for social promotion. But an exhortation to hard work isn't the only blunted arrow in his nebulous quiver. In response to what measures he might take, based on the report, he gravely intoned, "We will take every proposal seriously and will act in a timely fashion," which is Presidential Dismissal Speak for "Yeah, whatever."

The Baker-Hamilton Group's report was not the chronicle of clarity itself. It came to the considered opinion that…Iraq is messed up and, mostly, it's our fault. For this we spent a million dollars? Too bad they didn't have time to get into other blistering exposés, like the Pacific Ocean is moist. Mahogany is not your foremost option for conducting electricity. Red wine and peanut butter: not a match. The board goes back.

The president refused to comment on specifics in the report by dipping into his bottomless bag of vague generalities. "My message is this: I want to work with the Congress, I want to work with people in both parties." Yeah, sure he does, the same way a 5-year-old with a magnifying glass wants to work with ants. The bipartisan Study Group provided 79 recommendations for alleviating the chaos in Iraq. Unfortunately, none of them involved the president's and his entire Cabinet's resigning, proving that perhaps this study group should have studied more.

The Escargot Stratagem

Responding to the American public's mounting suspicion that either the White House is lying to us about how the Iraq War is going according to plan, or the plan really, really sucks, the Administration has decided that the problem is not their doomed policy but rather the slogan being used to sell it. So "the war on terrorism," has officially been ash canned and replaced with "the struggle against violent extremism." Which clears things up like a double-hulled oil tanker spill in a 9-inch kiddie pool.

Like a floundering hurricane losing wind speed over a land mass, the war has been downgraded to a struggle. I don't know about you, but I feel much better already. Hey, is that the cool refreshing breeze of a scheduled, steady troop withdrawal? Alas, no, it's Secretary of Defense Donald Rumsfeld propelling himself across another briefing room simply by igniting his own verbal flatulence. Again. Does the term "Band-Aid on a sucking chest wound" have any meaning here?

This particular scheme is something I like to call the Escargot Stratagem. Imagine being a charter member of the Snail Wranglers Antidefamation League back in the '50s. Tough gig, right? When most Americans would rather chew on pork lips and linoleum than consider sliding the paradigm of slime down their gullet. It wasn't till slugs with shells were marketed as a delicacy under their French moniker that people worked up the nerve to stab them with a fork, much less dangle them within spitting distance of their mouths. Of course, if you ask me, the guy from the Garlic Butter Advisory Board is the real genius here. Throw in "squid" and "calamari" and "Rick Santorum" and "distinguished gentleman," and you see where I'm going with this.

It's all about reframing, such as replacing the word "bribe" with "campaign contribution." The Nixon years were the Golden Era of reframing, most notably for Reframing Hall of Famer Ron Ziegler, who informed the press that his previous statements on behalf of the Nixon White House were "inoperative." Which, to this day, remains the best euphemism for "lied like a thieving corn weasel," ever.

The problem here is the word "war." Unfortunate term. Unduly contentious. Steeped in insinuations of antagonism. Indicative of an enterprise to be either won or lost. So, having yet to exhibit any of the signs normally associated with winning, like a lack of dead people, it's obviously time for a change. "Struggle" conveys more of the murky, lifelong commitment that fighting terrorism—excuse me, violent extremism—will require. Like a voluntary congenital condition. Nobody expects to win the war against genital herpes. You simply strive to coexist. And eventually become a better person because of it. Blah blah blah.

If this were 20 years ago, I would expect the "war on poverty" to become the "tussle against insufficient funds," but that war ended. And the poor lost. Or, more accurately, extremely wealthy politicians surrendered on their behalf. One thing you can be sure of, this nomenclatural deevolution will be shoved down our throats as long as we continue to swallow it, right up to the point that they try to call the president "Beloved Leader." I'm not sure there's enough garlic butter in the world to facilitate that.

FAQ: *General Petraeus's Testimony*

Frequently Asked Questions About
General Petraeus's Congressional Testimony

Q. How did General Petraeus's testimony in front of Congress go?

A. Pretty good. He emphasized that progress was being made in Iraq. The same way he talked about the progress being made in Iraq when he testified in the same room back in 2004. (He might be using the same script.)

Q. What's the difference between then and now?

A. Back then, Baghdad still had electricity and water and the wheel.

Q. Did General Petraeus speak about what the future holds for our Iraqi involvement?

A. He acknowledged the road ahead would be difficult. He also allowed that fire engines are frequently red.

Q. The general said we have raised the number of trained Iraqi security forces fighting alongside American troops. Is it a significant rise?

A. 60 percent. From five to eight.

Q. Five to eight brigades? Divisions?

A. No. Troops. Used to be five guys we could trust. Now it's eight.

Q. What happened to the Democrats' holding the general's feet to the fire?

A. Everyone except MoveOn.org scampered away like 12-year-old girls running from a big hairy spider.

Q. What did MoveOn.org do?

A. They ran a full-page ad in the *New York Times* spotlighting General Betray Us.

Q. Why?

A. How often do you get a rhyme like that? Once-in-a-lifetime shot; they took it.

Q. Doesn't the latest National Intelligence Estimate report Iraq's government is paralyzed by internal squabbling and petty partisan differences?

A. Yes, so if you think about it, we have planted the seeds of an American-style democracy.

Q. Did the general really respond to whether our intervention in Iraq was making America safer, by saying, "Unh, I don't know, actually"?

A. Yeah. So?

Q. Nothing. Just curious.

A. Well, move on. I mean, keep going.

Q. What does the general mean when he says security gains since the surge have been "uneven."

A. "Uneven" is traditional Pentagon-speak for "getting our butts handed to us on a paper plate."

Q. What about those benchmarks that were, oh, so important in January?

A. Turns out they weren't really all that important. What is important is other stuff. Stuff that looks good right now.

Q. The president called the insurgents in Iraq "Al-Qaeda" 12 times in his speech. What's up with that?

A. A small group calls itself "Al-Qaeda of Iraq," but it's not the same Al-Qaeda responsible for 9/11. Surfing off the credibility of the name. Kind of like terrorism knockoffs.

Q. Does fighting one hurt the other?

A. There used to be two teams in the Canadian Football League called the Roughriders. But if you beat one, it didn't mean you got credit for two victories in the standings.

Q. Whatever happened to "we'll step down when the Iraqis step up"?

A. Someone stole the steps.

Q. Was a timetable provided for reducing troops in Iraq?

A. Nothing clear-cut. Something to do with ice and Hell.

Q. And the upshot of the whole thing...?

A. General Petraeus asked for more time. He's hoping to come back in March with a new report.

Q. So, they're just going to keep kicking the dead cat down the road. Till when, do you think?

A. Does November 4, 2008, have any meaning here?

Q. Is that a question?

A. Sorry, no.

Darting Squirters

Four-star General David Petraeus spoke of George Bush's vaunted troop surge as having unintended consequences, i.e., the squirts. And no, I'm not kidding. By putting pressure on targeted segments of the bad guys we have caused them to, and I quote, "squirt out of Baghdad." That's right. We squeeze. They squirt. Those darn squirters. Clever little squirters, they.

Wonder if they dart as well. Darting squirters; that would be something to see. Definitely worth a two-drink minimum.

Army Captain Phillip Carter likened the surge to a water balloon. We push on one side, and the insurgents squish over to the other. Apparently, Iraq is a brimming bladder beset by the enlarged prostate of occupation. There may be no future in our Baghdadian misadventure, but there *is* an excess of liquid metaphors. For instance: Some people see our involvement as a glass half full of democratic promise, some see it as half empty of morals, and others see it as a heathen receptacle equally saturated with the toxic wastes of imperialism and the soul-searing venoms of greed.

Doesn't matter what you call whatever it is we find ourselves stuck in: a quagmire, a crapstorm, a bloodbath. Bush, come Hell or high water, is not about to abandon ship since democracy is too important to let some silly civil war rain on any corporate earnings parade. Besides, the president has ice water in his veins, and wields the IV of free enterprise. He's got his hand on the nozzle that leaks pipeline profits. And you can't throw the revenue baby out with the insurgent bath water.

Our efforts to push back the tide of Islamic fanaticism are as successful as spitting into the wind-borne drizzle blowing off the Gulf of Oman. All we're doing is adding gelatin to the Kool-Aid and getting sprayed by the hose of dogmatism. The downpour of liberty can't feed the freedom-irrigating rivulets of independence when the showers of democracy are doomed to be foiled by the ancient dams of religious fanaticism. And when it rains, it pours. Look at Arkansas.

We all know that if a drowning man wants to learn to swim, someone is going to have to get wet. You can lead a horse to water, but you can't make it vote to share its oil revenue with the Kurds. And let's speak of the forgotten liquid…that black, viscous stuff bubbling out of the ground in too great an abundance to ignore. Blood may be thicker than water, but oil is thicker than both. And whoever didn't see that coming doesn't have both oars in the lake, if you fathom my meaning.

We ignore the torrent of ill will spewing from the spigot of anarchy that our invasion turned on at our peril. Same with the boiling emanations of international outrage bubbling over the edge of the stew of chaos we've stirred up. Not to mention the geysers of fury caused by the steaming vapors of collapse. What I'm saying is...people are pissed. And no matter how soon Bush's scheme is deep-sixed, we will be cleaning up the debris of this tsunami of sorrow tossed off the Tallahatchee Bridge over troubled waters and washed up on the shore of regret spoiling the broth of $2 a gallon gasoline for a long time. Then again, that's just me. Being a wet blanket.

The Boogeyman

"If you don't watch out, the Boogeyman is going to get you." When we were young, every one of us suffered a grandparent or a creepy, weird uncle or a fat, pimply-faced cousin who tried to plant similar irrational fears in us. A psycho adult who got his jollies by gleefully magnifying the shapeless dread of monsters lurking in the dark to susceptible children. Monsters who waited to gobble us up and skulked everywhere. Under the bed, at the back of the closet and in pretty much the whole of the entire basement, especially behind the furnace. And still, that creepy, weird uncle continues to frighten us with tales of the Boogeyman. And that psycho adult's name is George Walker Bush.

For the last five years he has run his Administration on the frightening fuel of the fear of monsters. "If we don't watch out, the Boogeyman is going to get us." And who is the Boogeyman, to the president? Anybody different than him. Saddam Hussein was a Boogeyman. That president of Iran whose name he can't pronounce is a Boogeyman. Scientists are the Oogie-Boogiemen. And Democrats are the Boogiest of all men. In a full term and a half, the president's major accomplishment has been to plant amorphous nightmares in our national subconscious and to fertilize them with nightly doses of B.S.

Due to its cross-cultural prevalence in almost every country on the planet, scientists theorize that the concept of the Boogeyman has been handed down from our stoop-backed hairy-foreheaded ancestors who used such scare tactics to encourage their subanthropoid tots to hang around the relative protection of the cave, semisafe in the warmth of the tribe from the dastardly grasp of possible predators. And no, I'm not talking about Fox News and its obsession with Hillary Clinton, but if the monosyllabic snarls fit, grunt 'em.

This, however, is the twenty-first century. We're supposed to be smarter now. Yes, terrorism exists. But in Great Britain and Israel and a lot of other civilized countries, they reconcile themselves to that fact and manage to expend their energies trying to solve it like a criminal activity and not obsess about it full time, curled in a fetal position trembling like a Chihuahua in a wolf pen, fearful of the unknown. Of course, I am talking about countries where the term "intelligence agency" is not an oxymoron. Where staffs are manned by professionals, and not the buddies of ex-girlfriends' roommates' cousins.

America is tired of hiding from the Boogeyman. We're tired of being grounded for asking questions about him. "Why? Because I said so. That's why" is not a good enough answer anymore. We're tired of being kept in a dark so complete, not even the flickering glow of the truth can pierce it. Maybe, finally, this is the election when we climb out from under the covers, open the closet door, look under the bed and sweep a broom handle behind the back of the furnace. And start snapping the suspenders and poking the chests of the creepy old men scaring us with exaggerated tales about the Boogeyman. Fee fi fo fum, I smell the blood of some Republicans.

WMD–U.S. Intelligence: Not a Match

For those of you lying back in your recliner with your feet up, thinking that all the weirdness of 2007 had already unspooled and you had a couple of weeks to sit back, relax and let your blood pressure fall from tropospheric levels, I have news that will compel you to crank your footrest down to its upright perpendicular position, poised to jump from your chair and ram your head full speed into the opposite wall. Repeatedly.

Remember Iran's nuclear weapons program? Apparently, it doesn't exist. You know: the nuclear weapons program the president said the CIA told him that Iran not only had, but was going to use to destabilize the Middle East. Yeah. That one. Turns out they don't have it. Turns out the CIA was wrong. Again. Who knew? But the funny part is, here's the funny part: Because even when we did know that they *didn't* have a nuclear weapons program, we still kept talking about it. Like they *did*. We even talked about the irresponsible people running Iran and how they were in danger of precipitating World War III by continuing their dastardly pursuit of a nuclear weapons program, which we knew at the time that they were not pursuing. Well, not so much we, as he. And you know "he who."

A new National Intelligence Estimate reports Iran halted its clandestine nuclear weapons program back in 2003. But our intelligence community (and I use the term so loosely you should take precautions it doesn't slip through your fingers like puréed oysters left in the rain) waited to tell the president that Iran's nuclear weapons program was halted even though they had evidence that it was, because they did not want to make the same mistake they made when they told him that Saddam Hussein might have weapons of mass destruction about five years ago. Which he didn't. Which they also had evidence of, but the president didn't want to hear that and instead talked about Iraq's WMDs till the cows came home and were industrially milked and produced cheese curds of shock and awe. So instead of making the same mistake, they went out of their way to make an entirely different mistake.

They finally got around to telling the president about it in August. The whole Iran-not-having-the-nuclear-weapons-program part. And then when our president called Iran's president a liar for insisting that his country had no nuclear weapons program, which our president continued to insist they did, though he knew they did not, they said nothing. You still with me here? Although having been played as complete patsies in the Iraqi weapons debacle may have something to do with why we are finding out about all this now, complete with maps and dates and a big red YOU ARE HERE dot right where the double yellow presidency and incompetence lines converge.

Now the president is walking around telling everyone he was provided with faulty intelligence. Yeah, well, DNA is a bitch. The upshot of all this: Iraq—no weapons of mass destruction. Iran—no nuclear weapons program. Throw in the fact that since our Middle East misadventure began, we've misplaced 190,000 of our own rifles and weapons somewhere, who knows where, in Iraq, and I'm thinking maybe we should outsource our weapons location intelligence gathering because it doesn't seem to be...what you call it?...our specialty.

Eyes Only

This is EYES ONLY and, for God's sake, don't let those weasels Richard Clarke, Paul O'Neill and Bob Woodward see it this time. Jesus!

MEMO

From the desk of Secretary of Defense Donald Rumsfeld

To: President George W. Bush

Title: DAMAGE CONTROL

CC: Dick Cheney

Dubyah:

Hey buddy. Thought I better give you a heads-up on this whole
Abu Ghraib prison deal. I'm telling you, we had it nailed. It's
Rather and those damn CBS punks again, and of course,
ordinary grunts looking for souvenirs. Dammit, if only we had
stemmed some of that up-front looting, our boys and girls
would have had some classic art to take home and wouldn't
have to resort to snapshots. But hindsight is always 20/20, isn't
it? This is just a tragic case of bad timing, especially so soon
after the Dover casket photos. I compiled us a list of possible
damage control measures I intend on using in the hearings that
I hope will be useful in extricating ourselves from this tar baby.
Using a blend of message and media, we could turn this into a
win–win–win situation. And I'm just the guy to get it rolling.

- Go ahead and create that independent panel to investigate
  the abuses. Don't worry, we'll be in charge of who gets on
  the panel, if you know what I mean.
- Blame the prison. See if we can get Stephen King or that
  Straub guy to agree it could be haunted.
- Trot out that whole "we'll have our good days and less-
  good days" thing again.
- Doctored. The photos were altered. Not all of them. Simply
  planting seeds of doubt, is all.
- *You* got to apologize to the Arab peoples. But just to the
  Arabs. And just the peoples.

- Outline the difference between what happens when democracy tortures bad guys and when dictators do it to good guys. Nobody ever heard Saddam apologize for his torturing, right?
- Talk to Ashcroft, re: outlawing American ownership of cameras. Just in Iraq. Commission a study group to see if we can spin it as a safeguard against terrorism for citizens. Use whatever leverage we have left to get Kodak and Polaroid on board.
- Explain how, in a free market, everything is for sale, including moral authority.
- Continue to portray anybody who criticizes us as giving comfort to the enemy. Remember, we're in this together.
- Keep calling it just an example of high spirits, that's all. Battle-weary kids blowing off steam. Nothing you can't see in a Madonna video. A college fraternity prank. Call Rush.
- Kick me. Hard and loud. No, I mean it. Kick me. In public. Use really sharp-toed shoes.
- What do you think, any chance we can cover Clinton with the blame blanket again? Just thinking out loud.
- The old standby: "I don't remember. Can't recall."
- Money. Can't think of a sticky situation that money didn't grease, at least a little bit. There's got to be somebody we can bribe. Maybe the prisoners themselves?

Get back to me when you can.
And good luck on the deal with the guy and that thing.

Rummy

FAQ: *Plan for Victory*

Frequently Asked Questions About President Bush's Plan for Victory in Iraq

Q. President Bush recently announced his "Plan for Victory." What does this plan entail?

A. It's two-pronged. There is a short-term plan and a long-term plan.

Q. And what are they?

A. The short-term plan is to keep the Democrats from regaining control of Congress in '06.

Q. And the long-term plan?

A. Keep the Democrats from regaining control of the White House in '08. Or acquire photographs of Hillary Clinton in bed with a domesticated yak and/or a woman.

Q. So, nothing about Iraq, then?

A. Well, now that you mention it...there *was* something about the brave, freedom-loving Iraqis and how together we are winning the tough struggle against violent extremism, but it was just more "same old, same old," in an attempt to rescue his poll numbers from falling through the floor like an anvil constructed from dark matter.

Q. What is the "Plan for Victory" going to replace?

A. The "Plan for Quagmire" we've been following the last three years.

Q. Didn't he reveal a strategy for winning?

A. Yeah, but, you know what, so do the Chicago Cubs. Every spring. Don't imagine election-bound Republicans are looking forward to changing their slogan to: "We'll get 'em next year."

Q. What is their slogan now?

A. Lately, it seems to be "Incompetently Corrupt and Clueless Cronies 'R' Us."

Q. Didn't he also refuse to set a timetable for withdrawal, saying it would send a message to the world that America was weak?

A. Yes, he did. So apparently he's OK with continuing to send a message to the world that America is a big bad bully who will beat the crap out of you if we don't like the way you look at us.

Q. Don't we run the danger of alienating our allies if we just cut and run?

A. Cut and run? There's no running. This isn't running. This is walking. Backward. Really fast backward walking. Who knows, we might even walk backward really fast right into Iran or Syria.

Q. How does the president define victory?

A. According to a separate 35-page document accompanying the speech, titled "National Strategy for Victory in Iraq," victory means creating the conditions that allow us to leave.

Q. Is he saying that getting out of Iraq is our only path to victory?

A. No, no, no. A lot of victories await us. Tiny victories and little victories and medium-sized victories. Not to say we haven't experienced victories already. A couple tiny victories, a moral victory and an election victory. And if we string a bunch of these little victories together, it could add up to a nice medium-sized victory. Or a gaggle of little victories and a medium victory or a series of medium victories, coupled with one or two moral victories, could add up to a big victory. And two or three big victories could result in a humongous victory.

Q. What is that?

A. A Republican victory in November '08.

Q. What is the best-case scenario?

A. We try to incubate democracy in the Middle East, and whenever the political costs at home get too high we declare victory and depart, leaving our secret prison camps intact.

WMDS, or No WMDS? That Ain't the Question

"Ooops, my bad." Is that too much to ask? That's all I want someone to say. Not just the president. Anybody. I know the chances of prying an apology from a politician are about the same as extracting infected molars from a wolverine with a pair of chopsticks made out of egg noodles, but still, I have this burning desire to hear someone say it out loud. "Sorry, made a mistake." Now that it's clear no weapons of mass destruction will be found, the Administration claims never to have said the threat was imminent. To which I can only say, "Yeah, right, and Formica is edible."

The new party line is that Saddam *could* have had weapons of mass destruction. WMDs have suddenly turned into WMD "program-related activities." Which is a mite different than being able to "launch a biological or chemical attack in as little as 45 minutes." Of course, you got to remember this "could-have" information comes from the very same people who a year ago relished branding anybody with the temerity to disagree with their assessment as being nothing but substandard tools of the Dark Prince himself, and no, I'm not talking about Dick Cheney.

Back then, Saddam possessed voluminous amounts of weapons of mass destruction and was aiming them at us with his crazy, shaky fingers hovering over the atomic button. Pretty soon we'll find out our evidence comes from a waitress who found the words "mass," "weapons" and "destruction" doodled on the back of a Hooters menu in what some guy who went to Baghdad once thinks looks a little like Saddam's handwriting.

Bush had "no doubt" his intelligence was correct. Well, there's your problem right there. He never *has* any doubt. Grew up without doubt. No doubt he could get into the Alabama National Guard. No doubt his tax cuts for the wealthy were going to stimulate the economy. No doubt the deficit was going to magically morph into a surplus. No doubt we can take police officers off the streets and use the money to send a guy to Mars. If you ask me, the man needs to cultivate a little doubt. Unless he's the man going to Mars, that is. Hell, I'd hold a series of bake sales to fund that project myself.

You can almost smell the desperation when the Administration trumpets the fact that Bill Clinton also thought Hussein had weapons of mass destruction. Bush citing Clinton as a credible source? There you go. Like Pat Robertson buying a fringed leather skirt because it looked good on Christina Aguilera. Bush has even been forced to call for an investigation into his own intelligence, and we all know what's going to happen: They're not going to find anything.

FAQ: Cindy Sheehan, Peace Mom

Q. So who exactly is this Peace Mom woman, anyway?

A. Cindy Sheehan is a 48-year-old from Vacaville, California, who, in response to losing her son Casey in Iraq, is selfishly attempting to hoard the honor of being a Gold Star Mother all to herself.

Q. What?

A. She's against the war.

Q. Oh, OK, so why the hell is she hunkered down in a ditch outside the Texas White House bothering the president during his vacation?

A. Vacation? Hey, 35 days is not a vacation; 35 days is five weeks—36 hours short of a tenth of a year. Longer than the gestation period of most mammals. Where's my 35-day vacation? Where's *your* 35-day vacation? Where's the American public's 35-day vacation?

Q. Good point, but that wasn't the question.

A. I'm sorry, got a bit worked up there. What was the question again?

Q. What's she doing there?

A. She's camped outside the president's ranch to meet with him and she vows to stay till he tells her exactly what noble cause her son died for. And she doesn't want to hear "Freedom Isn't Free."

Q. Wouldn't you think a president this media savvy would just invite her inside for some cookies and lemonade and get it over with?

A. My theory is he's spent too much time grilling cheese sandwiches on the hood of his pickup and might be suffering from heatstroke. Besides, what kind of a man takes his family to Crawford, Texas, for a vacation?

Q. Are you saying West Texas in August is not what you call your garden spot?

A. I'm saying it's real similar to Hell, and that's only assuming Hell has winged insects the size of footstools.

Q. How has the conservative media responded?

A. You mean the right-wing smear machine?

Q. Whatever.

A. Bill O'Reilly jumped on Sheehan like an irritable gorilla stomping the air out of an inflatable life raft in order to fit it into the back of an overstuffed Cadillac Escalade.

Q. Any specific accusations?

A. You could say that. You could also say porcupine pelts make substandard day-care pillows. Cindy Sheehan has been accused of everything from unpaid parking tickets to the ultimate treasonous act: association with Michael Moore. Won't be long before rumors of a lesbian relationship with Hillary Clinton emerge.

Q. What about the claims that Sheehan has become a tool of the left?

A. "A tool of the left." That's a laugh. Fox News calling Cindy Sheehan a political tool. A lot like a cobra calling a mongoose annoying. Or a White House official complaining about the smearing of Karl Rove. You can't make up stuff like this.

Q. Any comment on the criticisms that the protest has morphed from a lonely vigil into pretty much just another gathering of the usual suspects?

A. Last I looked, Jesse Jackson hadn't yet made an appearance. Oh wait, there he is. Never mind.

Q. Any other notables expected to appear?

A. With gas approaching three bucks a gallon, it's only a matter of time before a parading convoy of SUV owners pitching gravel into each other's windshields joins the protests outside Bush's ranch.

9

11 04 08

Election day. Approaching. Looming. Lurching toward us like the shadow of a racing big-rig on the sparkling late-afternoon water seen from the bow of a boat below the bridge. A changing of the guard. Ch-ch-ch-changes.

Still don't know whom the Democrats will anoint, but if I were them, I'd be proud to enter the general election and lose with whichever of their two fine candidates is nominated. Remember, it doesn't matter for whom you vote, as long as you do vote.

Because if you don't vote, you can't bitch. And besides, if we don't exercise our electoral duty, how will we ever know how close the polls actually were?

Presidential Spring Training

The World Series of presidential politics may be 19 months down the road, but the players are already lacing up their cleats and playing pepper with fungo bats on the sandlots of Iowa and New Hampshire. Yes, my friends, it's spring training for the presidency. A spring training where fund-raising takes the place of calisthenics. And batting clinics are supplanted by fund-raising. And the closet full of Ace bandages is now packed with envelopes earmarked for...you got it, fund-raising.

With no sitting president or vice president running, for the first time since the days of penny postcards, the 2008 field promises to be more crowded than a trainer's table after the first day of wind sprints for pitchers and Molinas. Besides, this is America. Where any Dominican can become a shortstop and any American can become president, although when they coined that phrase I'm not sure they had George Bush in mind.

So here is our scouting report on some of the announced and presumed contenders for the upcoming political season in which everybody has faith that if just a few breaks fall their way, and a couple of opposing teams' managers get caught peddling steroids to preschoolers or bogus opposition research to the *Washington Post*, they got a shot. Except the Marlins and Dennis Kucinich, that is.

Democratic League: The Donkeys

7 to 2. *New York Senator Hillary Clinton.*

Like the Yankees she's a converted fan of, acts miffed that the nomination isn't just handed to her and instead has to actually compete for it.

4 to 1. *Illinois Senator Barack Obama.*

Might not be ready for hardball practiced at this level. Already got into a pimp-slapping contest with Hillary and lost.

7 to 1. *Former North Carolina Senator John Edwards.*

Clinging to trademark "Two Americas" pitch. Extra four years of Bush might help public catch up to message.

15 to 1. *Former Vice President Al Gore.*

Lurking on deck ready to bop someone on head with his Oscar, till Florida Supreme Court takes it away.

50 to 1. *Delaware Senator Joe Biden.*

Back on disabled list with persistent foot-in-mouth disease. A little too comfortable flossing with own shoelaces.

500 to 1. The Field.

New Mexico Governor Bill Richardson. In it for the vice presidency.

Connecticut Senator Chris Dodd. In it for the parties.

Former Alaska Senator Mike Gravel. Who? Gravel? Alaska? Cool. In it for Secretary of the Interior.

8,000,000 to 1. *Ohio Congressman Dennis Kucinich.*

Could lose Iowa straw poll to the straw.

Republican League: The Elephants

3 to 1. *Former New York City Mayor Rudy Giuliani.*

Highlighting commitment to traditional family values. Having had three wives just means he's extratraditional. Better chance to win Series than to get there.

9 to 2. *Arizona Senator John McCain.*

Wily veteran. Lost a few miles on his fast ball. Doubts persist as to whether he is up for long, grueling season.

6 to 1. *Former Massachusetts Governor Mitt Romney.*

Wearing Al Gore's oversized flip-flops. Also has Mormon thing to get past. Might be a positive. Public gets bored with First Lady, can always move on to Second Lady, then Third Lady and so on.

15 to 1. *Former Tennessee Senator Fred Thompson.*

Warming up in bullpen, if needed to relieve. Of course, America would never accept an actor as president. Oh.

200 to 1. *Former New York Governor George Pataki.*

Bad timing. Country not ready for another president named George. Severe third-degree George fatigue.

400 to 1. *Former Arkansas Governor Mike Huckabee.*

Bad timing. Country not ready for another governor of Arkansas as president. Arkansas fatigue.

5,000 to 1. The Field.

California Congressman Duncan Hunter. In it for 2012.

Texas Congressman Ron Paul. In it for Texas.

Kansas Senator Sam Brownback. In it for the babies.

Colorado Congressman Tom Tancredo. In it to get the illegals.

Former Wisconsin Governor Tommy Thompson. In it for the cheese.

And They're Not *Off!*

I startled some guy in the next lane at a red light when I shouted at my radio today. A big-time famous network newscaster (Gil Gross) had come on, opining how former Iowa Governor Tom Vilsack could easily take the 2008 Iowa caucuses as a favorite son, resulting in a subsequent focus on South Carolina, which is John Edwards territory, and this might all work out to upset the Hillary Clinton Applecart Express. *Aaiiieee!* The guy next to me barely missed a covey of walkers as he peeled out.

I mean, OK, I know, political projection is as predictable as a spilt glass of milk before nap time at a day-care center for hyperactive 4-year-olds. But for crum's sake, a little common human decency, por favor. We've barely finished showering off the crap flung in the midterms and need a moment or so to send our clothes and our souls out to the dry cleaners. Or burn and bury them, then buy new ones.

You'd think these pundits could use a bit of time off themselves. Enough slack to recycle a few lame sports analogies and plant a couple of specious rumors. At least till the New Direction Congress is inaugurated. The 110th doesn't even start work for more than a month. Shouldn't they be able to break the seal on their stack of monogrammed Post-it notes before we start talking about an event occurring at the very end of their term? I've seen jailhouse marriages with longer honeymoons. Just ask Duke Cunningham. Or Bob Ney. Or Mark Foley. No, second thought, best not ask Mark Foley.

Is it too much to ask to wait till a mere *22 months before* the election to start handicapping our next national foray into the depths of depravity and degradation and accusations that make up a presidential sweepstakes? Apparently not. I bet even the Cartoon Network has a show speculating on the '08 front-runners in the race to replace George Bush. Even though most of the supposed competitors haven't even taken off their sweats yet.

Yeah, yeah, yeah. The extraordinarily ambitious have been running since November 3rd of 2004 (does the term "Junior Senator from New York" have any meaning here?). Who cares? Let them. Let them rot in the frozen fields of Iowa and New Hampshire in the middle of this winter. But let them do it alone. Because, except for the poor, beleaguered citizens of Iowa and New Hampshire, it doesn't matter. Speaking for the rest of us, I have one word for all you long-term prognosticators: Shut up!

I don't care. If Bill Frist or Russ Feingold have dropped out. If Clinton or McCain or Edwards or Romney or Giuliani has or hasn't formed an exploratory committee. If Barack Obama pitches a tent on the South Lawn. Not only don't I know who Duncan Hunter is, I don't want to know. People, we're talking two whole years down the road. A lot of crap could hit the fan in two years. And you know these guys. They have a history of not just finding and flinging crap but splashing and soaking in it. Give them a wide berth. That's all I'm saying.

Hill Songs

We members of the CCJU—the Comics, Clowns & Jesters Union—can currently be found moping around, wearing an excess of black, plunged into a state of funk that can only be called "premourning" as we anticipate the end of what will surely be known as the Golden Era of political humor. The reign of George W. Bush is nearing an end. Destined to go down in history as the worst president *ever,* and that includes William Henry Harrison, the guy who gave a three-hour Inaugural Speech in the rain, caught pneumonia and served 30 days supine in a sick bed till becoming the first president to die in office.

The Bush Administration would give its eyeteeth to be looked upon as possessing that kind of successful legacy. He was, is and shall be for 20 more months, the Full Employment Act for Political Comedy. Like if Reagan and Quayle had a kid. He's Quagan, and sharing the first four letters with "quagmire" only adds to the fun.

So the end is near and woe is we, and in three or four years our careers will mostly consist of inquiring, "You want lids on these?" But wait. A glimmer of hope flashes on the hill. And yes, I am talking about *the* hill: Hillary Rodham Clinton. Who just offered up the choice of her official presidential campaign song into the hands of us, the great unwashed. And if you don't think that's the comedic equivalent of a batting practice fastball lobbed right into our wheelhouse, you wouldn't know a comedy premise from roasted sesame paste.

Of course, the Hillster has attempted to limit our selections to certain prescreened songs. "Beautiful Day" by U2. "Get Ready" by the Temptations. "I'll Take You There" by the Staple Singers. Smash Mouth's remake of "I'm a Believer." Five others. Bunch of typical lame-ass options, if you ask me. Little creativity and not much of a window for laughs. But that's why we get paid the big bucks. To open that window wide enough for all our fat lazy humor butts to squeeze through. Brace yourself. Open wide. Here goes.

Here are a few optional tunes that might goose the junior Senator of New York's campaign, not to mention help with the whole perception that she has a rod up her butt the size of the John Hancock Building.

Alternative Official Hillary Clinton
Presidential Campaign Songs

Why does Justin Timberlake have to be the only who's
bringing "Sexyback"? Hunh? Go for it, Hill. Or how 'bout
"You Can't Always Get What You Want" by the Stones? Let
your contributors down gently. Want to rekindle the past while
still grasping for the future? Alter Bill's old song into "Don't
Stop Thinking About Yesterday." Need an anthem? What better anthem is there than Gloria Gaynor's "I Will Survive"?
For some comic relief: "I Got Friends in Low Places," "Fat-
Bottomed Girls" or "It's Too Late, Baby." But no, better save
that last one in case Al Gore decides to jump in. I got it: "The
Theme from *Shaft*." Maybe too candid, as might be Elton
John's "The Bitch Is Back." But if Senator Clinton wants a little
payback with her pomp and circumstance, imagine the look on
Bill's face every time he's stuck on stage while the orchestra
introduces her, the candidate, by kicking out Mitch Ryder's
"Devil with a Blue Dress." Heh heh heh. Thanks, Ms. Hillary.
This looks to be the start of a beautiful relationship.

Me. Me. Me. Me. Me.

You know what's wrong with America? I mean, other than the
fact that we can be convinced to buy a headache medicine that
you apply to your forehead? Our national obsession with "me."
Me. Me. Me. Me. Me. Nobody ever thinks about "us" anymore.
It's all about "me." "You" are on your own. "We" is a conve-
nient umbrella for a collection of like-minded "me's," of which
"I" had better play a feature part and "they" and "them" are
simply obstacles to be steered clear of at all costs and knocked
down and run over with track cleats if unavoidable.

It's not totally our fault, as we are engaged in learned
behavior. We, the people, or rather, me, the people, and you,

the rabble, can legitimately claim to be magnificently obsessed with ourselves, because of the conduct we witness in our leaders. Dim luminaries observed daily giving less thought to what is good for the whole than an alligator gives to the mood of a brood of baby ducks before hungrily gobbling up the parents.

Take our presidential primary process. Please. Over 20 states will declare their '08 party preferences on February 5th, fore-shortening a six-month winnowing process to less than four weeks of industrial-strength filtering. Not front-loaded enough apparently, since Florida decided to sneak ahead of the pack by a week, a move compelling South Carolina to leapfrog ahead to January 19th.

Now, we know New Hampshire is more likely to offer Fidel sanctuary than give up their First in the Nation status; besides, they have a state law that says they *must* be first, so they will precede South Carolina, probably on the 8th. And Iowa is certain to supersede that, because they got caucuses, a totally different animal than primaries. (Don't ask.)

Financial considerations are obviously at stake, but mostly it's ego that is fueling this jump-starting mania. The survival of the primary process itself, or whether it is good for the country or even the political leaders participating, is of little if any concern. Cutting in line used to be considered the action of a bully; now it's on legislative fast track. We don't only want to have our cake and eat it too, we want to have it, eat it, save it, hoard it, clone it, shrink it and freeze dry it so we can carry the frosting around in our pockets for later, and the fact that nobody else ever gets a crumb just makes it more tasty.

Not only do we fail to see the big picture, nobody bothers faking the slight lateral movement of the head pretending to look for it anymore. People either are boarding up the big picture with the custom-cut plywood of self-indulgence or they're staring just to the side of where the big picture used to be, at that more fascinating rectangle called the mirror.

We're simply spoiled little kids who never learned to share our toys. And stay tuned: If one more self-centered ghost jumps through the primary machine, we could be looking at a Christmas caucus in the Hawkeye State this year. And if the thought of Dennis Kucinich and Ron Paul dressed in Santa Claus costumes doesn't scare the bejeesus out of you, some sort of headache remedy should be applied directly to your forehead. Like a mallet. But enough about the state of the nation, let's get back to me.

Rove Bye-Bye

Karl Rove, Bush's brain, quit last week. And no, he hasn't been replaced, so yeah, I guess you could say the cavity remains empty. To put it another way: Voldemort has left the building. Darth Vader has taken off his helmet. Proof positive that Satan had more than a passing acquaintance with the Pillsbury Doughboy, has exited stage right. This sudden shift of malodorous winds has caused liberals to shiver in separation anxiety, knowing they're going to have to look elsewhere to assuage their demon jones, as they no longer have the pale pudgy strategist as a target for their limp verbal projectiles.

Rove made his teary announcement at a joint press conference held on the South Lawn of the White House alongside the tenant whom he thrust into residency of that property with all the elegance and subtlety of an armor-plated freight train run off its elevated tracks onto a third-world flea market. The 43rd president of the U.S. visibly choked up saying "So long" to the man he affectionately called "Turd Blossom," as his alter ego was pried away from him for the first time in 14 years.

Rove scoffed at reporters' questions about future subpoenas in the federal prosecutor firings investigation leading to his abrupt retirement, referring to the inquiry as "pure politics." And, coming from the high grand master of pure politics, this should be considered the ultimate compliment. Then the man with the power to cloud men's minds shuffled off to Nowheresville City in what has been laughingly labeled as a desire to spend more time annoying his family.

But the furniture in his White House office had yet to be decontaminated when his family apparently grew tired of his company and kicked him out to spend the bulk of his new free time on various television news shows tossing fistfuls of scathing barbs at potential Democratic nominee Hillary Clinton, whom he described as "fatally flawed," which in Republican code means "colder than a witch's catcher's mitt hidden in the rear of a walk-in freezer under a crate of three-and-a-half-pound rump roasts."

These mouthy jousts have caused more consternation in Democratic circles than a turkey vulture circling at dawn during the annual Galapagos Island turtle hatchling race-to-the-sea. Hillary's people are trumpeting Rove's blasts as kind of a Bad Housekeeping Seal of Disapproval. You hate him. He hates her. Ergo, she's your girl. While Barack Obama's people maintain that by attacking Hillary, Rove is attempting to rally Democratic voters to the more vulnerable candidate. The reasoning goes that Republicans are really scared of Barack and are attempting to scuttle his candidacy by attacking her opponent, because they realize these assaults will be construed as an endorsement. It's all so Machiavellian, it's probably true. Although I have no idea what I just said.

If it does work, this could be the next big thing in political campaign strategy. Hiring public pariahs to pretend to support your enemy is *so* 2007. No more shots of a drunken Lindsay Lohan wearing an "I'm a Rudy Girl" T-shirt (obviously a ploy by either the McCain or the Romney camp). The next tactic will mutate into a double triple switch where you hire someone really vile to attack yourself and then reveal that the attack was a cooperative effort between your opponent and his even-eviler puppet master, and there's a sex tape of the two that gets shown on YouTube. I'm still working out the details, but you get the drift. Practice on your friends. If Karl Rove has anything to say about it, the Republicans will.

Generic Republican Speech

I want to thank all of you, the greatest ordinary folks in this country, for showing up tonight. For demonstrating your determination to do what you can to make this nation great for all its citizens, including the least fortunate of us, and for paying $5,000 a plate to hear me talk about how. First off, let me say I understand your concerns. And I assure you: I share those concerns. As a matter of fact, your concerns are *my* concerns. And with the grace of God, our good and loving Christian God, we will find the answers to those concerns. Together. Because, my friends, together we are strong. It is only when we are divided by the people who hate this country that we are vulnerable. And only together will we have the will to find the good and repel the bad.

And that, my friends, is what this country needs: more good. And less bad. Much less bad. And both you and I know what is bad. Terrorism is bad. Taxes are bad. And so are crime and cancer. Families are good and so are puppies and veterans. And health care. Health care is good. But only good health care is good. Bad health care is not good. Bad health care is bad. And bad health care is what my opponent is trying to give you. Not me. I know what you want, my friends. You want less government control over your lives and so do I. You want more of your money, and I want to give it to you.

And if, through the glory of God, you bless me with your

vote, I will control that control. For good. Not for bad. And I will tell you right now that my definition of "bad" involves the weird sexual antics of godless perverts who want to destroy the very fabric of our society. Because even though I've spent 30 years in Washington, I remain an outsider who knows enough of their career politician moves to bring these career politicians to their knees. I've always been a reformer who understands the concept of good reform as opposed to bad reform. I bet, just like me, you're tired of these people promising bad reform the same way you have to be tired of all this negative campaigning.

Not as much as me, my friends. Let me tell you, I am so sick of these negative ads my opponent is airing, when he's the one who was saved from conviction of felonious sexual assault on a minor only through an illegal payoff to an activist judge with ties to Al-Qaeda. I will tell you the truth, my friends: He is a liar who lies about his lying, and I refuse to stoop to that level of negativity, which is why you should vote for me and not him, that mud-slinging, pervert-coddling insider. It is time for America to be great again, and with God's grace and your help, I will do everything in my power to make sure that happens. Thank you, folks. And may God Bless America.

Generic Democratic Speech

I want to thank you, the greatest ordinary folks in this country, for showing up tonight. For demonstrating your determination to do what you can to make this nation great for all its citizens, including the least fortunate of us, and for paying $5,000 a plate to hear me talk about how. First, let me say I understand you have concerns. And let me assure you: I share those concerns. As a matter of fact, your concerns are *my* concerns. And with the grace of God, our good and loving Christian God, we will find the answers. Together. Because, my friends, we are all in this together. And it is only together that we will find the good.

Which, although I know I risk ruffling a few feathers by saying it out loud, is what we need in this country: more good and less bad. Much less bad. Taxes are bad. And so are crime and cancer. Families are good and so are puppies and veterans. And health care. Health care is good. But only good health care is good. Bad health care is not good. Bad health care is bad. And bad health care is what my opponent is trying to give you. Not me. I know what you want, my friends. You want less government control over your lives and so do I. And once you elect me I will control that control. For good. Not for bad. And my definition of "bad" involves the weird sexual antics of godless perverts who want to destroy the very fabric of our society. Because even though I've spent 30 years in Washington, I remain an outsider who knows enough of their moves to bring these career politicians to their knees. I'm a reformer at heart, who understands the concept of good reform as opposed to bad reform. I bet, just like me, you're tired of these people promising bad reform the same way you have to be tired of all this negative campaigning. Not as much as me, my friends. Let me tell you, I am so sick of these negative ads my opponent is airing, when he's the one who was saved from conviction of felonious sexual assault on a minor only through an illegal payoff to an activist judge with ties to Al-Qaeda. I will tell you the truth, my friends: He is a liar who lies about his lying, and I refuse to stoop to that level of negativity, which is why you should vote for me and not him, that mud-slinging, pervert-coddling insider. Thank you, folks. And may God Bless America.

Iowa—It's Winner-Tastic

The great thing about the Iowa caucuses is that even after they're over, nobody knows exactly what happened. They're best described as musical chairs without the music. And no chairs. On the Democratic side, people don't really vote. They attend, then move off into designated candidate corners, but if not enough people hang in your corner, you have to go somewhere else. So the campaign staff that corners the market on breath mints and deodorant could hold a huge advantage. Hey, there's worse ways to choose a candidate than by picking the one with the best-smelling followers.

People still talk about how great Hubert Humphrey's staffers smelled. Like winners.

That's another great thing about the Iowa caucuses—everybody is a winner. The whole damn state is littered with the detritus of winners. Iowa is winner-tastic. Obviously, Barack Obama and Mike Huckabee are winners because...well, they won. And that's what winners do: They win. But you'd also have to say that John Edwards and Mitt Romney are winners too, because even though they came in second, they called themselves winners, and since they're big-time national politicos you got to assume they know what they're talking about. Hillary Clinton is apparently a winner, because in her speech, after coming in third, she never gave the slightest impression she hadn't won, so maybe she knows something the rest of us don't, which is another characteristic trait of winners.

Fred Thompson won because he came in third after canvassing the state with the energy of a three-legged tortoise on reds. John McCain won because he spent no time in Iowa at all and still came in fourth. Which, in some books, makes him a double winner.

Ron Paul is a big winner by coming in a strong fifth, if there is such a thing, when most experts didn't even expect him to be able to find Iowa on a map. Rudy Giuliani, the Mayor of 9/11, won, because he spent no money in Iowa, which can now be used to frighten people in states with more foreigners. Bill Richardson wasn't really try to win anyhow, and he didn't, so he's a winner. Joe Biden and Christopher Dodd may be the biggest winners of all, because they don't have to do this anymore. Duncan Hunter is what you call a winner in reverse, since he polled just 500 votes. Which is only 500 votes more than you or I got, and we weren't even running. Which certainly makes *us* winners.

The pundits win because they got a lot to talk about.

And because of the writers' strike, people might actually pay attention. The caucus-goers win because their electoral muscles have been exercised. Young people are winners for having participated in unprecedented numbers. Britney Spears wins since people stopped paying attention to her. Hope wins.

Change wins. Evangelicals win. Chuck Norris wins.

African Americans win. The country wins. *Lot* of winners here. Not going to be the case in New Hampshire next week. Going to be a lot of losers there. But here in the Hawkeye State, the biggest winners of all may be the residents of the Great State of Iowa themselves—not just because everybody has already left them to themselves, but because as soon as they did, the temperature rose about 30 degrees.

Shadows Trump Hope

Listen my friends and you will hear a tale of a fateful night. It's a tale no other dare speak of. Not a matter of political correctness. It is shame. Of which I have little. If any. OK, none. So here goes.

What follows is the real and true story of how Hillary Clinton overcame a double-digit same-day deficit and won the New Hampshire primary. A tale of a race and of race.

We all know what happened, but like the knickers of a Guatemalan nanny bent over a laundry basket in the room just off the kitchen, we pretend not to notice.

Tom Brokaw knows. John King knows. OK, maybe Laura Ingraham doesn't know, but how is that different?

Hillary knows. Barack not only knows, he feels it in his bones like a creeping worm of osteoporosis every day of his life, but he'll never say a word.

It was not a polling glitch. It was not co-opting the mantra of "change." It was not Hillary's vulnerability in Saturday's debate nor her moist eyes in that Portsmouth coffee shop. It was not Bill turning into a 60-foot-tall George Bailey Transformer rampaging through Bedford Falls. It was a little bit of the teeniest kind of invisible fear. A form of prejudice detritus known as the "Bradley Effect."

In 1982, Los Angeles Mayor Tom Bradley, an African American, was 10 points ahead in the polls the day before his California gubernatorial election against George Deukmejian. A whole 10 points ahead. Day before the election. He lost. Sound familiar? Ding. Ding. Ding.

Give that man a kewpie doll.

To add insult to injury, Bradley led in the exit polls. Which means people not only lied about how they were going to vote, they lied about how they *did* vote.

Proof positive that something crazy happens inside the heads of white people when they get behind that polling curtain. But after two terms of George Bush, that ain't new news.

Why didn't the "Bradley Effect" rear its ugly head in Iowa? Simple. We're not talking about racism, we're talking about nervousness. A fear that attacks your marrow in the dark. In Iowa, everyone watches you vote. No curtain to hide behind in a caucus. You bunch in a corner in full sight of all your neighbors under bright fluorescent lights. In New Hampshire, it's just you and your demons. Your inner New England demons. And hope tends to dissipate in those lonely enclosures. No matter how warm the January night, it gets dark at five up there. Northwoods dark, where shadows trump hope.

The difference was women over 40. Which, forgive me, but in both New Hampshire and Iowa means white women.

In the Hawkeye State, they went with the black guy in the wide open. In the Granite State, behind the curtain, they chose the white woman. I know. I know. I know. Sacrilege! Implying that discrimination exists in America today. Blasphemy! Accusing Democrats of possible prejudice. Heresy! But it's not bigotry so much as it is dread. Obloquy! "What?" Never mind.

Suffice it to say that in the last six years, we've been taught to fear. *Bang!* Salivate.

One can only hope the Clinton campaign understands this and doesn't convince themselves it was their wacky emotional-leakage-weekend strategy that turned the tide, because that would mean 10 months of Bill shrieking and Hillary keening, and nobody wants that.

The only thing worse would be to go on pretending this Effect does not exist, because future opponents are already devising plans to ramp it up.

Balkanizing Reagan

Thinning the Republican herd in this year's presidential sweepstakes is proving to be harder than 3-D chess with transparent pieces. In their first three primaries, the GOP has mounted three different heads on their electoral wall. And yeah, that means I'm disregarding the great state of Wyoming, for the simple reason that they're responsible for Dick Cheney and deserve to be ignored, if not flogged en masse and shipped to China to be coated in a lead-based paint then towed to sea by the FDA and dumped. But the exciting part is if Fred Thompson breaks out of his somnambulant trance and wins South Carolina, and if Rudy Giuliani reminds enough withered, transplanted Floridians of the postsqueegee wonder years up north, the GOP could roll into Minneapolis for their national convention this September with an entire starting basketball team of prospective candidates posing as Ronald Reagan.

Because that, apparently, is the current fashion.

Parading around as spitting images of the 40th president, with an emphasis on the saliva. The problem is, they can't find the whole package in one guy.

They've Balkanized the Gipper. The Christian Right is genuflecting toward Mike Huckabee. The charm contingent is sidling up to his Rudyness, while the Screen Actors Guild wing is Clapping For Fred, Mr. *Law & Order* himself. Reagan Democrats are big fans of John McCain, and the conservative money boys from Wall Street love that Mitt Romney character. Romney went so far as to appropriate Reagan's bulletproof hair, undoubtedly garnering the Secret Service's endorsement due to the added protection his hard-candy shell would provide.

One has to consider Ronald Reagan lucky he's in the ground and doesn't have to watch these poseurs go through their paces, otherwise he'd be spinning in his grave like a rotisserie chicken during a power surge. Not to mention being royally pissed off about being buried alive and all.

Curiously, two names you never hear mentioned in these celebrity look-a-like pageants are "George" and "Bush." The president is studiously being avoided like a broken pallet of eight-penny nails in the center lane of the Beltway. It's a vacuum almost big enough to suck an elephant through. They hope.

Among the names that do crop up on the campaign trail more often than that of Herbert Walker's son are Barry Goldwater, John Wayne Gacy, and Bjork. And the Prez is returning the favor by ducking out of town whenever possible, leaving the field wide open for whichever of the Dutch wannabes can best assume the mantle of looking presidential. Of course, the impact of that little trick has diminished somewhat, due to seven years of exposure to it.

Playing the "Reagan=Good, Bush=Bad" game has become so popular that candidates are clambering over each other like blind lemmings outrunning a dam burst, with their claims to be the only one truly capable of bringing change to Washington. Living in the shadow of the last year of consecutive Republican presidential terms (5 out of the last 7; 7 out of the last 10), and all the Republicans can talk about is…change. You know what, that can't be good. Must be considered a backhanded slap at Dubyah. Unfortunately, it's just a figurative slap and not a real one upside the head. With a chain-mail glove. Which might be a more cathartic experience for the nation. And more deserved, too.

Democratic Slap Fight

It's like seeing an old friend. More exciting than skydiving strippers with dissolving chutes. Having the Democrats revert to the famous fractious form they sported in the bad old days of the loony left, I mean. Scratching at each other's eyes like drowning meth addicts scrabbling for the last piece of driftwood visible on a heaving horizon. It's kind of comforting to see them finally back to eating their young. A '60s dream. All the joys of an acid flashback with none of the messy chromosome damage.

For a while, they managed to throttle their self-destructive tendencies and maintain the flimsy façade of semicivilization, what with the whole winning of Congress dealie thing a couple years ago. But right when you thought they might permanently shed their propensity to commit ritual seppuku in public, their two top presidential candidates dug deep into the communal Party storage shed, pulled the Circular Firing Squad Machine out from under the purple paisley poncho, and began shooting each other's knees off at the very first sight of a blinking red camera light.

And yes, I'm talking about the most recent televised debate, or, more accurately, "candidate slap fight," that preceded this weekend's South Carolina primary. What some are calling "the Gurgle in Myrtle." Admittedly, that "some" consists mostly of me. But everyone does heartily agree it was a slam-bang smack-down with gloves removed and swinging roundhouses weighted with brass knuckles and clenched rolls of Sacagawea dollars.

First, Hillary Clinton accused Barack Obama of saying nice things about Ronald Reagan, which is the most heinous sin a Democrat could commit outside of peeing on George Bush if he was on fire. Uncle Ronnie will neither be forgotten nor forgiven for busting a cap into the electoral backside of Saint Jimmy, thereby plunging the Democratic Party into 12 years of wandering in the wilderness of irrelevance. Flashing hitherto unseen mettle by responding in kind, the junior Senator from Illinois indicted Her Hillaryness for serving on the corporate board of Wal-Mart, which for any liberal worth their ACLU card is like getting sprayed with a fine patina of evil antiunion juice.

The two studiously ignored John Edwards as if he were a chip in the paint on the side of the limo that drove them from the airport where their private jets idled ready to take them to another city in a more important state as soon as their face time was through here. But the Not-So-Bashful-Breck-Boy shoul-dered his way into the prime-time act by kicking whichever of the two front-runners he deemed to be down at the time.

This guy is such an opportunist, I wouldn't be surprised to find he has finagled the rights to a series of snowball kiosks in Hell. It's one thing to be a lawyer. It's another thing to always act like one.

All this went down on the same day our country celebrat-ed the birthday of Martin Luther King, Jr. You know, the guy famous for his big nonviolence agenda?

This is how we honor the man who sacrificed his life to preach peace and civility? Thank God there's no holiday to cel-ebrate the birth of Gandhi, or they might go on national telc-vision and beat each other into submission with baseball bats fashioned out of raw beef. Stay tuned, because it's only a matter of time before something just as wacky goes down.

Flinching Toward Babylon—'08

Hard to believe, but here we are smack dab in the middle of another election campaign. Let us pray. The American political process has been called a circus wrapped in a game show covered with poisonous weasel glitter. All right, maybe it hasn't, but it should be.

What it is, is a Wild West, free-for-all, three-ring big-top, featuring ethical geeks, moral contortionists, and a legion of corruptible nincompoops perched precariously on slack media wires dodging blinding blasts of ridicule and vilification.

It starts with the arcane Iowa caucuses on January 3rd. Caucuses. Famously described as standup comedy without the humor. And no chairs. A process that has as much to do with reality as atomic isotopes have to do with tuna melt sandwiches. The problem is none of the people with any idea of what's supposed to happen at these things is still alive. The best guess is it has something to do with throwing smooth runish stones that are read at candlelit séances held in a double helix of hollowed-out cow carcasses.

On January 4th, the caravan picks up its tent stakes and moves northeast to the granddaddy of them all: New Hampshire, whose state motto is "Live Free or Die, You Commie Pinko Yellow Rat Bastard." And the winner immediately assumes front-running position for his or her party's nominee to become the next president of the United States of America. Lucrative Nike endorsements may also be available.

The next primary is in Michigan on the 15th, but it doesn't really count, because they ran around the living room making a mess playing leapfrog when they were told to sit still and behave. Nevada on the 19th and South Carolina on the 26th, but they're on Saturdays, which seems wrong somehow, and then Florida on the 29th. But they were naughty too. (See Michigan.)

On February 5th, a contest popularly known as Super Tuesday ensues. It's named more for the quantity of participants than the quality, and all interested parties risk overdosing on undercooked chicken and lukewarm stump speeches in a last-ditch national sweep to cloud our collective minds.

If the winners aren't known by then, all hell could break loose, and the conventions promise to be scarier than a Rob Schneider marathon on TNT with a broken remote. Comfortingly, some things can be counted on over the next 10 months. It's a given that the two eventual candidates will climb out on that fragile political limb and declare his or her unequivocal opposition to...waste. Each will also claim to have a similar aversion to...crime, ignoring their own long records of heavy involvement in...organized politics.

We're as resilient to this format as fourth-generation cockroaches to watered-down insect repellent. To demonstrate just how familiar, I've compiled a political forecast of what we habitual exercisers of our electoral muscle can expect in the coming year. Clip and save. All dates are approximate. Your mileage may differ.

Late December 2007: In an attempt to promote their grassroots themes in Iowa, candidates scramble to gather contributors to $10,000-a-plate fund-raising dinners.

January 2, 2008: During a freak winter thaw, millionaire career politicians wade through muddy Iowa fields in tasseled loafers and $3,000 suits, expressing their solidarity and innate understanding of the farmers' needs. Later, many shoes are donated to the Salvation Army.

January 4, 2008: CNN explains how there are eight different ways to determine the true winner of the Iowa caucuses.

January 7, 2008: On a *Larry King Live* candidate forum in Manchester, one candidate talks about how it's time to treat the American public as responsible adults and offers up a comprehensive outline to reduce the deficit through a national program of shared sacrifice. He's never heard from again.

January 9, 2008: The day after the New Hampshire primary, the second runner-up holds a press conference claiming a moral victory, while silently behind him his staff weeps openly.

January 15, 2008: At a campaign stop in New Mexico, an anti-immigration candidate personally chases an illegal alien back across the border.

February 2, 2008: In the midst of a brutal Super Tuesday road swing, a contender addresses a group of supporters in Chicago with a rousing "It's great to be here in Cleveland." All three network newscasts close with the clip. He's never heard from again.

June 3, 2008: On a Sunday morning news show, a vice presidential front-runner defends his foreign policy by intimating that the richest country in the world should determine the global agenda. A challenger smirks, "Let's keep China out of this." He's never heard from again.

June 20, 2008: A flag factory in New Jersey bans all photo-ops by presidential aspirants in a desperate attempt to get some work done.

July 4, 2008: At a barbecue in a Southern swing state, a candidate's wife gets noticeably queasy after standing too close to the goat spit.

July 29, 2008: At the Democratic National Convention in Denver, the Democrats float a platform outline that endorses good and condemns bad.

July 30, 2008: Because of pressure from bickering factions, the platform fails to pass.

August 3, 2008: Immediately following the Democratic Convention, the liberal wing accuses the nominee of selling out the party.

August 2008: Absolutely nothing happens in August and it's reported upon at great length.

September 3, 2008: At the Republican National Convention in Minneapolis, the platform committee outlines a proposal to hunt the homeless for food.

September 4, 2008: The plank is unanimously approved.

September 5, 2008: Immediately following the Republican National Convention, the conservative wing accuses the nominee of selling out the party.

September 26, 2008: The first presidential debate is beaten in the ratings by a PBS rerun of "Hydroponic Farming in France."

October 2, 2008: So boring is the vice presidential debate, sleep deprivation clinics utilize tapes of it as a last-ditch resort. Later still, the DEA rules it illegal to play an audio recording of it in your car.

October 7 and 15, 2008: In an unusual move, neither presidential candidate personally appears at the last two debates. However, the networks prominently cover their spin doctors giving detailed answers as to how the candidate might have responded if asked a particular question in a certain way.

November 4, 2008: The public stays away from the election in droves after pollsters characterize the election as a slam dunk and discourage voters from wasting their time.

November 5, 2008: The losing party's vice presidential nominee calls the election a statistical aberration and fires the opening shot in the 2012 campaign. The synchronized national groan is detected on the Richter scale by Lawrence Livermore Labs.

The Pols, They Are A-Changin'

You change. I change. We all change. But politicians aren't like you and me. They're as different from us as tripe is from glue. One of the major distinctions between politicians and actual people is that politicos don't change. They might convert, or evolve.

Or perform an about-face from evil. Possibly rehabilitate an opinion-based itinerary. Perhaps they'll digress from a well-intentioned but disastrously misconceived, staff-engineered game plan.

But change? No. Unless change suddenly becomes the new currency of the realm. Then, look out. Because you don't want to be anywhere on or even near the road when they decide to take a running jump onto the Change Bandwagon. Like now.

"Change? You want change? Why didn't you say so in the first place? I've got your change right here. Anybody who likes change is going to love what I got. Not only do I get it, I have gotten it and will continue to get it for as long as my loyal constituents wish. My career has always been about bringing significant change. As you would discover by asking anybody who knows me, I'm a veritable sucker for change. Been a fan of change my whole life. First I was a changer, then I changed, and now I'm a changed man who's changing again. 'Change' is practically my middle name.

"Over the long, hard years that I've been in politics, it has been my good fortune to accumulate some decent change. I've always had good change. Who was the first person to bring good change around these parts?

"The answer would be: me. Wish I had known you were interested in change, because I would have said something earlier. Ask anyone who knew me back when; my attitude, my hairline, even parts of my face—they've all changed.

"But not ordinary change. That's not what I'm slinging here. Some off-the-rack, run-of-the-mill, street change here, either. No, sir, this is pharmaceutical change that I've got a connection to. Clean, uncut, sliced right off the key change. What I bring to the table is a change totally different than their kind of change. Change infused with experience. Old change.

"The best kind of change. You don't want that newfangled change. Nobody knows where that stuff comes from or if any of it works. No, my friends, if you're looking for change, you should at least have the right kind of change. Change that's been around the block a couple of times.

"Good change. As opposed to bad change. Because, as you know, not every kind of change is good. From the frying pan to the fire is change. A leopard changing his spots and a mole changing colors: Those are not good things. Babies often need changing and nothing smells like that. Small change is not the kind of change we're looking for.

"And you know what? If someone tells you there's a bigger agent of change than me, they're lying. I'm OC.

"Original change. But this kind of change I'm talking about is not radical change; it's consistent change.

"There's a big difference. Come closer. Hear that noise in my pocket? Know what it is? That's right. Change.

"At least four quarters in there; bunch of dimes. Good change. Which is what I have. Not bad change. Which is what my opponent is trying to sell you. But the most important change for me, is for you…to change your mind. And vote for me. The candidate of change."

Flippity, Floppity, on the Campaign Trail

"And just who, exactly, are you calling a flip-flopper?"

"I am calling you a flip-flopper, sir."

"Ha! I laugh at the ludicrousness of your silly allegation-ette. At the risk of repeating myself, allow me to say that all available evidence proves that it is you who both flips and flops."

"How ironic that you call me a flip-flopper, Governor, when it is patently obvious to anyone who has paid the slightest attention to what you laughingly refer to as your 'career' that it is you who are the flipping flip-flopper."

"I'll have you know, Senator, that the extensive injuries I received in the service of our military, defending this great nation of ours, physically prevent me from either flipping or flopping. Furthermore, I, along with the families of our intrepid troops—who are thousands of miles away putting their lives on the line every day to protect your First Amendment right to slander and libel me—resent the accusation that I am a flip-flopper, especially considering that it is coming from you, the flippiest of floppers."

"If the Honorable Gentleman would simply look at the record…. Any impartial judge would be forced to admit that you are such a flip-flopper, you're in danger of triggering a Stage 4 John Kerry Alert."

"The one thing I can say about you, sir, is that the Secret Service would love for you to become president, since you never assume a single position long enough to get a bead on."

"That's quite a statement coming from someone's whose up-and-down movement is the envy of every Yo-Yo Competition Club in North America."

"Oh yeah? Well, you flop more often than a French soccer team that has been surgically deboned."

"With your waffling action, I'm constantly amazed that syrup isn't shooting out of your ears."

"You, sir, skate over the facts so easily you can do a triple lutz on an almanac."

"Due to the amount of fence-straddling you've performed,

there's enough slivers in your butt to build a tree house in a redwood."

"Oh yeah? Well, you sure wear pretty suits for a man who blew his children's inheritance on the added dental work necessary for both of the mouths you are accustomed to talking out of."

"You, sir, are such a pussyfooter, I wouldn't be surprised to find out that Idaho Senator Larry Craig has you on speed dial."

"If ambiguity were an Olympic sport, you would anchor a five-time-gold-medal-winning relay team."

"We disagree. Sir."

"And isn't that what this country is all about?"

The George W. Bush State of the Union Drinking Game

What You Need to Play:

- A group of four taxpayers, including one rich white guy wearing a suit, tie loosened; two folks (any sex) wearing jeans, one in a blue work shirt, the other in a flannel shirt; and one person wearing clothes that look like they were dragged through the sluice chute of the Three Gorges Dam. All belts and shoelaces are secured in a safe place.

- One shot glass per person. Everybody furnishes their own, placing it on a coffee table in front of the television. Suit gets to choose first among the assembled shot glasses for use during game. Blue Shirt picks next, then Flannel Shirt. Suit takes last shot glass as well, and Rags must arrange to rent it from him for the evening or drink out of own cupped hands.

- Everybody antes up $10. Cash. Except Suit, who tosses in an IOU.

- Pot of Texas chili, and a bowl of guacamole in middle of coffee table with Kettle Brand Salt & Fresh Ground Pepper Krinkle Cut chips nearby. If any players are women, they have to prepare and serve the chili and guacamole. Otherwise, buy some premade stuff at Costco.

- Bottle of bourbon.

- Stopwatch.

- Old newspapers spread out on coffee table and in front of and on top of television.

- A large stash of beer, in cans. Rags gets whatever's on sale, like Old Milwaukee Ice Dry Light. Suit gets whatever import he wants. Players in jeans get domestic, but must pay for all the beer, bourbon, chips, and ingredients for the chili and guacamole.

Rules of the Game:

1. Whenever George W. uses the phrase "economic stimulus package," the last person to slap his or her hand to their own forehead has to drink two shot glasses of beer. Every time the president says "make tax cuts permanent," everybody must drink a whole beer, then throw the empties at the television. If can hits president's face, everyone else must drink one shot of beer.

2. Every time George W. talks about his deep-seated desire for "change," the last person to cough "*Hack!*" must drink three shots of beer.

3. If George W. even attempts to pronounce the name of Iranian President Mahmoud Ahmadinejad, the first person to stop laughing is exempt from drinking three shots of beer.

4. Every time Senators John McCain, Hillary Clinton, or Barack Obama are shown in the audience, you have 30 seconds to throw a chip of guacamole at the television, and if anyone makes a chip beard on one of the candidates, everyone else has to drink five shots of beer.

5. Every time George W. refers to General Petraeus, the last person to yell out "Surgin' General!" has to drink two shots of beer.

6. The first time George W. talks about a lasting peace in the Middle East, last person to smash three tortilla chips on his forehead has to drink one shot of bourbon.

7. If the vice president or the First Lady is caught napping, last person to sing "Wake Up, Little Susie, Wake Up" has to drink two shots of beer. If Senator Robert Byrd is shown without drool running down his chin, Blue Shirt and Flannel Shirt drink two shots of beer.

8. Everybody drinks two shots of beer if President Bush mentions Pervez Musharraf. Three shots of beer if he mentions Benazir Bhutto. Four shots of bourbon if he mentions Osama bin Laden.

9. Whenever George W. makes a reference to his faith getting him through tough times, or the Bible, last person to fall to their knees and shout "Hallelujah!" has to drink two shots of beer.

10. Whenever George W. talks about No Child Left Behind, everybody takes turn throwing chips of chili and guacamole at TV for 30 seconds. First person to cover an eye is exempt from drinking three shots of beer.

11. The first time George W. mentions the tragic events of 9/11, the last person to eat one dollop of guacamole off a tortilla

chip must drink three shots of beer. The second time he mentions the tragic events of 9/11, the last person to eat one dollop of chili off a tortilla chip must drink three shots of beer. Continue to alternate. Any player who "mischips" must drink two extra shots of beer.

12. Predict the number of applause breaks. After the speech, the closest to actual number *doesn't* have to drink two shots of bourbon.

13. Whenever George W. smirks during a standing ovation, take turns drinking shots of beer until the audience sits down. Do it double time if his shoulders shake with silent laughter. If George W. winks and points to someone in the audience, Suit has to drink out of beer-filled hands of Rags, who gets to dry his hands on Suit's jacket.

14. If George W. uses a heartfelt story of a touching recovery experienced by one of our brave troops, Suit gets to kick everybody once. Twice, if the brave soldier is a woman. Rags gets to kick the Suit if Bush reveals the subject of the anecdote to be in the audience. Twice, if the brave soldier is sitting next to an astronaut. Four times if the astronaut is wearing a diaper.

15. If George W. Bush mentions alternative energy, the last person to pretend to faint has to drink three shots of beer.

Extras:

- Before the speech, everyone writes down who they think is giving the Democratic Response. Anybody who correctly identifies the person doesn't have to watch it. No Googling allowed.

- Suit takes home all the money.

- Leftover beer, chili, and guacamole go home with Rags after he or she finishes washing the dishes and wiping off the TV screen.

Bill Clinton: Threat or Menace?

It's desperation time in Hillaryville. They're putting out fires faster than a Rocky Mountain ranger station during a lightning storm in the middle of an August drought. Due to the fact that a certain inevitability has proven to be highly evitable. And watching the nomination slip through their fingers has to be going down as easy as a deep-fried fork. Causing several revisions to what was previously a dead-solid game plan. Corrections that include, but are not limited to, banishment of key staffers to "integral" precincts on the outskirts of West Texas. Further attempts to wring blood out of contributors who insist on impersonating dried turnips. And the most difficult fix: figuring out how to get the candidate's husband to shut the hell up.

Yeah, right. Good luck. You'd have a better shot at using a plastic butter knife to spay a pit pull than trying to muzzle this old dog. I suggest a wolf snare or a tranquilizer gun as the best means to render the 42nd president of the United States docile enough to throw a choke chain around his neck. Interesting, how quickly the game changes. It wasn't that long ago that rival campaigns were complaining that Hillary had an unfair advantage, being married to a former president. "But he gets so much press!" And now it's Hillary's staff doing the complaining. "But he gets so much press!"

What was once a secret weapon is now an albatross tied by a frayed rope swinging wildly from the neck of the former First Lady. And because of his unique stature as biggest hound in the pound, Bubba isn't just a loose cannon, he's a loose aircraft carrier in high seas.

Rampaging down the campaign trail in the manner of a

Japanese movie monster stomping through downtown Tokyo, using his heat vision to blast opponents, and batting around members of the media like pastel bunnies off an Easter display shelf in a Hallmark Card shop. He must see himself as a guard dog protecting the henhouse, no pun intended. (Barack's camp accuses him of being the junkyard dog.)

And we can't have that. Because everybody knows that if Obama gets the nomination, the Republicans won't be mean. They'll roll over on their backs, begging to have their bellies scratched. Worst-cast scenario, they'll try to bruise him by throwing rubber bones at his head. Hah. I laugh. Hah. I laugh again.

You want to see negative campaigning? You wait until the junior Senator from Illinois gets the nomination, because you're going to see negative campaigning that will make what they did to Michael Dukakis look like pranks played during recess at a Catholic girls school.

Bill Clinton nuzzles and he growls. He's a boon and a bane. A southern-fried Jekyll and Hyde. Smoother than a puppy's fur, and more divisive than a flea-ridden German shepherd at a bat mitzvah. One problem is everybody continues to introduce him as "Mr. President," as if he were still in charge. That kind of thing can have an effect on a guy. If Hillary were smart, she'd sponsor a bill in Congress that would mandate that all former Chief Executives be referred to as "Mr. Ex-President." Kill two dogs with one stone. One dog being a certain George W. Bush, whom a lot of us can't wait to call...Mr. Ex-President.

Clear. Unclear. Lead Apron.

Disappointment, thy name is Super Tuesday. Maybe the celebrated day was intimidated by trying to live up to its own hype, like the New England Patriots, who were perfect for an entire season (minus the last 35 seconds). What I'm saying is, not very superlative for either of them. Like opening a bottle of 30-year-old Beaujolais and finding it more appropriate for use on your salad. Or discovering on your honeymoon that your new spouse suffers from narcolepsy. Or waking up on Christmas morning and being told Santa called in sick.

Oh sure, the Republicans winnowed themselves down to John McCain, the Last Rich Old White Guy Standing, due to their jerry-rigged winner-take-all primary rules.

Which could come back to bite them on the ass, as they managed to pick the one guy that real & true conservatives detest—but that was always in the cards, considering that former Arkansas Governor Mike Huckabee is only reviled 3 percent less by those real & true conservatives and a lot more by…oh, what shall we call them?, that wacky, evolution-believing cabal.

Super Fat Tuesday did provoke the candidate that real & true conservatives do pantingly long for former Massachusetts Governor Mitt Romney to up and quit.

Mostly because, even though he was running second, he had royally pissed off everyone. Did I say "everyone"?

Because I meant everyone. Including his five Stepford Sons, for squandering their inheritance by blowing $40 million of his own money for the right to wear the conditional crown of Mr. Inevitable for 2012, should the Last Rich Old White Guy Standing falter this November.

Super Tuesday's most spectacular failure was on the other side of the aisle. Instead of putting some separation between Barack and Hillary, the voting in 24 states ended up intertwining the two, creating a kind of candidate bouillabaisse. The perfect Mardi Gras concoction: a gumbo of equal portions of the Black Guy and the Woman.

What was supposed to be crystal clear wasn't very clear at all. To be perfectly honest, the only thing that's clear is that this fight to the finish is not over.

The fat lady has not sung. Oh, I'm sorry, we're talking liberals. What I meant to say is, the gravity-enhanced diva has yet to warble. As a matter of fact, I don't even think waiting in the wings yet.

Probably she's still hanging out in the dressing room smoking a cigarette, talking to her agent on a cell phone with her legs stretched out on the makeup table stuffing her mouth full of bonbons while one of the assistant costumers lets out her dress. Again.

I mean, after an election of this magnitude, the outcome traditionally provides you with either your clear, your near-clear, your unclear, your blurry, your muddled, your opaque, or your lead apron at the dentist's office with the hygienist safely ensconced in a room two counties away from the chair you're reclining in with a three-ton X-ray gun pointed at your jaw. And this…is definitely one of the latter. But relief is in sight. Because guess what? More primaries coming up. Yee-hah. Which means more fund-raising, more ads, and more pundits pompously pontificating. And translucent and transparent are just around the corner. One can only hope. But then, one has been wrong before—hasn't one?

Lumpy & Hucky

Just when you thought the Republican primary was all over but the shouting, along comes the *New York Times* with a potential bombshell about possible indiscretions that may or may not have involved John McCain and a woman who does not necessarily look unlike his wife. But don't let that fool you, the charges aren't that solid. Murkier than 8 mm footage of Sasquatch grilling on a Cayman Islands condo balcony filmed from a boat across the harbor on a foggy night. The only certainty is the Gray Lady managed to unite the Conservative Right to fight the reviled shared enemy they represent. Isn't that just like the liberal media elite? Throwing synthetic dirt on the hill to make Obama's comeback climb even more impressive.

McCain's response to the suppositious exposé about ostensible malfeasance did provide his wife, Cindy, with serious face time to demonstrate that she was more than just the blonde lady who looks like the head stewardess for Republican Air. And the fact that the lobbyist in question, Vicki Iseman, is her doppelganger, simply means John has really good taste in Stepford Wives.

Over at the Mike Huckabee camp, the shouting is tinged with desperation. But still this Energizer Razorback Bunny refuses to give up. As the former portly former governor from Arkansas says, we've entered the "survival of the fittest" phase of the election. Strange talk from a man who doesn't believe in evolution. From my perspective it seems more like a "gnawing off one of your legs to escape from the coyote trap" phase of the election.

The GOP is down to a man who believes humans and dinosaurs walked the Earth together and another who can refute that, since he was there. Huckabee explains away his Sisyphean perseverance by saying he doesn't believe in numbers, he believes in miracles. The hell does that mean? He's waiting for God to smite John McCain dead? Don't laugh. It could be working. I got to tell you, I'm worried about the good Senator from Arizona. He don't look so good.

Not just the deer-in-the-headlights grimace at his recent entanglement-denial press conference. I don't know if you noticed but the lump in his face that he had surgically removed a couple years ago is back, and it brought its big brother with it. Looks like he's hoarding nuts for the winter. That can't be good. Generally, I find people are rather disinclined to vote for a president who resembles a marsupial.

This is particularly distressing because, let's face it, Lumpy is not a young man. At 72, he'd be the oldest white man to ascend to the presidency. What does it say about a country when the president's motorcade continually holds up traffic doing 30 in the fast lane with their left blinkers on? State Dinners held at Denny's on Wednesdays to take advantage of the senior discount? His campaign slogan: "Hey, you punks, get off my lawn"?

The allegation by the *Times* could be a speed bump or a spike strip to the front wheels of the Straight Talk Express. After all, McCain's major attraction to independents is his credibility. And his steadfastness, best exemplified by his early support of the Iraqi surge and his expectation for us to be there for 100 years. No big surprise. We still have a base in Cuba: a residue from the Spanish-American War, which ended in 1898. Ask John McCain. He was there, too.

Super Duper Fat Tuesday

Chin up, me buckos. Be brave. Don't go all El Foldo on us here. This is no time to pull a John Edwards. Oh, I understand the temptation to succumb to the numbing forecast of further interminable debates, but we've come much too far to break down into deep racking sobs just yet. The good news is (yes, there is good news) it's almost over. The primary process, that is. And the voters of the 24 states venturing into the swirling eddies of Super Tuesday next week should end it, and if they don't, then it ain't going to end for quite a while and there will be time o'plenty to cry and weep and keen over the grisly fate that awaits us.

There is a consolation; if the unthinkable event does go down, with no winner emerging, we have six long months to arrange to have the dosage on our medication stepped up in preparation for the conventions this summer when the TV show

American Gladiators will be restaged in pinstripes. Oh yes. There will be blood.

But Tuesday should clinch it. They don't call it Super Tuesday for nothing, you know. Actually, they call it Super Tuesday more for the quantity of states voting and not for the quality of the participants involved.

And through an odd quirk of fate, it's not just Super Tuesday where 52 percent of the Democratic and 41 percent of the Republican delegates will be chosen; it is also, more importantly, Mardi Gras. Fat Tuesday.

So called because that's the last day Roman Catholics allow themselves to gorge on all the things they plan to give up for Lent. Like what we hope and pray occurs with us and the candidates. Please shut up. Cleverly, the state of Louisiana chose the following Saturday for its primary, four days after Super Fat Tuesday.

Proving their bacchanalian propensities are not so debilitating as to prevent them from scheduling a brief recovery period before flexing their electoral muscles. As opposed to the rest of us, who do the exact opposite. We vote, then we drink.

This Super Tuesday also holds the distinction of being the most Super of any Tuesday we've ever known. You could say it's the Superest Tuesday, because of everybody vying to be relevant in the partisan-picking processes. "But what about me?" Leading pundits have taken to calling it Super Duper Tuesday, or Tsunami Tuesday, or Giga Tuesday, or The Tuesday of Destiny, or Le Ultra Tuesday That Will Make Your Head Snap Back Like Someone Dropped a Load of Ammonia-Laced Concrete in Your Lap, and believe it or not, the only one I made up was the last one.

The bad news is (yes, there is bad news) this is merely round one. And once the parties have chosen their standard-bearers, this procedure will repeat itself all over again. Oh yes. There will be mud. The scariest part is realizing one of these gas bags is going to win. That's right. The Actor, the Mormon, and the Mayor of 9/11 have all fallen by the wayside.

Our choice for the next resident of 1600 Pennsylvania Avenue has boiled down to the Woman, the Black Guy, the Preacher, and the Prisoner of War. A prospect that should make all of us shiver like stowaways in the baggage hold of a 747 on a Seattle-to-Shanghai run.

Oh yes. There will be hypothermia.

Careful What You Ask For

This is a tale of two California gubernatorial elections whose seismic aftershocks can still be felt today. The first was circa 1966. Democratic California Governor Edmund "Pat" Brown was running for a third consecutive term. In June of that year, upon hearing that a former Screen Actors Guild president had beaten the mayor of San Francisco in the Republican primary, he and his staff were barely able to contain their glee. Yes, this was so long ago, the mayor of San Francisco was Republican. Back when gay meant festive. And the TV went dark at midnight after 4 out of 5 doctors recommended smoking Chesterfields.

Jerry and Kathleen Brown's dad's wishes had come true. His opponent was a veritable lightweight compared to the gray eminence that was George Christopher: all flash and little if any pan. Surely, this terrific news signaled that four more years of employment as the CEO of the Golden State was in the bag. Hopefully, he refrained from calling in designers to redecorate his Sacramento digs, because that particular assessment proved to be as premature as a high school sophomore's first lap dance.

On January 3, 1967, Ronald Reagan was sworn in as the 33rd governor of California. Reputedly, he went on to other political postings later in life, but whether you liked or didn't like what happened during his multiple reigns of error, the lesson to be learned from this ancient anecdote is to be very, *very* careful what you wish for. You just might get it.

Fast forward 42 years. The mainstream Republican machine is salivating at a Barack Obama candidacy like a Pavlovian dog at a grade school bell-testing lab. All during the primary process, right-wing talk show hosts gave the junior Senator from Illinois a wider berth than a unicyclist juggling nitroglycerin on a floor full of marbles. Instead they concentrated on slamming Hill and her hubby for a long list of past and present outrages such as the audacity to breathe the same air as good God-fearing folks and Clay Aiken.

Didn't matter what Senator Clinton did. If she demonstrated a mastery of policy, she was an Iron Maiden devoid of passion. When she got weepy up in New Hampshire, she was a weak-kneed sob sister who would break down at the first stern look from Putin. Initially, her husband gave her an unfair advantage, then he was a dead albatross tied by a frayed rope swinging wildly from the neck of the former First Lady. Saying the Clintons are a target-rich environment is like calling an Antarctic winter…brisk.

All the while, Obama skated. But now that the hand is played out and the nomination locked up, the Republican Cheshire Cat grin has started to reappear. Apparently, they think Barack is going to be an easier mark. Perhaps opposition research has uncovered more skeletons than are housed in a cadaver dog training-camp storage space.

Maybe the plan is to exploit his inexperience. Like the Democrats did with Bush. Or maybe, just maybe, they're counting on the Bradley Effect to take over. You remember Tom Bradley: African-American mayor of Los Angeles. Lost the 1982 California gubernatorial race to George Deukmejian, after leading in the polls by double digits the day before. He even led the exit polling. That's Britney Spearsian–level delusional.

But Tom Bradley was nearly three decades ago. And hopefully, we have matured enough to realize race and sex and age and creed don't make you who you are. Your actions and what kind of car you drive do. Of course President Bush has to get some credit for single-handedly proving that anybody, and I mean anybody, could fill the job. So, good luck, GOP strategists. Congratulations: You got the candidate you wanted. Go for the gusto. And maybe in November, you'll learn to be a little more careful about exactly what it is that you ask for.

Shut Up

Shut up. Please shut up. No. Really. Shut up. Shut Up. Shut UP. I know you think I'm kidding here, but I'm not. Pretty please. Shut the hell up. Honest to God, it's not funny anymore. Would you two kindly have the simple common human decency to close your pie holes and be quiet for half a minute? Is that too much to ask? The hell is wrong with you people, anyway? The horse is dead. He's starting to smell. Put the bats down.

Yes, I'm talking about the two remaining Democratic candidates, who just participated in their 20th debate but it seems more like their 8,000th. And if you made it through the latest wearisome exercise in drudgery (appropriately held in Cleveland), you know what I'm talking about; but if you didn't, you should immediately fall to your knees and thank your lucky stars along with every big-rig accident or burnt pot roast or sorting of your sock drawer that kept you from sinking into a hole of depression deeper than a vertical zinc mine once you came to the realization that you will never ever *ever* have that 90 minutes of your life back.

90 minutes. 5,400 seconds. 3/48ths of a day. Time enough to cook a four-pound chicken and eat it. To listen to Green Day's *American Idiot* twice. Read an entire Robert Parker book. Roundtrip from San Francisco to San Jose in the fast lane of I-280. One and a half episodes of *The Wire*. Three consecutive

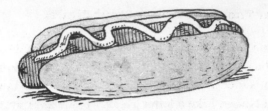

pizza deliveries from Dominos. 22 1/2, four-minute miles. 551 hot dogs at the rate that Joey Chestnut set the world record last July 4th on Coney Island.

Oh my living God, it was riveting. Like listening to golf on the radio in Mandarin. Made you pine for one of those mid '50s Soviet television documentaries on hydroponic farming in the Ukraine. You know that feeling you get when you've been driving 14 hours straight and are starting to nod off because it's 4:30 a.m. and you haven't seen a car in three hours and you figure you'll just rest one eye a little bit and then open it again real quick? Well, it was a lot like that, only with tedium.

Here's a news flash. We don't care anymore. You've broken us. Spending 18 minutes on two health care plans that don't have a gnat's pubic hair's worth of difference between them. Not just a discussion, but an actual altercation over the distinction between the words "reject" and "denounce"? You got to be kidding me. The two of you share similar opinions on every single policy issue of import and spend each of these interminable evenings sucking up to the same special interest groups agreeing with one another. That is not a debate. That's a swimsuit competition with pants.

Somebody, anybody, put an end to this misery. I'm begging you. Before one of us snaps and rushes the stage brandishing a turkey baster full of muscle relaxers. Save us. Please. Texas. Pennsylvania. If you have the tiniest scintilla of humanity hidden in the marrow of your bones you will stop this now. No. More. Debates. Until after Labor Day. And then, I'll personally furnish the bats. And the horse.

32 Short Thoughts About Ralph Nader

Ralph Nader. Officially threw his hat in the ring for president. Again. His fourth attempt. Shouldn't three strikes apply here?

Ralph Nader. The Dr. Kevorkian of presidential politics.

Ralph Nader. Like a lefter Dennis Kucinich minus the hot wife and massive groundswell of public support.

Ralph Nader. Liberal response: Good message. Bad delivery. Awful timing.

Ralph Nader. Conservative response: If you need any help with ballot access, let us know.

Ralph Nader. A retired two-term ex-president if hippies ruled the world.

Ralph Nader. Still serving life without parole if General Motors ruled the world.

Ralph Nader. First name is colloquial synonym for the rapid expulsion of stomach contents as a result of a series of involuntary muscle spasms whose appearance generally signals the host is sick or drunk. Not that that means anything.

Ralph Nader. Surname is homonym of *nadir:* which means lowest point possible. The opposite of *zenith.* Not that that means anything.

Ralph Nader. Makes Barack Hussein Obama look like a centrist.

Ralph Nader. Makes John Sidney McCain look vivacious.

Ralph Nader. Middle name is Moral Victory.

Ralph Nader. In '00, saw no difference between Al Gore and George Bush. Still denies missing repeated optometrist appointments.

Ralph Nader. Fervently believes the truth can effect change. Has yet to learn the American electorate would rather drink unfiltered haggis juice straight from the tap with their hands tied behind their backs with live copperhead snakes than confront the truth.

Ralph Nader. A Pisces.

Ralph Nader. Born in a Year of the Dog.

Ralph Nader. Not a socialist. But not unlike one, either.

Ralph Nader. Older than John McCain. Whiter than Barack Obama. More Y chromosomes than Hillary Clinton.

But all three were close.

Ralph Nader. Three-time recipient of the "Tony Orlando Coasting on Your Decades-Old Reputation" Award.

Ralph Nader. Michael Moore 19 years and 10 months hence.

Ralph Nader. When Bad Things Happen to Good People in Sears, Roebuck Suits.

Ralph Nader. Made the cars we drive safer and George Bush president. That's what you call your trade-off.

Ralph Nader. Yet to hold electoral office. Apparently not complicit with that whole "presidency should not be an entry-level position" cabal.

Ralph Nader. Like a scowling Ross Perot with a Harvard Law degree.

Ralph Nader. A saint, a visionary and a genius.

Ralph Nader. A fool with the same commonsense that God gave a bucket of claw hammers.

Ralph Nader. Harold Stassen for the MTV generation.

Ralph Nader. *Unsafe at Any Speed* is now him in a crosswalk.

Ralph Nader. Possesses the sense of humor of an end table.

Ralph Nader. Would rather be right in public than left at home.

Ralph Nader. People's lobbyist or Judas Goat?

Ralph Nader. Dramatically intones that if America is to become better, it first has to get worse. *News flash:* It's worse! We don't want worser. This is the worsest we can stand.

Acknowledgments

It would be exponential factor extreme remiss of me not to take a wee bit of a tad of time here to thank some of the insanely odd folks I've met over the years who have gone to the wall and sometimes through it believing in me and what I like to call my written stuff.

They include but are not limited to: Raymond Loesser. Jack Boulware. Leslie Crawford. Ruth Coniff. Matthew Rothschild. Denis Kitchen. Barry Weintraub. Rachel Clarke. Len Belzer. Julian Goldberg. Hut Landon. Larry Kramer. Bruce Brugman. Tom & Marilyn Auer. Howie Nave. Larry "Ratso" Sloman. Jim Finefrock. Rip Tenor. Jay Harris. Katrina Rill. Neil Genzlinger. Andy Valvur. Brooke Biggs. Michael Rosen. David Holwerk. Fred Dodsworth. Michael Bossier. Andrew Rougier-Chapman. Jerry Lubenow. Richard Halacz. Becky Bond. Michael Kieschnik. Bob Agnew. Don Hazen. Warren Hinckle. Chris Hunter. Cari Dawson-Bartley. Willie Brown. Alex Leo. Paul Krassner. Lois Kazakoff. Paul Wells. Dan Pasternack, and more. Many more. All the wacky wordsmiths at Ulysses Press: Karma Bennett, Bryce Willett and all the other smart ones I haven't met. An editor with the equanimity of Job's more patient older brother: Mark Woodworth. Special guilt must needs shine on Nick Denton-Brown, who initiated this madcap scheme. Eric Krebs, who believed in this material so much he produced an Off-Broadway show based on it. And last but so very not-at-all least, the funny member of Team Durst, my lovely wife, Debi Ann, without whom all of this would be just plain silly. OK. Sillier.

About the Author

Will Durst is a former margarine smuggler from Wisconsin who has written for the *New York Times, Esquire, George,* the *San Francisco Chronicle* and many other periodicals. This is his first book. With 400+ television appearances, he is a five-time Emmy nominee (no wins) who has been fired by both the *San Francisco Examiner* and PBS twice. He's racked up seven nominations for Stand-Up Comedian of the Year (no wins), co-hosted a morning radio show with former San Francisco Mayor Willie Brown and recently wrapped up a critically acclaimed Off-Broadway run of *The All-American Sport of Bipartisan Bashing.* His hobbies include pinball and the never-ending quest for the perfect cheeseburger, and his heroes remain the same as when he was 12...Thomas Jefferson and Bugs Bunny. He lives in San Francisco with his wife, Debi Durst, and their four-footed child, Annie. Readers are invited to go to *willdurst.com* for schedules and info and to win free prizes.